INSIDE THE CIRCLE:

A Historical and Practical Inquiry Concerning Process Groups in Clinical Pastoral Education

By

JOAN E. HEMENWAY, D.Min.

INSIDE THE CIRCLE:
A Historical and Practical Inquiry Concerning
Process Groups in Clinical Pastoral Education

Journal of Pastoral Care Publications, Inc.

ISBN: 0-929670-14-0

Dedication

With appreciation to colleagues, friends, and students

in the Association for Clinical Pastoral Education who

through the years challenged me to grow and learn.

This is my effort to give something back.

ACKNOWLEDGEMENTS

This book is the result of research and writing which could not have been done without the support and encouragement of many people. I want to especially thank my academic advisor, J. Earl Thompson, Ph.D., Professor of Pastoral Psychology and Family Studies at Andover Newton Theological School. Earl's commitment to faithful and self-directed intellectual inquiry inspired me to believe in my own abilities *and* reach for higher accomplishment during my Doctor of Ministry program. The tireless efforts and good spirits of the staff at the Franklin Trask Library at Andover Newton were instrumental in my procuring key books through their own collections and the interlibrary loan system. My participation in the doctoral program was supported by Rev. John K. Swift, Co-Director of Pastoral Services at Hartford Hospital where I served as Director of CPE training between 1984 and 1993. John's encouragement and flexibility allowed me to combine employment and study in a manageable way. I also want to thank the CPE supervisors in Connecticut and in the Eastern Region of ACPE. They have not only provided the inspiration and data for this study, but are an ongoing spiritual and professional community of central importance in my life. Finally, I want to thank Jennifer, whose patience and caring made all the difference in my being able to bring this work to fruition.

Contents

The main thesis of this study rests on two interrelated assertions. The first assertion is that in clinical pastoral education (CPE) work with individual students has been primarily influenced by the psychoanalytic tradition. The second assertion is that process-group work[1] has been primarily influenced by the humanistic psychology tradition. As a result, the educational methodology in CPE has been inconsistent, causing confusion among ourselves and our students. It is the intent of this study first to understand the problem and its ramifications, and second to propose a theory of group work which balances and integrates these two approaches and is consistent with the CPE historical inheritance, clinical practice, and commitment to theological education in the liberal tradition.

My initial interest in this subject was stimulated by some tapes of student process groups which were offered for peer review among a group of supervisors who meet regularly in Connecticut. My interest deepened through my work with supervisory education students who wanted to learn how to "do groups" from me. These experiences evoked my growing awareness (and uneasiness) that, even though as a certified CPE supervisor I had spent a considerable amount of time doing group process work with CPE students, I really had no group theory I could talk about in a coherent way. In fact, I was intrigued that I had apparently "gotten by" for nearly twenty years! I did know that the small process group experience always caused considerable initial anxiety and excitement in my students (and in me) and that, as the training unit progressed, the small group process became either the most highly valued and memorable part of the educational experience–or the most problematic.

As I dug more deeply into the subject, unsolicited comments came from others who had heard about my interest. One CPE Supervisor confessed: "I do not feel well-versed in group, nor do I work out of a consistent theory. So I would personally appreciate your efforts." After correspondence with another about the project, that person wrote: "Thanks for teaching me something–namely, that National Training Lab [Bethel, Maine] had something to do with developing our working with groups. I didn't know that! But I was actively involved during the early sixties in the group training stuff that came out of NTL through

---

[1] The reference is to unstructured group sessions variously known as IPG (interpersonal group), IPR (interpersonal relations group), "covenant group," "open seminar," or simply "group life."

the Episcopal Church." And a third commented: "I am sure some of us became aware that in our religious tradition small groups were very significant in our spiritual development. However, at least for me, I failed to succeed very much with small groups in my churches until I learned more about group process."

Nearly twenty-five years ago Malcolm and Hulda Knowles wrote a classic study entitled *Introduction to Group Dynamics*. In their concluding section they noted that social scientists have pointed out two important characteristics of modern life:

> (1) as life becomes increasingly complex individuals become increasingly interdependent and must inevitably do more and more of their work in groups and,

> (2) nothing can be more tyrannical than a group whose members are unsophisticated about its dynamics (Knowles and Knowles 1972, 86-7).

These conclusions are the basic concerns which underlie this current study–along with the conviction that clinical pastoral education, precisely because of its small group process, has something unique and necessary to offer in the training of effective and knowledgeable ministers for the church and society in the twenty-first century.

Recently clinical pastoral education has come under some harsh criticism. In "The Tragedy of Clinical Pastoral Education," an article published in *Pastoral Psychology*, the author, a seminary professor, focuses on the blurring of lines between supervision (education) and therapy. Among his several concerns is the quasi-therapeutic nature of the interpersonal relations (IPR) group. He criticizes the lack of confidentiality of this group work and the inappropriateness of the supervisor's written final evaluation of the students' participation in the group experience. He calls for limiting group work in CPE to case study and verbatim seminars, and then concludes:

> Personal evaluations may be a required part of such groups, but the focus of the groups should be on the students using such evaluations to help them understand and care for others, not on the students making changes in their personalities (Steinhoff-Smith 1993, 53).

A second critical article, "'They Had To Beg Us To Pray': Reflections on the Undesirability of Clinical Pastoral Education" recently appeared in *The Journal of Pastoral Care*. The author, director of a counseling training program in a mental health center, focuses on what he regards as the inherent weakness of process education (CPE) in which student-centered learning not only ignores conceptual knowledge but also presumes to claim that personal growth in self-knowledge, self-authentication and self-direction is sufficient to achieve professional skills for doing ministry. In the course of arguing his point the author notes that, since process education does not differentiate between transitory feelings and recurring (psychological) dynamics, "it can only circle regressively in upon itself" (Ahlskog 1993, 184). The author then concludes that

> the encounter with foundational principles of psychic functioning comes first. Processing these materials in order to formulate a ministry response comes second, along with personal growth possibilities (185).

It is the intention of this study to document three central claims: first, that the small process group presents a potentially powerful and unique educational element in CPE; second, that process-group work in CPE can best be done when it grows out of an adequate theory; and third, that the basic elements of an adequate theory can be found both in the historical development of small-group work in CPE and in its current efforts in theory and practice.

What exactly *is* a process group in CPE? First, what I believe it is *not*. It is *not* a didactic group session in which students gather to receive or share information or knowledge about a subject related to pastoral ministry. Second, it is *not* group supervision in which students gather as a group to learn pastoral skills from one another by reviewing a verbatim, case presentation, critical incident, or doing a role play. Third, it is *not* group psychotherapy (in the strictest sense) in which patients or clients meet together once a week with a therapist in order to seek healing for individual personality or emotional problems (pathology).

The small process group (SPG) is an *open agenda study group* placed within a clinically-based educational program (CPE) which employs an action-reflection-action model of learning as part of professional preparation for ministry. Anywhere from three to seven students and a certified CPE supervisor (or sometimes co-supervisors) sit "inside the circle." During a full-time unit of training the small process group usually meets for ninety-minute sessions three times a week for three months. During a part-time extended unit of training the small process group meets once a week for approximately seven months.[2] This dynamic small-group experience is intended to engage the student both experientially and reflectively, subjectively and objectively, affectively and cognitively, personally and professionally. The SPG experience is directly related to training for ministry not only because the church and society are filled with small groups which the pastor needs to understand and work with, but also because the group process itself is a powerful tool in helping ministerial students become more self-aware and more group-aware.

There is very little published material in book form on the supervision of process-group work in CPE. In *The Art of Clinical Supervision* (Estadt, Compton, and Blanchette 1987) there is one brief article entitled "Group Counseling: A Model for Teaching and Supervision" (Callahan and Davenport) which is actually about teaching group psychotherapy to pastoral counselors based on the work of Irvin Yalom. In *The Supervision of Pastoral Care* (Steere 1989), an article entitled "Group Supervision" by Bruce Skaggs (1989) reflects some of the current confusion. In his pastoral counseling training program (not CPE), Skaggs explains that he runs two types of groups: a "Super Group" (which he claims has a therapeutic focus and is modeled after the IPR group in CPE) and "Group Supervision" which has a clinical case focus (175). Another article (Smith 1989) shares seminary student responses to CPE, including the IPR experience, but does not go beyond descriptive reporting. Particularly disappointing was the recent publication of Kenneth Pohly's *Transforming the Rough Places: The Ministry of Supervision* (1993), which represents a sizable revision of his earlier work on pastoral supervision (1977). Though Pohly emphasizes the "critical need" for persons in ministry to have a peer group, skills in group supervision and group process are only a background element in his list of over fifty attributes needed to do effective (mainly individual) supervision of ministry students (1993, 86-87).

One of the hallmarks of the liberal Protestant tradition out of which CPE was born is its interest in engaging in dialogue with the behavioral sciences. It has done this in two ways. First, in order to fully grasp the complexities of the human situation it has turned to psychoanalytic thought. Awareness of primitive

---

[2] There are other models of CPE, especially regarding this type of group experience, including programs with minimal or no process group component. Further research is needed to determine current national and international practice.

urges, the need to repress, the presence of the unconscious, the fragility of the ego, and the possibility of some inherent "fatal flaw" all signal the essential aloneness and uniqueness of the human situation. Taking the dark side of life seriously and seeking partial healing through understanding and accepting illness and limitation were among these efforts. Such "pessimistic" ideas fit with our religious grounding in Calvinism as well as with what we experienced in our places of ministry among hurting people and a damaged society.

The second way in which liberal Protestantism and CPE have engaged in dialogue with the behavioral sciences has been through their attraction to American progressivism and humanistic psychology. Here has resided the optimistic belief in the innate goodness and limitless possibilities of the human enterprise. Here the opportunity to gain self-mastery and self-fulfillment, usually with the support and encouragement of a loving community, has predominated. What has been called "the psychological blossom theory" focused on the importance of receiving and giving nurturance in a warm and cohesive environment in order to assure and enhance relational growth and learning. If the first approach emphasized that we are "a little *lower* than the angels," the second approach emphasized that we are "a little lower than the *angels.*"

These differences have caused uncertainty through the years about the meanings of the words *educational*, *clinical*, and *pastoral* in clinical pastoral education. In general *clinical* tended to become identified with the psychoanalytic tradition; *pastoral* became identified with the humanistic psychology tradition; and *educational* floated between the two–caught up in controversies about the potential therapeutic value of the CPE learning process itself. *If* one subscribes to the validity and utility of *both* the psychoanalytic and humanistic psychology approaches (as this study does), then our *educational* enterprise in CPE includes not only dealing with learning problems but also problems in learning (countertransference). *Clinical* means not only the study of particular cases, but also the ability to look objectively at one's own self in relationship to those cases (or ministry). *Pastoral* means not only being a representative of divine love and acceptance just as we are, but also being a representative of divine judgment and forgiveness as we wish we could be but know we are not.

These differences also caused confusion about the nature and intent of the small process group experience in CPE. It is the contention of this study that under the influence of humanistic psychology in the 1960s the student group experience tilted toward becoming overly therapeutic, focusing almost exclusively on 1) interpersonal dynamics and 2) personal feedback in a cohesive group environment. This trend continues to the present day.

It is the further contention of this study that these two tasks of the SPG are secondary to, and subsumed under, a third task—experiencing and studying the group-as-a-whole process as understood in the psychoanalytic tradition. Work with students involving interpersonal dynamics and personal feedback in the small group always needs to take place within this larger framework. Otherwise the purpose of the small process group as an *open agenda study group* in CPE is compromised and the delicate balance between change (therapy) and knowledge (learning) inherent in this kind of experiential education is lost.

This book explores the history of process-group work in CPE as well as current theory and practice from the "inside." Through the use of a comprehensive literature review, a survey of current theory papers, and a review of videotaped group material, an effective three-part "fix" on the subject matter is achieved which demonstrates the current strengths and weaknesses of small-group work in CPE. Out of this groundwork, an integrative psychological theory is proposed which takes into account the CPE historical and psychological tradition as well as its continuing contribution to theological education.

The first chapter presents a brief history of the pastoral care movement with particular focus on the development of CPE and the Association for Clinical Pastoral Education within the liberal Protestant tradition. Chapters 2 and 3 summarize over eighty articles found in the literature. This material amply demonstrates the beginnings of small-group work in CPE and the variety of approaches, concerns, and tensions which emerged over five decades. Chapter 4 summarizes group theories and various issues concerning group work as these have been developed and refined in the fields of psychiatry, sociology, and humanistic psychology in the twentieth century. It concludes by pointing out issues of current concern.

Using a qualitative and phenomenological approach to research, chapter 5 summarizes the results of the author's reading of one hundred position papers written by candidates for supervisory certification in ACPE between 1988 and 1992. It also summarizes the viewing by the author of fifteen videotapes of small-group process work done by CPE supervisors in different training centers in the Eastern Region of ACPE during 1992-93. Chapter 6 presents the psychological foundations for an integrative theory for group process work in CPE based on the psychoanalytic tradition and object relations theory. Chapter 7 uses my supervision of one of my own CPE groups to demonstrate the need for such a group theory and its consequent application. This chapter concludes with a list of recommendations for CPE programs, CPE supervisors, and supervisory candidates. Chapter 8 places the significance of group process work in CPE in the larger context of religious experience based on current conceptual work in the field of psychology of religion.

In navigating our way through these waters, it is important to recognize and accept the fact that the specialized craft called CPE rides within the rich and sometimes rapid confluence of many different streams of influence: psychology and religion, education and therapy, experience (intuition) and knowledge (cognition), faith and culture, modernity and tradition, the individual and the group. Sometimes it steers too enthusiastically and quickly toward one particularly attractive shore; sometimes it becomes too careful or vague in order to stay afloat in the middle of the river; sometimes it overreaches itself and is in danger of tipping over or being swept out to sea. To successfully pilot the CPE craft–and especially exploration of its small process-group work–requires an ability to skillfully ride the waves and read the currents. It requires an ability to look below the surface and patiently map out both old and new contours. It also requires an ability to find the calm spots and enjoy some interesting scenery along the way. In the process the relative seaworthiness of our craft will become evident, as will the accuracy to guide it home.

1

CPE From a Historical Perspective

PART ONE: SETTING THE SCENE

With our late-twentieth-century eyes, it is difficult to imagine the immensity of social and economic change which took place in the United States between 1860 and 1900. These decades began violently with a deepening national crisis over the institution of slavery, leading to the slaughter of thousands in a civil war which tore the country apart. The same decades ended noisily with an industrial revolution which would bring both great wealth and productivity and also poison and deplete the country's natural resources. Bounded on one side by the publication of Charles Darwin's *Origin of Species* (1859) and on the other side by Sigmund Freud's *Interpretation of Dreams* (1900), these four decades marked a sea of change in how we were to understand the human situation–its origins, its meaning, its relationships, and its destiny.

There were a number of factors which contributed to the rapid change. The invention of the steam engine gave a new dynamism and energy to post-Civil War society. The mass influx of European immigrants during the 1870s forced a new social tolerance and religious pluralism. The rise of urbanization and technology, a nationwide railroad system, and a new class of entrepreneurs called Robber Barons created a Gilded Age known for its inventiveness and greed. Thus, the story of these four decades is filled with both wondrous tales of accomplishment and adventure as well as worried laments about dislocation, alienation, moral decay, and rapid change. Knowing all this, it is understandable that Henry Adams, eminent historian of the period, expressed his own sense of dislocation:

> My country in 1900 is something totally different from my own country of 1860. I am wholly a stranger in it.

1

Neither I, nor anyone else, understands it. The turning
of a nebula into a star may somewhat resemble the
change. All I can see is that it is one of compression,
concentration, and consequent development of terrific
energy, represented not by souls, but by coals and iron
and steam (Niebuhr, Williams, and Ahlstrom 1980, 250).

During this time of "the turning of a nebula into a star," the religious
world of American Protestantism was also changing. What has been called
"the essential unity of evangelical orthodoxy at mid-century" was breaking up
(Niebuhr, Williams, and Ahlstrom 1980, 251). From a theological point of
view, the providential nature and will of a transcendent God in special
relationship with His chosen (American) people was not as clear or compelling
a philosophical framework as it once had been. From a political perspective, a
people who had previously considered themselves to be "one [Protestant] nation
under God" was now faced with a sizable number of Roman Catholic immigrants
as well as nonbelievers in their midst. From a moral perspective, the growing
ravages of social ills and new excesses of material greed evident by the end of
the century had called into question long-accepted ethical prohibitions of a
Puritan nation founded on Christian principles. Apparently the delicate balance
between the will of God and the freedom and trustworthiness of human activity
shifted.

Growing differences in the ranks of the clergy accentuated the loss of
religious consensus. Evangelical ministers continued to preach salvation through
conversion in a revivalistic tradition, and were largely unaffected by and
indifferent toward the vast changes going on around them. Fundamentalistic
preachers insisted on biblical inerrancy, resisting pressures to respond to the
new developments in science and industry. In contrast, some urban pastors
aligned with social reformers were more open to worldly challenge, seeking to
enlarge the scope of the institutional church and its response to both social ills
and technological advancements by giving birth to an energetic Social Gospel
movement.

Among all these responses, it was the so-called liberal minister who was
most willing and open to the intellectual and emotional currents of the day.
This was not surprising since the guiding principle of liberal thought–whether
theological, philosophical, or political–was always free inquiry. A prominent
example was the Reverend Henry Ward Beecher, who delivered the Beecher
lectures at Yale in 1871. In contrast to the evangelical faith of his famous father
for whom the lectures were originally named, the younger Beecher made it

clear that engagement with the new scientific and technological spirit was now essential for theological relevance and a lively faith. Speaking to his fellow ministers he importuned:

> There is no class of people upon earth who can less afford to let the development of truth run ahead of them than you. You cannot wrap yourselves in professional mystery...you cannot go back and become apostles of the dead past, drivelling after ceremonies, and letting the world do the thinking and studying. There must be a new spirit infused into the ministry....We must be more industrious in investigation, more honest in deduction, and more willing to take the truth in its new fullness (Niebuhr, Williams, and Ahlstrom 1980, 257-8).

Such willingness to view both the Darwinian revolution and American industrial achievements as part of God's continuing evolutionary work on earth signaled a major shift in religious thinking. This "evolutionary teleology" (Holifield 1983, 166) assumed a developmental framework in which genuine achievement grew out of struggle and daily involvement. Instead of the *preacher* trying to persuade sinful people to conform to the will of a transcendent God, it was now incumbent upon the *pastor* to also point out and participate with his people in the divine impulse actively at work in the world. By the end of the nineteenth century, liberal religious leaders responded to these changes by shifting attention from a more or less exclusive focus on preaching and evangelism to an increasingly varied ministry, including the creation of outreach programs and social clubs within the church. Thus, a "natural style" of pastoral leadership began to develop in which there was growing interest in the dynamics of interpersonal relationships and the subjective experiences of people of faith (Holifield 1983, 166).

This shift resulted in a growing distinction in seminary education between the so-called practical and classical branches of the curriculum. Among the first to introduce the practical approach were the Hartford School of Pedagogy, Andover Theological School, and Boston University School of Theology. In his landmark study *A History of Pastoral Care in America*, Holifield comments that

> the purpose of pastoral theology [at this time] was still to teach more effective ways of appealing for a decision–

a decision to believe, to reform, or to face difficulty
bravely. But the pastoral writers now suggested that the
ministers' manner in evoking the proper responses was
almost as important as their message and that *a different
kind of clerical style could produce a different kind of
pastoral relationship*" (176; italics added).

The development of pastoral theology as a practical or applied discipline would
essentially open the way to a growing interest by religious liberals in human
development and behavior. This interest would find its locus in what would
become the full-blown field of psychology in the twentieth century.

Another development in the late nineteenth century which would affect
the world of religion was the growth of a distinct professional class. In 1878
the American Bar Association was formed and in 1901 the American Medical
Association was reorganized. Learned societies increased in number in the
universities, and public institutions became concerned with standards and
accreditation. Prior to the Civil War, ninety percent of college presidents had
been ordained ministers. This trend did not continue. In fact, between 1850
and 1895, while the total graduates of Yale University doubled, the number
who entered the ministry decreased by more than sixty percent (Niebuhr,
Williams, and Ahlstrom 1980, 279). Though lowering of academic caliber and
lessening of religious fervor were not necessarily the reasons for this situation,
the general decline of religious leadership in public and educational institutions
no doubt "intensified a long-standing sense of clerical insecurity," especially in
relationship to medicine and law (Holifield 1983, 172-3). These developments
also intensified the historic tension within the religious world itself between
ministry as a response to inner conviction and ministry as a profession requiring
specific education and training.

In 1902 William James, distinguished American philosopher and
psychologist, delivered the Gifford Lectures at Edinburgh which were
subsequently published under the title *Varieties of Religious Experience*. James
was already the leading philosophical proponent of pragmatism and voluntarism,
well known for his classic *Principles of Psychology*, which had been published
in 1890. In this new work James emphasized religious experience over dogma,
the essential unity of body and soul, and his conviction that by getting in touch
with the "subconscious," human energy is released that can lead to transformation
and healing –which he sometimes called "the More" (James 1958, 384). All
these "new" ideas contributed to the growing progressivism of American culture,

optimism within liberal religion, and interest in the relationship between the practice of ministry and the new science of psychology.

One of the first ministers to take seriously the relationship between psychology and pastoral practice was Elwood Worcester. Graduating from Columbia College in 1886, Worcester received his theological degree from General Theological Seminary and then earned a doctorate in psychology from the University of Leipzig. In 1904 he became rector of Emmanuel Church, the largest Episcopal Church in Boston. Convinced that spiritual healing was intensely personal and that the Social Gospel movement was inadequate in this regard, Worcester teamed up with several prominent physicians to offer classes and groups for those suffering from what were then called "functional nervous disorders"–hysteria, hypochondria, morbid fears, and worries. Interest in Worcester's efforts, which used a type of "suggestion therapy" based on hypnosis, quickly grew from several hundred clients to several thousand. With the resulting national publicity, the Emmanuel Movement was born as "the first American venture between clergy and doctors in the cure of souls" within historic mainline Protestantism (Stokes 1987, 25). It was the precursor to what would become the religion and health movement in the United States.

Though the Emmanuel Movement itself was to be short-lived, Freud's visit in 1909 to Clark University in Worcester, Massachusetts, certainly came at a propitious time. Interestingly, the invitation was extended by the pioneering President of Clark, G. Stanley Hall, a graduate of Union Theological Seminary who, like Elwood Worcester, had studied psychology in Germany.[1] In the United States, the medical profession had only recently distinguished between functional and organic mental illness. In 1906 a separate category for psychotherapy was included in the official index of medical papers for that year. While ideas of the subconscious as part of an untapped creative energy in human nature were widely known, Freud's idea that an *unconscious* is formed out of repression of chaotic infantile sexual instincts was revolutionary, not only to the medical profession but also to those engaged in pastoral work. It was William James who at the time predicted that "the future of psychology belonged to Freud" (Holifield 1985, 195). However, it would be well into the twentieth century before the far-reaching implications of Freud's ideas would be fully realized.

It was out of this increasingly fertile mixture of religious and psychological nutrients within the American soil of pragmatism and rapid change that the clinical pastoral education (CPE) movement would be born. A sign of the

---

[1] Hall received the first American doctorate in psychology from Harvard University in 1878.

coming times occurred in 1913 on the floor of the General Convention of the Protestant Episcopal Church when the Reverend William Palmer Ladd, a prominent Boston clergyman, suggested that the church should require some kind of clinical training for its seminarians. This development reflected the spreading interest in various sectors of the church and the culture for new types of education and training for ministry.

In addition to these influences, the Social Gospel movement and the new field of sociology would also have an impact on pastoral practice. In the early 1900s Graham Taylor, a Dutch Reformed minister and sociologist, held the first chair in Christian Sociology in the United States at Chicago Theological Seminary. One historian recounts that in his inauguration address,

> he told the students that their chief textbooks would be people, the men and women of the shops, the factories, the streets. He said he would establish a clinic similar to those used by medical students, where they would study the cause and cure of poverty, intemperance and crime, and the relationships of heredity and the environment and their influence on the making of character...[In the clinic] his students met with him and his staff and compared notes on their week's activities...Discussion follows each student's presentation of his facts gathered at firsthand, questions are raised, the next steps planned, and Professor Taylor draws the meeting to a close by showing the relation of their work to the up-building of the kingdom of God on earth (Kemp 1947, 155-6).

By the 1920s field work and clinical training similar to Taylor's earlier vision would begin to appear as part of the curriculum in a number of theological seminaries.

The intellectual influence of John Dewey (1859-1952), philosopher, educator, and proponent of democracy, contributed its own momentum to the increasing experimentation and change which was taking place in American educational institutions. His *Democracy and Education* (1916) outlined education as a process which reconstructs experience and leads toward growth. By encouraging a kind of utilitarianism, Dewey emphasized that knowledge was a useful tool rather than an abstract endeavor, that the evolution of truth arrived at by doing (i.e., through actual experience) is at the heart of the educational endeavor. The idea that how to think (process) was more important than what to think (content), that method affects outcome, would become foundational to subsequent developments in training for ministry and theological education (Hall 1992, 3).

The field of liberal religious education, increasingly attracted to psychology and evolutionary science itself, welcomed Dewey's ideas. In 1909 George Albert Coe became professor of religious education at Union Seminary in New York and next-door neighbor to Dewey, who was teaching at the Teacher's College of Columbia University on Morningside Heights. Increasingly aware of the therapeutic implications of his approach to religious education, Coe did not hesitate to talk about "the care of souls" and the need to "assist in self-realization" as germane to the educational task (Holifield 1983, 225). Accordingly, it was actually the early religious educators who first "became known as 'psychologists' within the seminaries and churches...[and] set the stage for the appearance of a 'modern pastoral psychology'" (Holifield 1985, 225-26).[2]

Thus, as the first two decades of the twentieth century were completed, the worlds of psychology and liberal religion were intersecting and influencing each other in some unusually creative and unexpected ways. Driven by such basic American cultural values as emotional optimism, educational utilitarianism, technological pragmatism, and the belief in scientific progressivism, the country saw a major resurgence of idealism and renewal of growth which was only temporarily curtailed by the tragedy of World War I. Increased commitment to self-understanding through the influence of both education and psychology had caused a theological shift as well. Moving from a previous dependence upon achieving salvation for one's sinful soul through the gracious intervention of an all-powerful God, the focus was now upon expectations for self-realization through active engagement in the world and within human experience where God's presence was manifest. It was out of this shifting theological milieu that a new type of training for the preparation of future ministers would be born in the 1920s.

---

[2] Harrison Elliott, who followed Coe at Union Seminary in the 1920s, based his own religious education course work on Freud, Sullivan, and Adler. Carl Rogers was one of Elliott's students, as was Seward Hiltner.

PART TWO: THE FOUNDING

In his classic study *Professional Education for Ministry: A History of Clinical Pastoral Education* (1970), Edward Thornton names three "fathers" as the actual founders of clinical pastoral education. Thornton points out that although each of these men was quite different in their interest, motivation, and situation, "in each instance the new profession emerged as a result of the creative interaction of a theological educator and a concerned medical doctor" (40). The close relationship between the health professional on the one hand and the religious professional on the other, continues to the present day as a key pattern in the clinical pastoral education movement. A second collaborative influence which served as both bridge and impetus came from the emerging field of social work.

William S. Keller, a physician from Cincinnati and active layman in the Episcopal church, was convinced that people in ministry had much to learn from the fields of social work and community organization if they were to be effective in bringing about improved social conditions. A great believer in learning by doing, he joined forces with Dean Samuel Mercer of Bexley Hall, an Episcopal seminary in central Ohio, in order to institute a program of clinical training. In the summer of 1923 Dr. Keller housed five theological students in his home. They were assigned to work in various social agencies (mental hospital, human relations court, public welfare agency) in the Cincinnati area. On the weekends they reported to Keller on their work and explored its relevance for the ministry (Thornton 1970, 43). What came to be known as the Bexley Hall Plan quickly grew to include Episcopal students from other seminaries and as many as thirty-six social agencies. In 1927 Keller engaged an Episcopal priest to help him with student supervision. This interdisciplinary model of supervision would come to be highly valued in clinical pastoral education.

In the mid-1930s this summer program expanded to year-round and was established as the Graduate School of Applied Religion (GSAR) with its own buildings and Dean, the Reverend Joseph Fletcher. Within a few years most theological students at GSAR were engaged as social caseworkers by Cincinnati's Family Service Society, which provided the clinical settings. Within ten years an effort was made to relate GSAR more closely to theological education by making it part of the Episcopal Theological School in Cambridge, Massachusetts. As the clinical training movement increasingly emphasized individual healing and quality pastoral supervision rather than efforts in social engineering and community organization, the School of Applied Religion diverged from the mainstream and eventually closed in the mid-1960s. It is important to note that the desire to bring about social change was part of the initial agenda for ministry preparation in these earliest years. The story of GSAR illustrates some of the tensions in clinical pastoral education between the private and the public, the pastoral and the prophetic, individual growth and the wider social good. Efforts to address this lack of balance are reflected in growing concerns about public issues within the pastoral care movement since the mid-1980s.

The second father-founder was Richard C. Cabot, a prominent Boston physician at Massachusetts General Hospital and a Unitarian. Cabot is noted for his introduction of social work into that hospital in 1905. He was among those in the original group which began the Emmanuel Movement with Elwood Worcester. An interview with Cabot which was featured in the Boston *Post* on December 27, 1908 was entitled "Physician and Minister Must Work Together to Cure the Sick." It reads in part:

> Therefore, the work of helping a patient belongs to others as well as to the doctor. It belongs to someone who can doctor his moral as well as his physical ills. A physician specializes on the body, and the minister makes his specialty the human soul. The two should co-operate. There ought to be a school somewhere which would take up the subject thoroughly, and ministers should take the course (Billinsky 1954, 15).

When he reached the age of fifty, Cabot left the field of medicine and accepted a chair at Harvard University in the field of ethics. In 1925, long concerned with professional education in both medicine and ministry, Cabot suggested to some "theologs" from Episcopal Theological School that they approach Anton Boisen, the newly hired Chaplain at Worcester State Hospital, for a summer course of "clinical training." This is considered to be the first official unit of clinical training.

Cabot worked with, and at times financially supported, three key pastoral/theological leaders in the Boston area who were interested in "clinical theology" and on-the-job training for ministry: Anton Boisen at Worcester State, Philip Guiles at Andover Newton Theological School, and Russell Dicks, who became chaplain at Massachusetts General Hospital. Cabot had a particular interest in "the growth of souls" and coined the term *growing edge* as a personal and spiritual concept. He used metaphors from medicine and biology to make his point:

> Not many years ago it was discovered that we can
> cultivate a bit of human muscle or kidney outside the
> body and watch the details of its growth. The tissue
> puts out new columns of cells like the rows of bricks
> added as we build a brick wall...The growing edge,
> jagged and irregular, is the surface out of which new
> cells sprout. Something like this happens in the sapwood
> of a tree just beneath the bark and at the edge of every
> fresh leaf. The soul has a growing edge. It can advance
> only from the point where just now it is (Cabot and Dicks
> 1936, 13-4).

Among the plethora of Cabot's contributions to medicine and clinical
education, none has been more lasting than his Clinical Pathological
Conferences. In these learning labs he would challenge students to make
differential diagnoses based on their reading of the record and listening to
autopsy reports. Cabot would make his diagnosis on the spot while listening to
histories but without reading the medical record. At the end of the conference
the official diagnosis was shared by the pathologist.

This method of using case histories combined with professional self-
exposure in the clinical training of medical students became a key element in
clinical pastoral education. It developed into a tool called the verbatim, a written
record of the pastoral conversation originally developed by Chaplain Russell
Dicks in the early 1930s and based on his earlier experience in the Clinical
Pathological Conference. The partnership between medicine and ministry is
no better exemplified than in the Cabot/Dicks alliance. Their influential book
The Art of Ministering to the Sick elucidated such key ideas for the minister's
"kitbag" as directed listening, rituals of the sickroom, the use of silence in
pastoral visitation, and "notetaking as creative work." Such basic helps could
be of benefit to any chaplain working in the modern hospital today.

The third father-founder, and probably the most beloved by succeeding
generations, was Anton Boisen (1876-1965). Boisen was raised in Bloomington,
Indiana, in a family of educators and ministers in the liberal tradition. He
began a career as a language teacher, switched to forestry, and in 1905
experienced a call to the ministry. He writes about his entry into Union Seminary
in 1908: "There was no provision in its curriculum for the consideration of the
subject in which I was especially interested, the psychology of religion as
interpreted by William James" (Boisen 1960, 60). Happily for Boisen, George
Albert Coe was to arrive at Union the next year. After graduating from the

seminary, Boisen did rural survey work for the Presbyterian Board of Home Missions. He also held short pastorates in a number of rural churches. However, Boisen was not to find his true vocation until well into mid-life.

Boisen had suffered the loss of his father when he was seven years old and the loss of his grandfather when he was twenty. In addition, Boisen was always a shy, introverted man who experienced lifelong jealousy toward his vivacious, younger sister. From age twenty-two on, especially during times of vocational uncertainty, Boisen underwent a series of mental breakdowns, some worse than others. He was often obsessed with his unfulfilled love toward a woman, Alice Batchelder, whom he first met in 1902.[3] When a serious psychotic episode occurred in October 1920, Boisen spent three weeks in Boston Psychopathic Hospital. At this time Fred Eastman, a classmate and friend from his Union Seminary days, sent Boisen the *Introductory Lectures* of Sigmund Freud. In a letter to Eastman, Boisen reports being "very excited" by this material (Asquith 1992, 6). It was out of this experience that Boisen decided to study his own mental illness. He had become convinced that it held the key to his understanding of the human/divine situation.[4]

Boisen's focus from the beginning was on research into the human condition, specifically the terrors of mental illness as a religious problem rather than solely as a medical concern. He was convinced that psychotic episodes were emotional efforts to reorganize and heal the soul, and therefore, no serious student of religion could be in the pastoral field without an understanding of this phenomenon. After the death of Alice Batchelder, Boisen was able to write his remarkable book on the phenomena of mental illness entitled *The Exploration of the Inner World* (1936).[5] Boisen was passionate in his commitment and radically experiential in his approach:

> Not in any revelation handed down from the past, not in anything that can be demonstrated in test-tube or under the microscope, not in systems found in books, nor in rules and techniques taken over from successful workers would I seek the basis of spiritual healing, but in the

---

[3] Boisen never married. One person has commented: "Emotional celibacy was his answer to his anxiety over affection" (Cedarleaf 1987, 5).

[4] Few people know that Milton Erickson was Boisen's therapist at Worcester State Hospital in 1930. One author attributes Boisen's positive attitude toward the healing potential of his own unconscious material to Erickson's therapeutic approach of reframing (Close 1981).

[5] The culmination of Boisen's personal integrative efforts is chronicled in his autobiography *Out of the Depths* (1960).

> *living human documents* in all their complexity and in
> all their elusiveness and in the tested insights of the wise
> and noble of the past as well as of the present. To the
> ability to read these human documents in the light of
> the best human understanding, there is no royal road. It
> calls for that which is beyond anything that books or
> lectures or schools can impart and to which only a few
> can attain (1936, 248-9; italics added).

Boisen's quest for healing and understanding led to his taking a course on the clinical case conference method from Richard Cabot at Harvard and, fortuitously, being hired by Superintendent Dr. William A. Bryan as the first chaplain at Worcester State Hospital in 1924.[6] The next five years saw steady growth in the clinical training movement with several students in Boisen's first groups becoming organizational and inspirational leaders: Philip Guiles at Andover Newton Theological School, Helen Flanders Dunbar, M.D., in the New York area, Carroll Wise as Boisen's successor at Worcester State, and Russell Dicks at Massachusetts General. In January 1930 the Council for Clinical Training of Theological Students (CCTTS) was officially organized. Among those to sign the papers were Richard Cabot, William A. Bryan, and Anton Boisen. The central importance of Cabot to these developments is signaled by the use of his home address in Cambridge on the incorporation papers. But shortly thereafter there would begin an unfortunate and extensive period of fragmentation and competition within the fledgling clinical training movement.

The first problem occurred because Richard Cabot had never been able to accept the psychosomatic or functional understanding of the genesis of mental illness and was, therefore, deeply at odds with Boisen. When Boisen's mother died in the early 1930s and he experienced another serious psychotic episode, Cabot decided he could no longer give his support (financial and professional) to Boisen at Worcester. As a result, by 1932 Anton Boisen was to take a position as chaplain at Elgin State Hospital in Illinois, combining this with the part-time teaching post at Chicago Theological Seminary he had held for over a decade.

The second problem occurred when the charismatic Philip Guiles and strong-willed Helen Flanders Dunbar, out of growing personal animosity, were

---

[6] Bryan's response to criticism from his medical peers about this innovative decision has become legendary. "He said 'he would be perfectly willing to bring in a horse doctor if he thought there was any chance of his being able to help the patients!'" (Boisen 1936, 9).

no longer able to work together. Dr. Dunbar's response to this situation was simply to move the headquarters of the Council to New York and change its name to the Council for Clinical Training (CCT). With the decision of Carroll Wise to go with the New York group despite his position at Worcester State Hospital, plus the continued strong presence of Richard Cabot in the Boston area, the New Englanders decided to focus their training efforts in medical rather than mental hospital settings. Guiles, with financial help from a family foundation, developed a new organization, the New England Theological Schools Committee on Clinical Training. Though this group would not be officially incorporated as the Institute of Pastoral Care (IPC) until 1944, substantive differences between the New York and Boston educators grew deeper throughout the 1930s.

A number of authors have elucidated these differences (Thornton 1970, Powell 1975a, Holifield 1983, Hall 1992). First, the New England group kept their training programs more closely connected to theological schools, both in spirit and administratively. A seminary president or dean was usually named president of the Institute. In their clinical programs the New England Group focused on the student-patient relationship. They were primarily interested in the development of pastoral skills, the application of theological concepts to pastoral care, and in training people for parish ministry. Their supervisors tended to hold a graduate academic degree beyond the basic theological degree and were trained to search for an integration of the conceptual and the practical in what was called "clinical theology."

In contrast, the New York group was increasingly influenced by the medical (that is, psychoanalytic) rather than theological tradition, believing that it was only through a psychodynamic understanding of one's own emotions that pastoral competence could be achieved. Freedom for such work necessitated an administrative organization separate from the influence of the seminaries, complete with its own standards for training and supervision. The institutionalization of this approach became one of the major contributions of the CCT to the movement. Another contribution was the expansion of training programs beyond mental hospitals into correctional and veterans' hospitals.

At a deeper level, the Boston and New York supervisors were torn between two conflicting views of the self, both of which grew out of the progressivism and liberalism of the times (Holifield 1983). In his cogent article on clinical pastoral education published in the *Dictionary of Pastoral Care and Counseling*, Edward Thornton summarizes these differences. He points out that the New Englanders basically lived out of the optimistic once-born religious experience described by William James. Here a combination of rational discourse, common sense and hard work could overcome self-deception and immorality and lead to purposive growth and ethical formation. This attitude, along with trust in an immanent divinity, would "carry one to health and meaning in life" (Thornton 1990, 178). In contrast, the New York group understood the self as being fraught with conflict and irrationality and potential chaos. This was the pessimistic twice-born view of William James in which freedom and self-actualization could only be achieved by understanding and working through inner conflicts and rigidities and, in the process, undergoing a conversion or enlightening experience–by the grace of God. The publication in the same year (1936) of both Cabot and Dicks's *Art of Ministering to the Sick* and Anton Boisen's *The Exploration of the Inner World* gave dramatic evidence of the basic divergence of these two points of view (Thornton 1990, 179).

The introduction of the clinical method of learning was not unique to theological education. Similar developments were occurring in other professions which influenced seminary curricula. As early as the 1870s, the case-study method had been introduced into law schools. With the appearance of the Flexner Reports in 1910 and 1912, the medical profession was forced to upgrade its training in response to scientific developments already occurring in the universities. At the first meeting in 1918 of the Conference of Theological Seminaries (later to become the American Association of Theological Schools or ATS), one session was entirely devoted to the responsibility of seminaries to provide professional education. Another session focused on the use of the case-study method.

The Kelly Study in 1924 was theological education's wake-up call. Inspired by the Flexner Reports in particular, and the pervasive influence of progressive education in general, the Kelly Study was based on a social survey of 161 theological schools of which at least half, according to the outspoken author, could not qualify as educational institutions (Thornton 1970, 25). At the end of the report special commendation was given to those few theological schools which sponsored supervised field work programs. The result was that by 1930, even the deans of prestigious Harvard Divinity School and Chicago Divinity School were in agreement on the need to modify the traditional classical curriculum in favor of a more professional approach, including greater contact with the behavioral sciences. Though barely a decade had passed since that first training unit with Boisen at Worcester, in 1936 the Committee on Supervised Training of the Association of Theological Schools made special note of "the high value of clinical training" toward which it felt "not a single doubt" (Hall 1992, 5).

The situation in liberal Protestantism which gave such welcome to these developments was not without its critics. Troubling social events during the early 1930s, beginning with the Great Depression, challenged the optimism of theological liberalism and its easy tendency to identify with educational progressivism and achievements of the culture. H. Richard Niebuhr's translation of Paul Tillich's *The Religious Situation* presented an early critique of true religious faith as antithetical to culture. Niebuhr himself emphasized divine revelation as essentially judgmental and critical of human endeavor. Along with his theologian brother, Reinhold Niebuhr, this new group of theological realists was beginning to recover "a traditional doctrine of sinfulness that the liberals had forgotten" (Holifield 1983, 256) and which would be confirmed in the years ahead by the onset of World War II.

In 1939 Rollo May, a pastor and part-time professor at Garrett Theological School in Chicago, published *The Art of Counseling*, based on the work of Freud, Adler, Rank, and other European psychoanalytic thinkers. This book was immediately popular and became largely responsible for the general spread of psychoanalytic ideas among many liberal clergy in the United States. Anton Boisen described the book as an "enlightened" presentation of psychotherapy for religious workers (Holifield 1983, 251). In line with the theological realists, May was less optimistic about the possibilities for growth and achievement, and more aware of the basic conflict between freedom and determinism.

In reviewing developments among clinical pastoral educators at the end of the 1930s, it has been noted that beyond the political differences there were at least three strands present in the pastoral care and training movement. There were those who wanted training to focus on pastoral formation and skill development, those who wanted to focus on the study of sin and salvation in the "living human document," and still others who were primarily interested in the psychoanalytic approach as a means to inner liberation and readiness for ministry (Holifield 1983, 258). This tripartite division epitomized well the growing differences between Cabot and Dicks in the New England group, Anton Boisen's original intentions, and the approach of Dunbar's New York group.

It was Seward Hiltner who first began to pull together the frayed strands of the early clinical training movement. Having met Boisen while attending the Divinity School at the University of Chicago in the late 1920s, Hiltner did CPE first with Don Beatty at Maywood Hospital in Pittsburgh and later with Carroll Wise at Worcester.[7] After earning his Ph.D. in religion and personality

---

[7] A delightful piece of poetry entitled "Doggerel Days in CPE" recounts these early years (Hiltner 1980).

at Chicago, Hiltner became executive secretary to the Council for Clinical Training in 1935, working closely with Helen Flanders Dunbar.[8] He was also a mainstay in the little-known but highly influential "New York psychology group" which met weekly to discuss issues of religion and mental health and included such notables as Paul Tillich, Rollo May, Erich Fromm, and David Roberts (Stokes 1985, 109-42).

Hiltner went on to work with the Department of Pastoral Services of the National Council of Churches and eventually returned to the Divinity School at the University of Chicago to become Professor of Religion and Personality (1950). It was his intellectual contributions which most helped to establish pastoral psychology and clinical pastoral education as legitimate theological and pastoral enterprises. It was toward Hiltner, long considered a centrist in the differences between Boston and New York, that Philip Guiles turned in order to suggest that representatives from the two organizations meet. As a result, in June 1944 the first national conference of clinical pastoral educators convened at Western Theological Seminary in Pittsburgh. This meeting heralded the development of the clinical pastoral education movement as it is known today.

PART THREE: COMING OF AGE

It was significant that the 1944 gathering took place immediately following the annual meeting of the American Association of Theological Schools and that twenty-seven of the fifty participants were seminary representatives. The keynote speaker was Everett C. Herrick, President of Andover Newton Theological School. He emphasized the focus of the conference on the relationship between clinical training and theology:

> I would like, therefore, to consider not the place of clinical training in a theological curriculum, but the place of theology in a clinical curriculum. What we are really dealing with is a clinical theology. There is a practice of theology for the cure of souls, just as truly as there is a practice of medicine for the cure of bodies...This is the kind of theology that every pastor needs...It is the affirmation and expression of our Christian faith made

---

[8] They were not always in agreement and in 1938 Hiltner was replaced by Robert Brinkman, a CCT supervisor with a decidedly psychoanalytic approach.

available for the deepest needs of the human soul. As the medical schools send out men to practice medicine, so it is the function of our seminaries to send out men to practice theology (1945, 79, 81).

Charles Hall in his recent book, *Head and Heart: The Story of the Clinical Pastoral Education Movement* (1992), identifies "clinical theology" as a dialogic process which was to become the fundamental rubric of clinical pastoral education. Engagement in the process leads to shaping a theological and pastoral foundation which is uniquely "open to new insights about God and humans" (xv). In Hall's retrospective view, it was precisely through the dialectic inherent in clinical theology that the differences between New Englanders and New Yorkers, theologians and clinicians, theory and experience, head and heart would be experienced and eventually resolved.

The most significant accomplishment of the 1944 meeting was a statement of agreement about CPE by the three major organizations offering training: the Council of Clinical Training, the Institute of Pastoral Care, and the Graduate School of Applied Religion. Issues around which consensus developed included supervision by an ordained and trained person, student work in a clinical situation, student notetaking which is discussed with the supervisor, didactic instruction, and integration of the training into the seminary curriculum (Hiltner 1945, 56-7). Their work together was formalized by an official vote and made possible continuing exchange between people and ideas from each group throughout the 1940s and beyond.

The movement was indebted for this accomplishment to Seward Hiltner, who was "wise in the use of strategy"–that is, he did not press the psychodynamic agenda of the New York group (Hall 1992, 52). But outside pressures were also influential. On a practical level, theological schools interested in CPE for their students were not interested in internal disputes among the clinical educators. Second, as the post-war years dawned there was a surge of interest in clinical training. The more than 8,000 chaplains who had gone off to war had discovered that people in need wanted to talk and that such in-depth listening required learning new pastoral skills. Third, a new spirit of cooperation was generally in the air, bringing forth such organizations as the United Nations and the National Council of Churches by the end of the decade. In the field of pastoral care in 1946 the College of Chaplains became a division of the American Protestant Hospital Association and the Lutherans created their own endorsing agency for chaplaincy. The Association for Mental Health Chaplains formed their own organization in 1948. Most importantly, publishing efforts among leaders in the clinical training movement joined forces. Although in 1947 the CCT and IPC each established their own journals, by 1949 they would agree on joint sponsorship of *The Journal of Pastoral Care*. This development assured not only a professional locus for communication, but also ongoing cross-fertilization of ideas between the two differing organizations in the years to come.

The post-war years heralded the emergence of psychology as a significant influence in American culture. Career counselors, personality tests, and industrial psychologists proliferated and were helped along by congressional legislation, especially the 1946 National Mental Health Act which provided clinics and services under government sponsorship. Among clinical educators and seminary students new methods of counseling were greatly enhanced by Carl Rogers's book *Counseling and Psychotherapy* (1942). Briefly a student at Union Seminary in the 1930s, Rogers went on to become a proponent of a new kind of "nondirective" counseling in which a supportive environment and "reflective listening" were purported to be effective pastoral skills which enhance psychological health and personal growth. Carl Rogers's client-centered approach would continue to have a strong influence upon pastoral theology, pastoral care, and a student-directed approach to learning for the next fifty years in clinical pastoral education.

Even more than the realists H. Richard and Reinhold Niebuhr, Paul Tillich was to exert a major influence on the field of pastoral psychology and its clinical pastoral educators. Using his method of correlation, Tillich sought connections between the psychoanalytic and the theological, the immanent and transcendent. In his popular book of sermons, *The Courage To Be* (1952), Tillich's theme of accepting the unacceptable (i.e., justification by grace) reached deep into the hearts of clinical educators and Protestant ministers alike. Tillich's fascination with making both the depths of psychological experience and the heights of theological doctrine cohere within the human situation marks him as the major influence within the modern pastoral care and counseling field.

In the clinical training movement, the 1950s turned out to be "a time of intense dialogue" focussing on the work of a group which came to be called the Committee of Twelve (Hall 1992, 69). This leadership group was formed in response to the Lutheran Council's desire to be included in any possible merger between the IPC and CCT. The Committee was composed of three representatives each from IPC, CCT, the Lutherans, and the Association for Seminary Professors in the Practical Field. During the 1950s the Committee of Twelve convened annual national conferences of pastoral educators, formulated the first set of Standards (1953), and presided over increasingly heated discussions concerning joint (i.e., agreed upon and shared) accreditation of supervisors. Other lively issues included debate about CPE as education versus CPE as therapy, training for specialization vs. training for parish ministry, sorting out issues of program content (accreditation) vs. the dynamic process of interpersonal supervision (certification), and administrative location of programs. Reverberations from these themes continue to the present day.

The 1956 Conference held in Atlantic City featured six major presentations by theologians and supervisors, including papers by Paul Tillich and James Gustafson. During the conference Frederick Kuether, a CCT supervisor, presented an apt summary of the movement up to that time. Kuether saw early founders in the 1920s asking the question "What must I *do* to be of help?" With the advent of the case study/verbatim method and emphasis on skill development in the 1930s, the question became: "What must I *know* to be of help?" During the 1940s a shift of focus to the dynamics of the student-patient relationship focused on, "What must I *say* to be of help?" And finally, with the pervasive influence of psychodynamic psychology in the 1950s, the question became: "What must I *be* to be of help?" (Hall 1992, 98-100). Though probably too facile and no doubt reflective of the tilt toward the therapeutic among CCT supervisors, Kuether's address nevertheless gave a sense of theoretical integration and historical perspective which was much needed. By the end of the 1950s, despite the lack of organizational unity, there were 117 training centers and forty theological schools related to clinical training efforts throughout the country.

It would take ten more frustrating years for the clinical training movement to accomplish organizational unification. Over these years, the Committee of Twelve gave way to an Advisory Committee, which in turn gave way to an Executive Committee. Among the many leaders, Ernest Bruder of St. Elizabeth's Hospital in Washington, John Billinsky of Andover Newton Theological School, and Karl Plack of the Lutheran Advisory Council gave generously of their time and expertise, but not without occasional conflict among themselves and suspicion from the membership. The impetus to establish a national organization came from the increasing interest on the part of various denominations in having an influence on clinical training, the formation of the Southern Baptist Association of Clinical Pastoral Education in 1957, and the growth of reputable, independent training centers.[9] However, it soon become apparent that despite

---

[9] For example, Reuel Howe's Institute for Advanced Pastoral Studies in Detroit, and Thomas Klink's Program in Psychiatry and Religion at the Menninger Clinic in Topeka.

these many pressures, political unification could only come about after agreement on the most basic element of all–the certification (then called accreditation) of CPE supervisors.

In 1962 Charles Hall of the CCT and Richard Lehman of the IPC, respective chairs of each organization's accreditation process, called a joint meeting of their committees. To the surprise of many, the committees were successful in working together in consulting with several students seeking certification. Talk of possible merger suddenly mushroomed! A promise of significant help ($100,000) from financier Clement Stone fueled hopes, and prompted the official appointment of a national Merger Committee. By 1965 the Joint Standards Committee presented a comprehensive document outlining standards for three levels of CPE with greater development of the supervisory component than ever before. This document "symbolized the implicit agreement (between IPC and CCT) that supervision is the key element in this type of experiential theological education" (Hall 1992, 132). An array of implicit agreements and actual accomplishments through these years finally led to tangible decision making at the Uniting Conference held at Kansas City. There, in the fall of 1967, the Association for Clinical Pastoral Education (ACPE) was officially incorporated.

By this time "the culture was seemingly awash with therapeutic possibilities" (Holifield 1983, 308). A new humanistic psychology flourished in which the fulfillment of one's full personhood was the chief goal. This so-called human potential movement was giving birth to numerous popular therapies and a burgeoning of small groups. Amid this veritable onslaught of therapeutic efforts, the pastoral theologians and clinicians moved in three directions (Holifield 1983, 313 ff). A first group, using developmental theories from psychologist Erik Erikson based on psychoanalytic tradition, rooted (and limited) hopes of self-realization in developmental (historical) realities. A second group influenced by Gordon Allport, Abraham Maslow, and Karen Horney, believed that the innate power of growth within the individual could not be overemphasized. These differences were reflective of the old New York/Boston split and persist to this day. Interestingly, both groups agreed on the importance of a third approach, that of a "new" field of interpersonal and social psychology including the work of Harry Stack Sullivan who wrote the influential *The Psychiatric Interview* in 1952. This latter development, in tandem with the whole field of humanistic psychology, would play a key role in the development of small-group work in CPE.

The distinction between pastoral care and pastoral counseling has not always been clear. From the beginning, both Seward Hiltner and Wayne Oates insisted on establishing pastoral care in the context of the church's ministry and theology. Pastoral counseling referred to counseling work done one-on-one by a pastor trained in psychology and usually located in a pastoral counseling center. For some, including Hiltner, this latter type of professional activity by clergy was highly suspect. In 1963 Frederick Kuether, director of the American Foundation for Religion and Psychiatry in New York, wrote a letter to clergy who were doing pastoral counseling asking them to a national meeting. Out of this gathering, with the financial support of Clement Stone and the organizational determination of Howard Clinebell, the American Association of Pastoral Counselors was formed–a story which has recently been told in Van Wagner's *The AAPC in Historical Perspective 1963-1991*. Many of its initial members were supervisors trained in the psychoanalytic tradition of the old CCT under Robert Brinkman. The AAPC has since become the major accrediting and certifying agency for the pastoral counseling field.

During the 1950s and 1960s the theme of spiritual emancipation of the individual from the strictures of mass society became a theological concern as well. Books by Danish theologian Soren Kierkegaard added depth and *angst* to the quest for human fulfillment. The martyrdom of young Dietrich Bonhoeffer (once a student at Union Seminary in New York), who died protesting the rise of Nazi Germany, gave stirring proof that there were no absolute moral laws in society or government except the divine law of love. Martin Buber, eminent Jewish philosopher, would add spiritual momentum to the importance of the interpersonal dimension of life with the publication of *I and Thou* in 1958. Erich Fromm, Jewish psychoanalyst and social critic with a lifelong interest in religion and ethics, had a particular influence on pastoral theologians with the publication of his enormously popular *Escape from Freedom* (1941). Fromm's critique of authoritarianism and the dangers of mass culture were consistent with much of the thinking among clinical educators in the nascent ACPE.

For Protestant theologians in the liberal tradition, the relationship between psychology and theology, the human situation and divine initiative, was most creatively explored by an American movement called process theology (Holifield 1983, 336). Based on the complex writings of philosopher Alfred North Whitehead, which were clarified and extended by Henry Nelson Wieman (Divinity School, University of Chicago) and Daniel Day Williams (Union Seminary, New York), process theology insisted on the divine participation in all events, people, and processes. In this way it made connections between

fields had become "religious." In the field of psychology, developments cluster around the growth of family systems theory, the extension of psychoanalytic thought through object relations and self psychology, and the creative critique from women's voices and viewpoints.

Meanwhile the world of theological education has begun to question the professional model of training for ministry and express its dissatisfaction with the widespread development of competing academic specialities among its faculties. In response to Edward Farley's influential *Theologia* (1983), which called for a turn to a sapiential knowledge of God as the locus for all theological education, regional forums among theological faculties have been held and the Association for Theological Schools (ATS) has sponsored a program called Basic Issues Research. With these efforts there is a developing consensus that theological education must change, but it is not clear how.

Much of the controversy swirls around the relationship between academic learning and practical experience in graduate education and training for ministry. In *Christian Identity and Theological Education* (1985), a study sponsored by ATS, Joseph Hough and John Cobb disagreed with Farley that the professional clerical paradigm was the problem. Here the authors sought to bring theory and practice more closely together, insisting that the churches be the unifying locus and take major responsibility for educating the minister-to-be as a *reflective practitioner*—a term first used by social scientist Donald Schoen (1983).

Beyond Clericalism: The Congregation as a Focus for Theological Education (Hough and Wheeler 1988), a follow-up study to the ATS report, presented the various responses of professors from academic disciplines to the proposition that theological education be rooted in the local congregation. In concert with this general direction, James Poling and Donald Miller had claimed in *Foundations for a Practical Theology of Ministry* (1985) that the goal of ministry is community formation, whether in the seminary or the parish. This knowledge is the special purview of the field of practical theology. Before the decade ended, Max Stackhouse reported in *Apologia* (1988) on extensive faculty conversations at Andover Newton Theological School about such key issues as the relationship between care of individuals and societal transformation, and the tensions to be inclusive and responsible in an increasingly pluralistic and global world. Pushing to reinstate Farley's orthodox theological point of view, Stackhouse writes:

> Surely one of the particular responsibilities of theological
> education, at least as it takes place in seminaries or

departments of theology, is to lead people to know something reliable about God (131).

Though CPE supervisors tend to be relegated to the sidelines of this ongoing theological debate among practical theologians in the seminaries, they are keenly interested in the problem of the relationship between theory and practice–especially as this is played out in the supervisory certification process.

As the 1990s unfold, the world in general and the world of ACPE in particular seem to be getting smaller and larger simultaneously. On the one hand, an international movement in pastoral care and counseling has opened up training opportunities, multicultural issues in supervisory methodology, and increasing contact with Third World countries. In particular, the Pastoral Care Network for Social Responsibility (PCNSR), led by Howard Clinebell of Claremont School of Theology, has played a major role in connecting people in the field of pastoral care with world-wide justice and political issues. In contrast, supervisors in the United States have become increasingly specialized in their approach to clinical education, dependent on medical facilities to support their training programs, and separated from developments in seminary-based theological education. Due to deepening budget cuts in the health care field and instability in seminary enrollments as the mainline Protestant churches shrink, these chaplain educators are becoming cautious and insecure about the future, uncertain how to respond to training ministers for the next century.

The governance of the ACPE has recently "downsized" with the elimination of the General Assembly (successor to the House of Delegates) and centralization of power in a Board of Representatives. It is too soon to tell if this will be administratively and financially an effective way to do the business of the organization, notwithstanding the politics involved. In the last five years or so, a small group of (mostly male) supervisors has reacted negatively to the loss of the old camaraderie and reforming vision of both ACPE and AAPC. Their creative protest has resulted in the formation of yet another training organization, the College of Pastoral Supervision and Psychotherapy (CPSP), complete with its own standards and programs. Concern runs deep about this development, which is understandable in the light of the historic struggle for unification in ACPE.

In November 1992 at its national meeting in Oakland, California, the ACPE celebrated its first twenty-five years of existence as an independent organization. Five-hundred pastoral educators, chaplains and CPE students celebrated together with a combination of balloons and banners, music and dance, prose and poetry, memory and hope, critique and appreciation. One person summarized for all in the look behind and ahead: "This community has been my salvation. When I was lost it found the real me. When I was depressed, it helped me to release my anger and be free...I can only stay on this path if you are with me. We can only birth the next generation of this Association if we do it together" (ACPE Anniversary Celebration Play Premieres 1993, 8).

2

GROUP WORK IN CPE

Three distinct types of student group work have developed in clinical pastoral education: structured learning time for lectures and other didactic presentations; semistructured group time for supervision of case and verbatim presentations; and unstructured group time for participation in an interpersonal or psychodynamic small-group process. While the focus of the present inquiry is primarily on the third type of group work within CPE, this chapter and the following one will show the interweaving and intermingling of these three approaches as they developed in CPE over time and the unique historical and cultural forces which influenced the development of the interpersonal group process itself.

Unfortunately much of the history of the origin and development of group work in CPE is stored in supervisory files and student evaluations, skewed by the oral tradition, lost to individual memory, and often obscured by the more immediate programmatic or political issues of a particular time. The tendency of group life to be a steady background element, important yet unexamined, too complex to figure out or analyze, too varied and unpredictable to control, is as true in clinical training as in any other educational endeavor. To further complicate the situation, published historical documentation is limited to a few major books about the history of pastoral care and CPE, presentations and workshops from national meetings through the years, and an assortment of articles published primarily in *The Journal of Pastoral Care*. Though there are some rich sources of information in this material, the work of collection and recollection also involves catching a few glimpses or oblique views hidden behind a more prominent historical foreground.

The history begins with Joseph Hershey Pratt, a physician from Massachusetts General Hospital, who is considered to be the founder of group psychotherapy in the United States. Pratt was among those physicians who joined Elwood Worcester at Emmanuel Church in Boston in 1905 in an effort to connect the cure of bodies with the cure of souls. Applying "suggestive therapy" to the groups of patients with tuberculosis who first streamed into his hospital clinic, and later into the church, Pratt discovered that his weekly "classes" elicited a special kind of group support which was useful in combating the individual depression and isolation which comes with serious illness. In addition to the reporting of weight gains and sharing of weekly journal entries, personal testimonies during the group sessions would encourage and inspire downhearted members of the class. In retrospect, it is interesting to realize that the Emmanuel Movement, precursor to the religion and mental health movement as well as the beginnings of clinical pastoral education, is also connected with this first effort to offer group therapy.

The first explicit mention of group work within the "prehistory" of the clinical training movement is found in William Keller's program in Cincinnati in the early 1920s. The Bexley Hall Plan included groups of from five to eight students gathering in Keller's home on weekends to report their experiences in ministry. Group meetings during the training included lectures on social problems and seminar discussions of "the correlation of lectures and direct experiences in the community" (Thornton 1970, 43). Through the use, adopted from the field of social work, of case studies, the students were encouraged to "observe the interaction of social and spiritual variables, and perhaps thus to discover for themselves some of the bases of ethical reasoning" (Powell 1975a, 6). From the earliest days, the action-reflection model of learning in the small group setting was part of clinical training for seminary students.

Keller's case-study approach to student learning was no doubt adopted from Richard Cabot's earlier development of this particular method of learning in his Pathological Conference. One historian notes that in this way Cabot provided "meaningful encounter between the [medical] students and two other forms of living human documents: the student's peers, and his clinical instructors" (Powell 1975a, 6). Though there is no documented evidence to suggest that learning from peers and supervisors was a conscious method or goal of Cabot's work in these early days, it was at least a natural by-product. Certainly Cabot's charisma and energy contributed to lively group experiences all around. The extent to which this dynamic interpersonal focus was carried over by Dicks or Boisen into their CPE student groups during subsequent verbatim sessions is not clear.

While Cabot and Dicks focused on teaching students pastoral skills, Anton Boisen was initially more concerned that his students minister to the forgotten on the back wards of the mental hospital and learn about the religious experiences of the emotionally troubled. To this end, his "theologs" at Worcester State worked as attendants on the wards, organizers of group recreation efforts, and leaders of worship services. From the beginning Boisen valued the case-study method which he had learned from Cabot, though he tended to use this method to understand the religious experiences of the patients rather than to develop the pastoral skills of his students. There were also other elements in the program. In a promotional piece (1930) Boisen wrote:

> By thus cutting the required routine work to eight hours a day, the student has left sufficient time and strength to do the special case work, to write up his notes, to do the reading and attend the ward walks and staff meetings and the special conferences which are held twice each week for the benefit of the group, all of which are essential if the student is himself to profit by his experience....We also seek to give each student some part in the research work which has now been going on for six years in the religious and social factors in mental disorders (29).

These "special conferences...for the benefit of the group" were probably the two didactic seminars held each week on "the interrelationship between religious experience and mental disorder." These were under the direction of the assistant superintendent at Worcester State (Thornton 1970, 203). This interdisciplinary and collaborative educational approach became one of the hallmarks of Boisen's program and continues to this day as a highly valued part of the CPE experience.

There is evidence that a certain group spirit did develop right from the beginning under Boisen's leadership. One student from the 1929 group at Worcester State Hospital wrote in his recollections more than forty years later:

> The most vividly recalled event of the summer was our first meeting together as theological students from different seminaries. Mr. Boisen had us meet him in a room high in the tower of the main building. After we introduced ourselves and said a little about what interested or concerned us most, he talked a bit, and then he turned the meeting into an Episcopal communion

service. Several students remarked later on the strong
emotional effect on themselves as the chalice went round
the circle and came to them. It was partly Mr. Boisen's
reserved and quiet manner. The effect on me was most
unusual. I had been losing my faith during the previous
Spring at the Seminary and had decided to enroll...for
graduate work in psychology....Receiving the chalice
made me realize how much I would miss religious
living...that communion service made us instantly a team
as nothing else could have done–not all the welcoming
speeches nor all the picnics nor all the seminars in the
world (Powell 1975a, 29, #69).

It is generally known that Boisen was not a particularly effective group
leader or "people person." In an article based on personal interviews with
Boisen's former students, one investigator summarizes:

[Boisen] was often too preoccupied by his own view on
the matter to freely acknowledge and utilize the ideas
which came up in the discussion. He often left the group
members free for twenty or thirty minutes without
interruption. If he felt that the discussion had moved
too far away from his own ideas, he delivered a short
monologue and let it go on from there.....He hardly paid
attention to what the students had said. It is clear that
Boisen was much more a teacher than a supervisor and
that, although he had discovered the power of the case-
study from Cabot, he was not able to make it the sort of
interchange between students and teacher which Cabot
had in mind (Nouwen 1968, 170-1).

A CPE Supervisor who was a former student of Boisen's at Elgin State Hospital
in 1943 remembers:

Anton was a single issue, research-oriented theological
scientist. His primary focus was his "case"....This
singular focus tended to detach Anton from the student
group. For example, he was minimally interested in the
contents and conflicts of our daily lives....If we really

required a listening ear, a student assistant sometimes
gave us a few minutes (Cedarleaf 1987, 6).

Though Boisen never considered his work with theological students under
the rubric of interpersonal group process or group therapy, it is interesting that
he took some of the same educational methods and used them in his work with
mental patients. He then called *this* "group therapy." In an article published in
1954 in *Pastoral Psychology*, Boisen notes his efforts to create a therapeutic
milieu on the wards at Elgin State Hospital date as far back as 1932. In what he
called "formal meetings" with small groups of selected patients, Boisen came
to use the case-study method as part of his therapeutic program. He explains:

> Asking [the patients] to assume that they are the medical
> staff, I present the case as graphically as I can and call
> upon them to figure out what the trouble is, what is likely
> to happen and what ought to be done about it....There is
> often lively discussion which reveals surprisingly good
> insight and develops a warm, friendly spirit (36).

Boisen was also clear about the limits of what could happen in a group situation:

> It is obvious that in discussing the case under
> consideration each patient will be thinking of his or her
> own problems. Some will want to tell the group about
> those problems. This, however, is not encouraged. We
> ask such persons to wait and talk with the leader
> individually...*Group therapy* is thus a valuable adjunct
> to individual therapy (36; italics added).

In addition to these formal sessions, Boisen held weekly open meetings
on the wards, beginning them with a period of singing followed by the case
approach for questions and teaching, and concluding with general concerns
about life on the ward. On Sunday there were ward worship services which
were also considered to be a form of group therapy (Boisen 1948; Jackson
1950). Boisen even put together his own hymnal, deleting potentially violent
or destructive religious images which might evoke paranoia or anxiety among
the patients (Boisen 1948).

On the more disturbed wards, Boisen used "informal conferences" in
which "frequently we are able to draw out one or two of them for the benefit of

the others" (1948, 37). In explaining the function of group therapy in the institutional context, he comments:

> In our general plan of religious ministry in this institution these group therapy conferences correspond roughly to the Bible classes in the normal church set-up....Our objective is the same. Our aim is the furtherance of fellowship among our people and the exchange of experience regarding the laws of the spiritual life (1948).

In all of his work Boisen is clear that "soul cure" through group experiences was precisely what the church should be about. "The Christian Church with its class meetings and services of worship may thus justly be said to constitute down through the ages the outstanding exemplification of group therapy," for

> on every side we have evidence that man is a social being, that his primary need is that for love and fellowship, and that the major evil in non-organic mental illness is not to be found in anxiety and discontent with one's present achievements, but in the sense of estrangement from the inwardly conceived fellowship of the best. Salvation, or cure, is therefore to be found, not in lowering the conscience threshold and thus getting rid of inner conflict but in release from the sense of isolation (Boisen 1954, 37- 38).

This statement picks up several key themes in Boisen's work. First, he never separated the *sociological,* in the sense of social roles and social learning, from the *religious*, in the sense of individual mystical experience. Thus, Boisen's understanding of group (social) life was always in the context of a religious (forgiving, saving, loving) community, whether he was working with his students or with his patients. In the Boisen tradition, the religious-social perspective shapes and informs the uniqueness of the clinical training experience from its earliest days.

Second, though Boisen benefitted greatly from reading Freud and using psychological concepts, he never totally agreed with the psychoanalytic approach to understanding human nature. Instead of inner conflicts and libidinal drives being the source of mental anguish, Boisen viewed human social isolation as the chief cause of suffering. Thus, effective therapy involved renewed contact with one's fellow human beings, increased socialization, and an experience of being loved by others. The interpersonal context for both learning and healing was key to Boisen's thinking, though he made this more explicit in his work with patients than in his work with students. Unfortunately, his own search for "liberation from his sense of isolation" would be lifelong.

Third, Boisen placed great importance on what he called "the fellowship of the best," though it is not exactly clear what this meant to him. In a speech given on the occasion of the Silver Anniversary Conference of the clinical training movement in 1950, Boisen remarked:

> The aim of psychotherapy is therefore not to get rid of conflict by lowering the conscience threshold, but to remove the sense of alienation and enable the sufferer to feel himself restored to the fellowship of the best, thus setting him free to strive for his true objectives in life....I believe that love is the paramount human need and that there is a law within which forbids us to be satisfied with any fellowship save that of the best (16).

In all likelihood, Boisen's idea of "the fellowship of the best" has roots in the thought of Josiah Royce (1955-1916), an American philosopher who taught at Harvard University and from whom Boisen may well have taken courses (Snyder 1968). Royce believed that the natural order of the world was a moral order and that human ethical obligation to this order takes the form of loyalty to the greater society or "Beloved Community." Like Royce, Boisen thought that the internalization of conscience was primarily a loyalty phenomenon based on caring from and for significant others. The Beloved Community, or fellowship of the best, is an atoning community "not in the sense of demanding a victim...but in the sense of being willing to go through the pains of hell alongside a person" (Snyder 1968, 182). Conscience, for Boisen, made possible close identification with his fellow sufferers in the hospital. In fact, the hospital would become "the place where Boisen's life," whether as a patient or as a chaplain, " was most in touch with the universally human" (Snyder 1968, 182). It is not surprising to learn that, after his retirement in 1942, Boisen continued to live at Elgin State Hospital until his death in 1960.

Since Anton Boisen did not remain active as a chaplain educator, it is impossible to know how some of his ideas about the therapeutic value of the group experience and the faithful striving to be reconciled with the fellowship of the best might have influenced his work with ministry students doing clinical training–or how his students might have influenced him.   According to one author, Boisen always held firm on his original ideas for clinical training. When called upon as an educational consultant in later years, he "was especially critical of those centers that focused heavily on psychoanalytic theory, group dynamics, or techniques of counseling as opposed to the in-depth study and understanding of human experience" (Asquith 1992, 8).

During the 1940s documented evidence of interpersonal or psychodynamic group work in clinical pastoral training programs remains meager. In the formal agreement reached between the Council for Clinical Training and the Institute of Pastoral Care in 1944, there is no evidence of interpersonal group process work as a distinct element in the learning experience. In his presentation on behalf of the New England Group, Philip Guiles noted seven basic components present in most clinical pastoral training programs: service as orderlies, training in listening, experience in observing others' work, note-writing, special reading, seminar discussions, and personal conferences.

Under the topic of seminar discussions Guiles clearly refers to structured didactic sessions:

> The sixth provision is the seminar period each week. The content of these class sessions varies in our New England group with the different supervisors or instructors....It serves as the common meeting place and the one unifying experience for the group (1945, 48).

In the section on personal conferences Guiles notes that "person-to-person teaching is still perhaps the most valued type of education." He then makes an intriguing reference which reflects some of the emotional impact occurring in training programs:

> I would suppose that our small groups in our clinical training schools come as near including in a modern parallel the New England Divine and his reverent student, as any recent development in the field of education (49).

At this same meeting Rollin Fairbanks, who followed Russell Dicks as Chaplain at Massachusetts General Hospital, indicated two new developments in his own training program. The supervisor was making regular visits to the floor to directly observe the work of the student chaplain, and the group was now engaging in role playing as a way of practicing pastoral skills. In doing this latter activity "the instructor assumes the role of a troubled person" while the student is cast as the pastor and seeks to administer pastoral assistance. Fairbanks notes that, while "the experience is more intensive to the student assigned to the problem, the entire group is silently participating in the role of what they would do if in a similar situation" (1945, 39-40). Clearly the rich possibilities for peer learning in the semistructured group environment were growing naturally out of the training experience itself.

Though the Institute and the Council were increasingly taking different approaches to clinical training, the one emphasizing the application of theology in developing pastoral skills and the other giving priority to understanding theology through a psychodynamic understanding of human experience,[1] by the early 1940s they both could agree on the importance of the supervisor and supervised experience. Thus, when it came to summarizing the focus of the Institute's training for the conference attenders, Fairbanks listed four key components:

1. The work performed shall be of a *pastoral* nature.
2. It shall be done *under supervision*.
3. It shall be *recorded*.
4. These notes shall be *submitted for criticism*

(1945, 38).

At the same conference, the New York group made its presentation under three categories which reflected its own growing contribution to the movement: standards for selection of supervisors, standards for length of the training period, and standards for content of the training programs (Brinkman 1945, 23-30). Though there is no mention of group work in the CCT document, the bottom line for agreement between the CCT and IPC is there: "The Theological Supervisor is the key person in the operation of a training program....The heart of the program, of course, is the supervised student-pastoral relationship with people in trouble" (Brinkman 1945, 23,26).

By the end of the 1940s there was a shared perception that those involved in clinical training were in some sense mavericks in relationship to both the church and the seminaries. Not only did the uniqueness of the training experience draw students and supervisors together in some powerful ways, but there was

---

[1] It is important to remember that Boisen agreed with neither of these approaches in his emphasis on learning about theology through studying the living human document.

also developing a shared identity as participants in a larger movement for reform within theological education and the church. A certain amount of student nonconformity hearkened back to the earliest days when some of Boisen's "theologs," after their experience in clinical training, became enamored with the empiricism of the medical world and chose careers in psychiatry and medicine–instead of ministry (Beatty 1965). Others, upon their return to seminary, began to question the academic rigidity of an exclusively doctrinal, biblical approach to preparing for ministry. Though the New England group located its clinical training programs administratively in the seminaries, the New York supervisors were more autonomous and free spirited. This latter approach tended to further loosen some of the historic ties and attract less conventional students.

Henri Nouwen, in an unpublished manuscript entitled "Anton T. Boisen and the Study of Theology Through Living Human Documents," confirms this situation:

> The result of all this [rebelliousness] was that the clinical training centers received many adventurous students, men who wanted something, were mad somewhere and willing to fight somebody, especially authority. They were received by supervisors who knew what their students were talking about and who were able to identify (Powell 1975a, 19).

This sense of identification was among the elements which paved the way for the students themselves to become the living human documents under study during the clinical training experience. Thus, out of the supervised student-patient relationship, clinical training began to focus more on the student himself (all male in those days), his motivation for ministry, blocks in his learning, his attitude toward authority figures, and so on. This change would be reinforced by the growing interest in pastoral counseling and the general emphasis on the psychodynamic approach to individual supervision in the 1950s.

Summary

During these early years there is little evidence of the presence of a distinctive interpersonal group process in clinical pastoral training programs. What is clear is that the early training programs engaged students in important ministries, confronting them with an array of physical, emotional, social, and personal problems to which they were to respond. In the process, the students were to learn ministry by doing ministry. It is clear that the earliest student groups, whether under Keller, Boisen, or Dicks, used the case-study method (and later the verbatim) to learn pastoral skills and reflect together about their pastoral efforts. Theological and ethical reflection was probably a natural outgrowth of this process. By the mid-1940s both the Boston and New York educators involved in offering clinical training could agree that it was: 1) a shared learning experience, 2) over time, 3) which focused on professional functioning, 4) under the watchful eye of a more experienced person, 5) in a setting receptive to ministry efforts. These five elements were fundamental criteria for the earliest clinical training programs and remain so to the present day.

Anton Boisen added a sixth element to this mix when he made a connection between experiences in the small group and his desire to join "the fellowship of the best." Though this religious connection may have been more explicit in his therapeutic and pastoral work with groups of patients than it ever was in his educational work with students, Boisen's abiding sense of the healing potential of social (i.e.,group) interaction was key to his efforts in ministry and, by extension, clinical education. Though the church was one such fellowship, there was a universality about this concept for Boisen which extended well beyond one specific institution. This religious dimension was among the most distinctive and pervasive elements in the clinical training movement.

There were a number of problems inherent in the developments of these early years which would challenge the next generations of students and supervisors. For example, out of the Boisen legacy comes confusion about the relationship between his group therapy done with patient groups and the supervision done with student groups. Was this the same case method simply applied to people in different situations? To what degree would the psychotherapeutic focus of chaplain-run patient groups in the mental hospital setting be carried over into supervisor-run student training groups? And to what degree would the emphasis on skill development in the medical setting set the tone toward increasing professionalization of training and chaplaincy in those CPE programs? Further, as the focus shifted onto the student as the living human document, how would the balance be maintained between student-centered learning, pastoral ministry, peer group experiences, and the relationship with the supervisor? What would be the dynamic interface between the student-supervisor relationship and the group process itself? More broadly, what general theory of interpersonal group work would inform supervisory practice and why?

Out of the rich legacy of the early founders of clinical pastoral education came many questions which would set the direction for the future of clinical pastoral education, and set the scene for this current study.

PART TWO: THE BURGEONING (1950-1962)

Though little direct mention is made of interpersonal group work in clinical training in the 1940s, by the early 1950s it is clear that a great deal was actually going on behind the scenes. In the spring of 1951 the then-fledgling *Journal of Pastoral Care* contained a number of articles from the movement's Silver Anniversary Celebration which give both indirect clues and direct evidence. In an effort to help others get inside the CPE experience, the issue begins with the sharing of a typical supervisor's evaluation and a typical student evaluation

The supervisor, who ran a program in a general hospital, focused on a descriptive analysis of the student's work and made no mention of any group experiences in the training. In contrast, the student, who trained in an unidentified mental hospital setting, mentioned "seminar discussions" as one of three important elements (the other two were supervisory conferences and patient contacts). According to the student, these seminar discussions most often focused on a *case history* drawn from the supervisor's file which was *"used as a point of departure from which to discuss theology and one's self"* (A Student 1951, 33; italics added). As it turned out, the group experience was key to the student's personal learning:

> In our seminars, I found a greater degree of love than I had previously known. Here was a group who watched me grow angry and withdraw, which listened to me tell them they didn't know what they were talking about, which discovered the really basic flaws and weaknesses in my personality–and none of these things made any difference in our relationships. I was still liked and kept as a welcome member of the group. Of course, this was a gradual process. But as time passed, I saw ever more clearly that I did not have to do anything special to win their favor. I did not have to agree with their opinions. I did not have to pretend I was always right. I did not even have to be pleasant. No matter what I did, or how I acted, or what they found out about me, they did not

exclude me from the fellowship. They accepted me just
as I was. It was as simple as that (31).

It would be hard to find a more eloquent expression of the personal benefit of
the group experience in clinical training.

Clear evidence that group work in clinical training was beginning to come
of age is signaled in this same issue of the *Journal* with the article, "Growth
Through Group Interaction," written by Robert C. Leslie. Leslie, a graduate of
Boston University School of Theology and an ordained Methodist minister,
had done his doctoral research on group therapy as a method for church work.
First serving as an Army chaplain in the war, Leslie afterward became Protestant
Chaplain at Boston Psychopathic Hospital (1947) and Boston State Hospital
(1948), where he worked as a group therapist and taught theological students in
clinical pastoral training in programs sponsored by the Institute of Pastoral
Care.

In a reminiscence written in 1968, Dr. Paul Johnson, longtime Professor
of Psychology of Religion at Boston University School of Theology, explains
the origin of Leslie's involvement in clinical training and group work. In 1945
Dr. Harry C. Solomon, a professor of psychiatry at Harvard University and
superintendent at Boston Psychopathic Hospital, invited Johnson to bring his
theological students for training at his hospital. Two years later Johnson co-led
a student clinical training group with psychiatrist Dr. Robert Hyde in which
Robert Leslie was a member. But even before this Johnson (and Leslie) had
been involved with working with patients and learning group psychotherapy.
As Johnson explains:

> In 1946 Joseph H. Pratt, M.D., founder of group therapy
> in 1905, invited me to lead his famous classes in applied
> psychology at the Boston Dispensary. Robert C. Leslie
> and James H. Burns became co-leaders, and our students
> actively participated in group sessions and interviews,
> evaluated by a clinical team of psychiatrists, physicians,
> social workers and pastoral counselors (1968, 228).

Thus, the close connection between group therapy efforts in the psychiatric
setting and group experiences for seminary students doing clinical training can
be traced back to these connections beginning in the mid-1940s at Boston
Psychopathic Hospital. Leslie's article outlines for the first time a full-blown
theory of interpersonal group work which focuses unabashedly on personal
growth of the theological students and the therapeutic (i.e., healing) nature of

the group experience. Leslie views the group experience as "natural" and "normal" since "man is basically a social animal and needs the company of others to reach his highest development" (1951, 37). From evidence in the article, there is no doubt Leslie was influenced both by the group psychotherapy tradition within psychiatry as well as the new developments in field theory and social psychology spearheaded by Kurt Lewin and others in the 1940s. Unfortunately Leslie makes little effort to trace the historical or theoretical bases for his ideas.

Leslie used his work with a group of ten trainees at Boston State Hospital: six theological students, one full-time pastor, one university chaplain, and two YWCA executive directors. Leslie notes conditions necessary for growth in the group experience. First, the group needs a "special atmosphere" which comes about largely through the efforts of a "non-autocratic leader who accepts hostility without retaliation," thus creating a trusting environment which "stimulates the group members to analyze their own ways of interacting with others." Second, discussion is to "arise spontaneously without predetermined plan." After mentioning "the scapegoating mechanism," Leslie concludes this section:

> The goal of the group is then to seek out the deeper, more personal implications of each topic discussed. Contacts with patients suggest the topics for consideration; interaction within the group helps to make possible a personal application of phenomena observed in the wards (40).

It is interesting to note here the implied parallel process between the student's personal work in the group and application of learnings in ministry efforts on the wards, and vice versa. Using the group process in this recursive way has continued to be a fundamental approach to interpersonal group work in clinical training.

The second section of the article focuses on stages in the group process itself: testing-out, resistance,[2] acceptance, and responsibility. It also outlines the stages in the personal development of the members as defensiveness, anxiety, increasing expression of personal feelings, introspection, and spontaneity. Leslie concludes with a section on the role of the leader who is "the key figure" because

---

[2] Resistance is expressed in hostility toward the leader. Leslie comments: "This hostility is a normal part of the group process when responsibility for directing group activity is placed with the members instead of leaving all accountability with the leader. The hostility is best understood as being resistance to the unexpected method" (Leslie 1951, 41). Leslie's "unexpected method" was probably influenced by the work of Wilfred Bion.

"it is in working through the relationship with the leader that the movement toward higher stages in the group process and in personal development is made possible" (43).

According to Leslie, the leader is to seek clarification, penetrate areas of greater dynamic significance, and seek the more personal implications of the behavior of students in the group setting. The leader relieves tension by humor, permits conflict but discourages excessive hostility, refuses to interrupt a process which needs working through, and deals with an individual student's excessive anxiety by meeting in an individual conference. Interestingly, Leslie notes, "at one point in our group, the leader was asked to halt the group process with a prayer in order to relieve an 'un-Christian' situation" (44).

Leslie concludes by noting the future need for evaluation of the group process, increased use of psychodrama and role play, the need for research on group dynamics, and the need for leaders to experience group therapy themselves "and thus know from firsthand contact the tremendous satisfactions of a therapeutic group experience" (45). All in all, there is no doubt that Leslie's comprehensive presentation articulated and legitimated the interpersonal group experiences which had already been occurring in clinical training programs. His article is often cited as marking the "official" start of group-process work.

In 1951 Reuel Howe, then professor of pastoral theology at the Virginia Theological Seminary in Alexandria, delivered the keynote address at the national conference. Howe shared his theological reflections about clinical training over his own fifteen years of involvement. In a memorable and much-quoted passage about the training itself, he insisted:

> I want [the students] "dunked"–plunged deeply into life, brought up gasping and dripping, and returned to us humble and ready to learn. Until all students are faced with the tragedies, the contradictions, and the stark questions of life, they cannot understand the need for redemption or God's redemptive action. I want my students to lose, as soon as possible, their easy faith, their ready answers; and I want them to lose any hope of ever again having an easy faith or a ready answer. I want them to lose their personal conceits and their illusions about themselves, their illusions about their fellow men and their illusions about God. I want their assumptions about the ministry and their assumptions about how they are going to conduct their ministry completely destroyed (1952, 5-6).

Howe went on to comment on the experience of one of his students who was "finally able to face the truth about himself" with the help of his peer group:

> He was one of five students working in a center where the supervisor was consciously or unconsciously using the group as a resource for training....As soon as he found himself in a group...that could accept him and support him, then suddenly [the student] had the courage (faith) to face the truth. The deepest meaning of his experience was theological instead of psychological. It began to dawn on him that he had experienced the real predicament of all men, that man cannot face the truth about himself as long as he is alone (8).

"Incidentally," Howe then concludes, "I wish more supervisors would make use of the student *group* as a resource for learning" (8).

In the same issue of *The Journal of Pastoral Care* in which Howe's speech appears, Ernest Bruder, a CCT-trained chaplain supervisor from St. Elizabeth's Hospital in Washington D.C., contributes an article which explores the differences and similarities between training and therapy. In this instance, Bruder's "total group" was comprised of fourteen students and three supervisors who apparently met all together as well as in three smaller subgroups. For Bruder, the importance of the student's interpersonal experiences with his small peer group is assumed. Especially valuable is the sharing of negative feelings leading to deeper acceptance of self and other (1952, 15). This piece is followed by four student evaluations.[3] Each mentions the importance of the peer group:

> My relationships with my fellow students have been the most meaningful of all. I came here as a fellow who had not been used to having close friends. I came here as a person who could not imagine what others thought of him and I am leaving here with the feeling that I am beginning to meet myself (Student "A" 1952, 19).

> As the summer progressed I became more and more aware of the dynamics of relationships. I feel that the psychodrama sessions in which this theory was presented and then the sessions in which we saw it work out were

---

[3] It is not clear whether or not these students were in Bruder's program.

of the most value....I was wary at first, because I did not know if I would be able to find a place in this group....As I look back at the group relationship and my part in it I am thankful that I was able to have a part in a situation in which individuals revealed more of their true selves than any other group with which I have been associated (Student "B" 1952, 23).

Relationships within this group and my participation in the group as a whole have given me a greater appreciation than I have had before of the Church as a fellowship of Christian people. I have thought of this group this summer as the Church in microcosm, a unity in diversity....Most of my time and attention this summer have gone into self-exploration and the exploration of individual and group relationships (Student "C" 1952, 26-7).

As more time went on I found that I wasn't making as many [pastoral] interviews as I started off making, but was getting more personally involved in discussions and was doing considerably more thinking about myself....And so my attitude toward the program changed from one of objective study to one of subjective study....After about the seventh week, when I began to allow myself to become involved, and after I saw that I always destroyed the continuity of a discussion by my jokes, I came to feel more a part of the group than I had before. By letting *me* enter the discussion, I found that I came to know not only myself better, but the other members of the group (Student "D" 1952, 30-1).

These quotations give ample evidence of the central importance of the peer group experience, the growth in self-acceptance, student awareness of group dynamics, the experience of group intimacy and cohesion, and the theological connection with the religious fellowship of the church. There is also evidence of increasing self-reflection, even to the point of self-absorption, and consequent decreases in ministry efforts.

In this same 1951 issue of the *Journal* Robert Leslie contributed an article on the use of "group therapy" in the church. This is probably a distillation of his previous dissertation material. Here Leslie emphasizes that the small group is a "laboratory for life" which "repeats the family situation" (1952a). Comparing the situation to the twelve disciples gathered around Jesus, Leslie writes, "Religion has meant the most to those who have actively experienced it in intimate fellowship groups where study and worship and work have been combined" (58). Leslie is interested in how such support or study groups conducted by trained ministers could treat "psychoneurotic" people in the church. "It is the purpose of this paper," he summarizes, "to consider how church groups can be used to supplement therapy groups and to help in preventing personality disorders" (56). Leslie's article reflects considerable optimism about the healing potential of the group experience. But in the process he confuses and blurs the lines between a support group and a therapy group in the church setting. This same confusion would also occur in clinical training programs.

The April 1955 issue of *Pastoral Psychology* honored Robert Leslie as Man of the Month and presented a veritable feast of articles about group work in the church, though none was directly connected with clinical training. In the introduction to this special issue, editor Paul Johnson mentions three pioneers in the field: Joseph Pratt in group therapy, Jacob Moreno in psychodrama and role play, and Kurt Lewin in group dynamics. This is the first mention in the pastoral care literature of these influential leaders in the group field. A lead article by Leslie, now professor emeritus of pastoral psychology at the Pacific School of Religion, defined the unique aspects of a therapeutic group in a church setting: a clear therapeutic purpose; a basic concern for the expression of feelings (verbal and nonverbal); a focus on current activities and relationships both among members and between members and the leader; a leader who is in an active role of acceptance and permissiveness and who has an ability to deal with emotionally charged material (10-13).

The idea of therapy groups in the church had also been developed from a psychoanalytic point of view by Clifton Kew ("head psychologist" at Marble Collegiate Church in New York) and Clinton Kew (Rector of St. James Church, Youngstown, Ohio). Basing their ideas on such concepts as free association, transference and countertransference, resistance, dream analysis, analytic interpretation, and working through, the brothers Kew advocated training in psychotherapy for all ministers and the establishment of church groups for "recovery" (i.e., treatment). For ministers who were less trained or did not want to go as deep, dream analysis would not need to be included (Kew and Kew 1951/1955).

Another article written by a professor of psychology at the University of Chicago focused on the importance of "the group-centered leader" (Gordon 1955). By creating a warm and accepting atmosphere through non-evaluative responses, leadership of the group is extended to all its members. Thus, "the task of the group leader is to lose his status or authority....If he can accomplish this, then the group members no longer need to submit to him or fight him" (Gordon 1955, 21). The result is the creation of a "democratic" group that is "strong enough to withstand an attempt of domination by an authoritarian leader" (24). Credit is given to Kurt Lewin, Carl Rogers, and the Tavistock Clinic for this combination of ideas.

Judson D. Howard had followed Robert Leslie as chaplain at Boston State Hospital, continuing the tradition of a training supervisor being involved in group work. Howard's article in this issue of *Pastoral Psychology* begins by stating that therapy groups should be called interpersonal relations groups. He then goes on to describe his own experience as a member of such a group which was run by a psychiatrist. He shares his struggle with expressing warm feelings (which cause embarrassment) and angry feelings (which cause hurt), dealing with an absent member, and dealing with his own "difference" (deviance) as a clergy person. He includes an intriguing description of the group leader and group norms:

> Before telling of our feelings, a brief word should be said about how our leader acted. He told us that we could talk about anything we wished except our personal histories, that the focus of attention would be on "what went on," that from time to time he would participate and comment on what he saw (28).

Howard is clear about the value of the experience, especially in terms of his feelings about the authority of the leader:

> we felt him to be a strong father...one whose sole purpose was to fulfill the goals of the demos, us...It was good to have a father around while I did some growing up–a father who knew what he was doing" (34).

This issue concluded with an article by a local pastor on how to work with church youth in a therapy group. The article included verbatim material, was clearly oriented to an interpersonal process, and mentioned initial group "shadow boxing" (social conversation) and some of the dynamics around inclusion needs for newer or younger members. All in all, this issue of *Pastoral Psychology* was quite remarkable. In the back was an apology for taking up so much space with special articles that there was no room for the regular monthly features. Clearly something new was afoot.

Throughout 1952 every issue of *The Journal of Pastoral Care* contained at least one article on some aspect of group work. One interesting development was initiated by Robert Hyde, psychiatrist and assistant superintendent at Boston Psychopathic Hospital. Hyde began to offer group therapy for ministers under the leadership of a psychiatrist or chaplain. This "dynamic therapy course" was separate, at least at first, from clinical training per se. It met for thirty sessions in which the group went through various stages, struggled for leadership, became aware of resistances, and learned the difference between affect and intellectual content. The goal was to introduce ministers "to the principles of dynamic group leadership through personal experience which can be applied directly to their church groups" (Hyde and Leslie 1952, 23). An accompanying article by Hyde explored the further ramifications of expressing feelings in a group setting (Hyde 1952).

The next issue of the *Journal* contained an article by Robert Leslie explicating the role of the chaplain in leading patient groups in a mental hospital setting. Such groups, reminiscent of Boisen's early work, fall somewhere "between the large worship service and the small analytic group...a type we shall call the activity group" (1952b, 44). Leslie outlines the work of this "person-centered group" as focusing on three elements: reconciliation, reality-testing, and rehabilitation. "For the patients," he concludes, "the group may well be thought of only as a social and/or religious club, but for the chaplain it can be a significant group counseling experience" (46).

During the early 1950s there were increasing efforts by leaders in the pastoral clinical movement to come up with some national standards for what was now being officially called clinical pastoral education (CPE). Intensive conversations prior to the 1953 national meeting allowed for sharing of ideas by chaplain educators from various parts of the country.[4] Participants included such diverse leaders as John Billinsky from Andover Newton, Seward Hiltner from Chicago, and Wayne Oates from the Southern Baptist Theological Seminary in Louisville. Ernest Bruder was especially convincing during these conversations in expressing concern of the Council for Clinical Training that

---

[4] These are recorded on audiotape and are in the ACPE archives.

emphasis in any set of standards be placed "on the interpersonal relationships involved in the dynamics of the thing." He went on to say:

> If there is a specific emphasis [in CPE] as far as the Council is concerned it would be on the inter-relationship...for example, we used to talk about studying cases, studying patients, and so forth. Now the emphasis has changed considerably in the Council. *It is not a study of the patient but a study of the interpersonal relationships* (Hall 1992, 72; italics added).

Apparently Bruder was not alone in his perception of this change. The first line of the first set of official CPE *Standards* approved in 1953 by attenders at the national conference reads: "Clinical pastoral education is an opportunity for a theological student or pastor to learn Pastoral Care through interpersonal relations in an appropriate center" (Bruder and Barb 1958, 132). Among the "Minimum Essentials of Clinical Pastoral Education" are listed a supervised practicum in interpersonal relations (#1) and adequate provision for group discussions, seminars, and other group activities (#5) (Bruder and Barb 1958, 84).

Ernest Bruder delivered the keynote address at this 1952 conference. He spoke with great conviction about the deeply personal effect which clinical training has on each student chaplain and publicly proclaimed the importance of the peer group experience. He explained:

> We have developed within our programs what we have chosen to call "group concerns seminars" the purpose of which is frankly stated to be that of ventilating any and all concerns the individuals may have and which have been precipitated by the training experience. The therapeutic value of these group sessions (one and a half hours each, twice a week) is quite remarkable and has been attested to by such pioneer reporters as Dr. Robert C. Leslie (1954, 138).

However, this development also served to highlight the continuing concern about how to differentiate clinical pastoral education from either individual or group therapy. Bruder himself was not all that clear:

> Further, in both seminars and personal conferences a
> considerable directiveness is offered. The student is not
> encouraged to ventilate personal feelings or simply to
> "free associate," but to concentrate on patient or other
> relationships which have raised some questions for him.
> We conceive the essence of the supervisors' function to
> consist in clarifying with the student how he relates to
> others...if we find that students cannot avoid a
> preoccupation with personal concerns, strictly training
> objectives are dropped, and the student is either worked
> with in a counseling relationship, or he is referred for
> therapy (142).

Bruder then makes one of the few references to group work of the past by
noting, "the values originally recognized by pioneering supervisors in *'free
discussion' seminars* are preserved [today] in the group concerns seminars"
(142; italics added).

Bruder concludes his seminal presentation with an extensive theological
section about the spiritual emancipation of students through the clinical training
experience. He emphasizes such Tillichian categories as the courage to be,
self-acceptance, and unification with the Ground of Being. Finally, Bruder
compares the group experience to the Body of Christ:

> When a group meets together in a common purpose, to
> know something about another area of human living,
> and shares with itself the feelings involved in this new
> exploration, there is indeed a new creation. Something
> unique has happened—account for it as you will. When
> the individuals of this group come together not only to
> know about this new area of experience, but in
> relationship to the Ultimate which is devoutly and most
> certainly believed--and affirm this in terms of the living
> faith of the Lord Jesus Christ, –then the Body of Christ
> is alive...we are met together in His name. And there
> He is also! This we most surely believe! (Bruder 1954,
> 145).

Bruder's paper was the object of much discussion at the 1953 conference.
Critics maintained that talking about individual experience and interpersonal
relationships had little to do with the classical theological doctrines of sin, evil,
eternal life, atonement, and God. Proponents maintained that "God's qualities

can, in part, be experienced through relationships." Engaging in such dialogue was certainly part of the doing of clinical theology inherent in the clinical training movement. From an historical perspective, the significance of this head-versus-heart discussion was that, for the first time, it did not divide along the traditional CCT and IPC lines (Hall 1992, 92).

In the next two or three years several interesting articles referring to group work were published in *The Journal of Pastoral Care*. In "Group Dynamics and the Church" Rev. Theodore Wedel, Canon at Washington Cathedral, writes about his experience as the first clergy person to attend (in 1949) a laboratory in group dynamics at Bethel, Maine. There, over 150 people from secular professions were divided into groups of eighteen which met for three weeks with mostly silent leaders and the single directive, "Become a group!" (1954, 203). Wedel's eyes were obviously opened by the experience and he pleads in his article for the church to take note:

> And if it be true that the contemporary Church has also fostered fellowship-starved individualism or merely membership in an impersonal collective, though this devote itself to pious exercise, the problem of reviving community ought be for the Church a major concern (205).

Within the decade, the "new religion" of the group dynamics movement would sweep through many mainline Protestant churches.

In 1956 a key article by Ernest Bruder and Marian Barb summarized the results of a ten-year survey (1945-55) among the 140 students who had done clinical training at Saint Elizabeth's Hospital. With an eighty-three percent return rate, the survey confirmed, among other things, the central importance of the interpersonal group experience to clinical training:

> of those responses naming specific program aspects, a high percentage mentioned those activities, such as psychodrama and seminars, which are highly charged interpersonal situations as conducted in the training group (93).

The authors encouraged more research on group process by analyzing transcripts of actual sessions of the Group Concerns Seminar (94).

The proceedings from the Fifth National Conference of Clinical Pastoral Training, held in Atlantic City in 1956, were published in 1958 in a volume entitled *Clinical Education for Pastoral Ministry*, edited by Bruder and Barb. This was the first time since 1945 that the clinical training movement had offered such a wide-ranging collection of published material. With Paul Tillich as the keynote speaker on the theology of pastoral care, and many other notables (Hiltner, Klink, Gustafson, Loomis, Kuether, Fairbanks, Dicks, Billinsky, Bruder, and more) writing in depth and in detail about the goals and methodology of their clinical training programs, this volume became a rich source of information and influence in the pastoral care movement.

It is clear by the late 1950s that intensive interpersonal group work had become an accepted part of many clinical training programs throughout the country. Again, a presentation by Robert Leslie emphasizes the basic three-fold interpersonal purpose: students can measure their growth against others, share their hopes and frustrations, and struggle for deeper self understanding (Leslie 1958). In response to Leslie's paper, Wayne Oates is alone in expressing some concern. He comments, perhaps a bit tongue-in-cheek, that "Professor Leslie...has caught [in his paper] the grandeur of the well nigh-mystical experience of the small-group educational processes going on in clinical centers." Oates goes on to wonder whether the student's relationship to the setting (i.e., ministry to patients) is not being cut off in favor of the student's personal growth in the training experience (1958, 36). Keeping the proper balance between working on personal growth and doing pastoral care continues to be a challenge to the present day.

A presentation by a younger supervisor, Thomas Klink from Topeka State Hospital, received considerable attention. In his own effort to distinguish between education and therapy, Klink cites the "cross-grained experience" within clinical training in which anxiety aroused by unfamiliar situations signals repressed emotional conflicts within the student. Klink makes it clear that, rather than deal with these conflicts, the supervisor should keep the student based in reality (1958, 109-10).

Klink goes on to explain that in his program the group hour (held three or four times each week) "is an extension of supervision...and perhaps the most significant exposure that the student will have to the experience of the group process dimension of human living" (106). Its purpose is to help the student minister on the ward and in the church as a whole, rather than just to individuals. Klink concludes with his understanding of group leadership, and in the process seems to re-cross the line between education and therapy:

> In my ideals the function of the supervisor in the group
> hours is to participate in the discussions with a "third
> ear" attuned to the covert meaning of the discussion.
> This covert meaning will be sought in terms of the
> gradually evolving social entity called "the group." The
> expression of this "third ear" hearing will be some
> affirmative variation of the question, "What causes you
> to raise that with the group, now?" (106).

[handwritten marginal note: What are they not saying]

Among the presentations at the conference was one by Judson Howard. His group dynamics seminar at Boston State Hospital has a decidedly different "feel" to it–and seems to have evolved out of Hyde's former course for ministers. In meeting three times weekly for an hour and a half, he explains, "emphasis is placed upon understanding the group process, relationships, and problems; not upon the student's personal past or his characteristic traits or his role functioning in the group" (1958, 113). It is noteworthy that Howard's approach was focused on a group-as-a-whole experience. This needs to be distinguished from the primarily interpersonal approaches of Leslie, Bruder, and Klink.

Howard highlights important issues which occur in the group: expressions of hostility, differing leadership styles, absent or silent members, forming a group culture, relationship to authority, the phenomenon of scapegoating, and the work of expressing feelings. Sometimes the leader even takes the scapegoating role himself to show that "he is against the usual method of securing homogeneity by excluding the opposition." Howard comments that "at least thirty sessions seem to be necessary before there can emerge a therapeutic orientation, i.e., the group conclusion that the interests and needs of every member are vital to the whole group" (114), and he concludes:

> The students find the group experience to be the most
> interesting and stimulating of all [the program
> components]. I would also rate it high, for, besides the
> experience of coming to see basic group processes and
> the side effects of personal analysis, the student sees
> very graphically the difficulty of giving and receiving
> warmth and affection, processes which are basic to his
> Christian calling (114).

An article by Frederick Kuether in *Clinical Education for Ministry* entitled "How are Supervisory Skills Transmitted to New Supervisors?" revealed some interesting organizational patterns involving student groups and the training of new supervisors.[5] Working with one assistant supervisor, Kuether's thirteen summer students were divided into two groups. Students were supervised individually by one supervisor and met three times a week in seminar sessions with the other. The students were to choose which supervisor for which activity. (The groups met altogether once a week for a worship seminar.)

> We also agreed that each supervisor would feel free to drop in and observe the other's conduct of group discussions. We found out very quickly, however, that the group leader could not possibly keep good notes on the discussion. Therefore, after the third week we recorded all seminar sessions for each other (Kuether 1958, 82-3).

Not only does this material indicate a serious effort to learn from the group experience itself, but by this time there was considerable experimentation with leadership configurations in supervisory training.

In Kuether's program, when he was away one week, the assistant led his group. In the ninth week they traded groups for three sessions with no discernible adverse effects. In his conclusion Kuether likens the supervised group situation to mice in a cage whose behavior can be directed by food pellets. "For a certain number of hours each week the students and the supervisor are confined to this cage. The food pellet is an emotional one. It is the verbal response of the supervisor to the random statements made by the student" (88). In this way, students are encouraged to deal with self-revelation, anger, grief, or whatever, directed by their unconscious need for the supervisor's approval.

Enthusiasm for using the small-group experience to achieve a deeper sense of inclusiveness and acceptance spread to the national organization. In planning the 1958 national conference, the Advisory Committee came up with an entirely new format:

> The conference was divided into ten discussion groups, distributed in such a way that each group contained representatives from the five major disciplines: 1) theological educators, 2) chaplain supervisors of clinical training programs, 3) pastors functioning in the parish

---

[5] Kuether's article explains the origin of the term *Acting Supervisor*, which was used in ACPE until 1984. An assistant training to be a supervisor was to "act as if he were the supervisor" both with the students and with the training supervisor (Kuether 1958, 83).

setting, 4) church administrators, 5) institutional
chaplains, not necessarily operating training programs
(Hall 1992, 105).

Group discussions during the conference ranged from the application of
psychodynamic principles to social problems, to the contribution CPE has made
to the theological understanding of redemption. Audiotapes of the conference
reveal excitement about "the feeling of a community of faith" which was present
at the meeting and a growing sense that the movement was making a significant
contribution to both theological education and new church leadership (Hall
1992, 105).

Interest began to build in trying to understand and empirically measure
the interpersonal group process in clinical pastoral training programs. In 1958
a clinical psychologist and a chaplain supervisor at South Carolina State Hospital
attempted to measure group dynamics and the effectiveness of clinical pastoral
training. The study involved identifying four levels of behavior and sixteen
interpersonal variables through using the Minnesota Multiphasic Personality
Inventory (MMPI), Interpersonal Check List (ICL), Thematic Apperception
Test (TAT), and Idiosyncratic Method for the Measurement of Covert Group
Dynamics. A group of four ordained ministers and their chaplain supervisor
were given the tests at the beginning and at the end of a three-month training
period.

The tests revealed that initially members of the group viewed each other
as generous and responsible individuals based on "the public interpersonal
behavior projected by members of their group." By the end of the course they
described each other as "less friendly and more managerial"–though assignations
were still somewhat bland and generalized (Gynther and Kempson 1958, 213).
The testing did reveal the presence of many covert negative feelings about
individuals in the group. The authors concluded that therefore only a preliminary
stage of group development had been achieved.

The rivalries, power struggles, and symbiotic dyadic relationships so
frequently found among individuals placed in a new situation were present, but
for the most part unexpressed and definitely not worked through or resolved.
This lack of mutual understanding and group cohesion probably interfered with
the training process. The blank picture derived from the overt ratings of others
also suggests that the interactions were superficial and guarded (Gynther and
Kempson 1958, 218).

The article is accompanied by a two-page chart of results and footnotes citing previous articles by Ernest Bruder. In the final analysis the ambitious tone of the study is somewhat muted by its negative findings.

The Fall 1960 issue of *The Journal of Pastoral Care* contained a major article by Judson Howard entitled "Interpersonal Group Seminar: A Training Method in the Pastoral Care of Groups." Howard, who was now known as the guru of group work in CPE, makes it clear that this seminar at Boston State initially grew out of the hospital's training program for leaders of group psychotherapy dating back to 1946. It involved thirty sessions of one-and-a-half hours each and was intended to help ministers understand group process so that they could "become conversant with the basic issues in the pastoral care of groups" and thus work more effectively with groups in the local church (Howard 1960a). The seminar seems to have been offered to both local pastors in a separate course *and* as part of the clinical pastoral training program. Though its historical development may be somewhat serpentine, Howard is clear about its purpose:

> A common misunderstanding for the group-therapist-to-be is to view the purpose of the group as therapeutic rather than didactic, that is, he views the group as one whose purpose is to effect therapeutic change in the behavior and attitudes of its members rather than to study group processes (161).

Howard also makes clear that his conceptual framework is based on the work of W. R. Bion and Kurt Lewin. He focuses on themes of exclusion and inclusion, individuation and conformity, responsibility and dependency in the life of the group. Howard differentiates between the maintenance activities of a group and the task of a group. He concludes his article by driving home his basic intent and concern:

> The student needs a conceptual framework within which he may look for the processes which are important to the pastoral care of groups as contrasted, for example, with the processes important to the leader in group dynamics or group therapy (166).

By 1960 Howard's emphasis is on learning about group process rather than participating in interpersonal dynamics or having a personal therapeutic experience. Thus, he takes group work in CPE in a different direction which in subsequent years came to be known as "the peculiar approach." It is also important to note that his effort to maintain a pastoral focus is also consistent with the general approach to CPE in New England.

The "peculiar" approach to group work at Boston State Hospital received additional impetus by the arrival of chaplain supervisor Emil Hartl and graduate student William Ramsden. Hartl began recording all his group sessions, and this led Howard to procure a group room with a one-way mirror and built-in sound equipment. In the summer of 1960 Ramsden helped record all group sessions which "were then replayed for the whole staff to hear and to comment upon" (Howard 1960b, 83). Both Hartl and Ramsden made presentations on their research at the 1960 Fall Conference of the Institute of Pastoral Care.

Ramsden uses sociometric measurement to assess the social configuration of the interpersonal group (Ramsden 1960). Each member is asked at three different points in the program to rank himself and the others on dimensions of aggressiveness, leadership, contribution, involvement, cooperativeness, and friendliness. Then he was to rank the others according to how he liked them, how much he felt he resembled them, and how much he would be willing to follow them (87). Ramsden found high levels of agreement and intercorrelation among the group members and evaluated group development based on the degree to which members were appreciated for contributing to a work group (task) orientation rather than an enjoyment group (maintenance) orientation.

Hartl was even more ingenious in his approach. Using a system of categorizing people by body types (endomorphic or rotund; mesomorphic or muscular; ectomorphic or linear) and temperament (viscerotonia, somatotonia and cerebrotonia),[6] Hartl took sets of photos of the students, conducted interviews and asked students to rate themselves based on certain characteristics. Using statistical analysis, he determined "the somatotypic distribution of this group with respect to the descending strength of the endomorphic component" (1960, 99). He then correlated student temperament and body type with behavior in the group in an effort to study "the whole man" (106).

Other presentations at the conference confirmed the impression that group work was becoming more self-conscious and "studied"–at least among supervisors trained in the Institute of Pastoral Care. One program had group sessions four days a week for an hour at 4 p.m.

---

[6] Categories developed by Dr. William H. Sheldon.

> As we sat around the table in group sessions we noted
> such things as the student who sat at the side of the table
> and turned his back to the group leader. At times when
> anxiety producing situations arose he would turn
> completely around so that his back was toward the table.
> We watched this and other students for clues as to their
> attitudes toward authority, toward one another and
> toward the group as a whole....We watched tone of voice
> and agitation of movement for clues to anxiety, guilt,
> and fears....We used group sessions among other things,
> as an opportunity for evaluation of individual students
> (Rogers 1960, 46).[7]

In another program, the students

> eat together, sleep together, work together, and live
> together. They each have private rooms, but all adjoin,
> and one cannot retreat from interpersonal interplay if
> he would....Situations occur in living together which are
> often discussed when they arise. The feelings of the
> moment are examined. Many of the bull sessions turn
> out to be group therapy sessions....One hour a day is set
> aside for group dynamics....While students jokingly refer
> to the process as group dam-nimics or group dam-antics,
> they really regard it as the most helpful experience in
> clinical training" (Klinkman 1960, 63-4).

Despite what may have become excesses in group work in certain training
programs by the end of the 1950s, it was also through the increasing facility
and confidence regarding group dynamics that the Gordian knot of the two
founding organizations was finally loosened. In 1962, with the encouragement
of the Joint Executive Committee, the powerful Accreditation and Training
committees of the CCT and IPC met together during a free afternoon at the fall
national conference in Craigville, Massachusetts. Charles Hall, chair of the
CCT committee, writes:

---

[7] This same author notes: "Changing supervisors every four weeks had the advantage of giving
the student contact with a different personality. It also resulted in keeping a student from getting
too deeply involved therapeutically with his supervisor. While we wanted to help the students
to be sensitive to their way of relating to patients, we also wanted to keep a training program
rather than a therapy program" (Rogers 1960, 50).

I shall never forget that first meeting. Although the chairs had been arranged in a circle, all members of the Institute sat on one side of the room and all members of the Council sat on the other. We were lined up as if we were adversaries....Then, suddenly realizing that the group needed a process dialogue, we [Hall and Richard Lehman, chair of the IPC committee] made a suggestion: we should share the perceptions we had of each other, the stories we had heard about how each group conducted the certification of supervisors (1992, 122).

The participants quickly discovered that their stereotypes about each other were simply not true.

The more we talked, the more ludicrous it sounded to ourselves, for we could not pin these impressions on any specific persons. We had inherited an oral tradition that said we were different, and we supposed these descriptions fit others but not, in all probability, the persons in that room." (122).

The next day the committees met together to do some student consultations, and the following year began to meet jointly to "accredit" supervisors. This breakthrough was one among several accomplishments which paved the way for the eventual establishment of a unified organization of the Association for Clinical Pastoral Education in 1967. Charles Hall concludes, "Making use of the CPE educational methods of group process and the interrelationship of concept and feeling certainly facilitated our successful functioning together" (135). So much so that at the first official meeting of the House of Delegates in 1967, Edward Thornton functioned "as an observer in a group dynamics process" and reports in detail on the discussions (Thornton 1970, 192).

SUMMARY

The 1950s saw a huge growth in the intensity, importance, and variety of unstructured group work in clinical training programs. Articulation of this work was initiated by Robert Leslie at Boston Psychopathic Hospital in his 1951 article in *The Journal of Pastoral Care*. Leslie's interpersonal approach emphasized the importance of group warmth and cohesion, the sharing of negative feelings, working through relationship to authority, and experiencing personal growth and acceptance. In the process it was assumed each student would also learn something about interpersonal group dynamics. Both Reuel Howe and Thomas Klink would affirm and develop this basic approach.

At the same time, a second approach was being developed in New York where traditional psychoanalytic concepts were being applied to group work in the church (Kew and Kew 1955). Though counselors in the field of pastoral psychology were interested in this psychotherapeutic approach (as were some local church pastors), it is not clear to what degree it was taken up by chaplain supervisors running clinical training programs. It is clear that chaplain supervisors in both Boston and New York were interested in what they could learn from the field of psychiatry in working with groups of patients and, by extension, students.

Toward the end of the 1950s a third approach to group work evolved at Boston State Hospital, where all students participated in a clearly delineated psychodynamic "group seminar" as part of their training program. The purpose of this experience was to learn a theory of group process through participating in that process. The goal was to teach ministers-to-be more effective ways to care pastorally for groups-as-a-whole in the local church. Particular attention was given to issues of authority and leadership in this group training. Through the writings of Judson Howard, this approach (based on the work of Lewin and Bion) was publicized and became influential, but was not always understood or appropriately applied.

A unique element in group work in CPE programs was emphasized by Ernest Bruder. In the tradition of Anton Boisen, Bruder viewed the student group as a kind of small church in which ventilation of feelings led to experiences of profound acceptance by and reconciliation with others and God. These experiences in training would affect one's life, one's theological view, and one's ministry. Though leadership of this interpersonal group process was not necessarily based on specific psychotherapeutic concepts, its results could be intensely therapeutic (that is, changing and healing) for students. Within this process the interplay between psychological insights and theological convictions was expected to be a focus of reflection.

A major issue being worked on during the 1950s was the relationship of clinical training to therapy. The development of a more self-conscious interpersonal process-group component in training programs raised this question quite forcefully. Other themes to be heard from this decade include awareness by individuals in a therapeutic group of repeating patterns from their family of origin (Kew and Kew 1955); increasing influence of the T-Group or sensitivity training movement and how it might contribute to church life (Wedel 1954); a reference to the group experience as a process which leads to awareness of the larger system and development of a group culture (Klink 1958); and some creative efforts to do research (Gynther and Kempson 1958: Ramsden 1960; Hartl 1960). All in all, it was clear by the end of the decade that, despite considerable differences in approach and theory, the small-group experience had become a vital and dynamic component among the descendants of the founders of clinical pastoral education.

mental Hospital

Boisen

What must I Know about people

Boston Acute Hospital

Dix

New York

Theology/Union

Hiltner

Tillich

3

GROUP WORK IN CPE (CON'T.)

Interest in small-group work during the 1950s continued to spread to the more liberal churches. In the early 1960s several entire issues of *Pastoral Psychology* were devoted to such themes as the therapeutic dimensions of small groups in the church, small groups and church renewal, and ethical dimensions of small group leadership in the church. What had previously been called group psychotherapy now appeared in a modified form and was called "group pastoral counseling" in the church (Holt and Winick 1963). These counseling groups focused on the individual problems of the members, dealing with such issues as faith shaken by a family tragedy, infidelity in a marriage, and job loss.

Ministers who would be "group therapists" were advised to select members carefully (no drug addicts, alcoholics, psychopaths, exhibitionists), begin and end each meeting with prayer, establish a norm of confidentiality, watch out for contagion of affect, take notes, and be aware of the effect of his (sic) position of authority on the group. Unconscious material was usually out of bounds, and "the minister must foster a climate in which unconscious material [dreams mainly] is repressed or suppressed, since he is not a psychoanalyst and is not equipped to deal with such material" (Holt and Winick 1963, 19).

But not much else was out of bounds. Ministers were encouraged to comment on sexual dynamics going on in the group, push nonparticipating members to participate, use other church activities as therapeutic assignments for reticent group members, expect indirect attacks in the form of anger at the church itself or religion, and much more:

> In response to the situation or need of a group member,
> he [the minister-leader] may visit a home, talk to an

61

employer, or otherwise intervene in a group member's external situation (Holt and Winick 1963, 20).

Members stayed in the group for as long as it took them to solve their particular problem.

As the therapeutic dimension of the small-group experience began to make its way into the churches and popular culture, there were only scattered references in the literature to unstructured group work in clinical training. This is in marked contrast to the flurry of previous articles. Much of the focus during the 1960s was on the clinical training movement itself– unification efforts within the organization, challenges that called for training to be less focused on therapeutic change and more focused on social and community ministries, increasing emphasis on the contribution of clinical pastoral education to theological education, and the growth of CPE supervision as a distinct profession or specialization within the field of ministry.

One article in *The Journal of Pastoral Care* by Clifton Kew, now clinical psychologist and director of group psychotherapy at the American Foundation of Religion and Psychiatry in New York, focuses on how to teach group psychotherapy to pastoral counselors. Kew focuses on the role and effect of student transference and teacher countertransference on the group process (Kew 1965). This is apparently Kew's first effort to move from didactic teaching of group psychotherapy to a more experiential model. He is careful to point out that his theoretical sources are from the fields of social psychology and psychiatry. A brief review by Charles Hall of an article from *Social Casework* appears in *The Journal of Pastoral Care* in 1966 and highlights the interrelationship between content and process in therapy groups (Hall 1966). The general impression is that during these years professionals involved in pastoral counseling and clinical pastoral education were searching for reputable (nonpopular) theoretical bases on which to ground their practice of small-group work.

In the meantime, Robert Leslie was continuing to present his own approach based on his work with theological students. A major piece entitled "Education in Group Methods: A Working Paper" appeared in *The Pastoral Counselor* (1967). Interestingly, this material was originally presented at the American Association of Pastoral Counselors (AAPC) annual meeting. It outlined the therapeutic intent of group work and the role of leadership, and included long sections of student testimony regarding the group experience. The material reflects Leslie's background in group psychotherapy as well as influences from the growing sensitivity training movement. Leslie's presentation also reflects the growing interest of pastoral counselors in group work.

In 1967 chaplain supervisor Lowell Colston visited fifty-seven clinical pastoral education centers in eighteen different cities. His purpose was to substantiate the ways in which clinical pastoral education might be different from traditional theological education. Though his report was never published, Colston made some important observations. For example, he saw that the theological method used in CPE had three unique characteristics: it was developmental, existential, and phenomenological in nature:

> Developmental because the focus is on process-learning rather than upon the impartation of content; existential because the concern is for present experiencing in which the student's self-consciousness is expanded and enhanced; phenomenological because the student's own uniqueness, the struggle for his own identity is at the heart of this educational enterprise (Thornton 1970, 232).

Since the report is not available, there is no way to know whether Colston had some specific observations about interpersonal group work and its contribution to these three foci. Nor is it clear exactly how the methodology generic to CPE might be affecting theological education in the seminaries. What is clear from Colston's report is the presence of a general enthusiasm for the reforming spirit of the clinical pastoral endeavor, a spirit which harks back to the beginnings of CPE.

By the time of unification in 1968, clinical pastoral education consisted of four primary elements which would remain constant for the next twenty-five years. First, programs focus on supervised ministry to persons in crisis in which pastoral skills and theological reflection are learned. Second, appropriate didactic and theoretical information is provided in order to assist the student in this learning. Third, a peer group "enables students to support and confront each other as persons and as ministers [and] provides opportunity for group supervision of pastoral work and opportunity for students to become aware of how their own emotions and their personalities affect their relationships" (Hall 1992, 162).[1] Fourth, the relationship with the supervisor helps the student integrate his/her training experience.

---

[1] This definition seems to encompass both semistructured and unstructured group work.

The 1968 summer program at Worcester State Hospital was outlined in detail by Edward Thornton in his *Professional Education for Ministry* (1970). Thornton chose Worcester State in order to contrast their current program with the first training unit in 1925 under Boisen. By this time the Worcester program was accredited by the Association for Clinical Pastoral Education and run under the auspices of Andover Newton Theological School. Chaplain John I. Smith, with the help of four assistant supervisors and four course assistants, enrolled twenty summer students. The goals of the program were to help students understand people, develop effective pastoral skills, work cooperatively with professionals in other disciplines, and be stimulated to do research (205). Among the various components of the program was the following:

> Students in the 1968 Summer School participated in
> small group meetings with an Assistant Supervisor and
> Course Assistant four times each week. One of the four
> sessions was used for a case seminar with material being
> presented by the student, and the other three sessions
> were *unstructured* (208; italics added).

Smith also met twice weekly with his assistant supervisors and twice weekly with his course assistants for a "group time." Various didactic sessions were given to all students with the following four offered on a regular basis: Interpersonal Relations, Adolescent Behavior, Group Psychotherapy and Group Work, and Phenomenological Theology. All but the last one (which was done by John Billinsky from Andover Newton) were given by psychologists or psychiatrists (207).

While unstructured group time seems to be a regular part of CPE training in the 1960s, in contrast to the earlier decade there is significantly less published documentation regarding how these sessions were being experienced by the students and conducted by the supervisors. Further, by the later 1960s some troubling questions were being raised both privately and publicly. In September 1968 an editorial appeared in *The Journal of Pastoral Care* entitled "Dealing with Defenses in Clinical Pastoral Education." It was written by Carroll Wise, who had trained under Boisen and followed him at Worcester State Hospital and then became professor of pastoral theology at Garrett Biblical Institute. Wise raises some delicate issues:

> In talking with students who have just returned from a
> quarter of clinical training one sometimes becomes

aware that they have been in a group where the supervisor
used a technique of aggressive attack on their defenses.
This aggressive attack began very early in the training
quarter and continued throughout the quarter (171).

Wise noted that in response to the consequent anxiety and depression from the
group experience, CPE students often got into individual therapy for support
during the training.

In some cases psychotherapists have raised a question
about the qualification of the supervisor for this job....In
talking to some supervisors about this one often receives
a very defensive answer. They are not willing to examine
their techniques, but rather are confident that they are
handling situations in the proper way. Some have said
that they have to prepare advanced students to respond
to the demands of accreditation committees that the
students may have to face in the future (171).

Wise goes on to ask that some distinctions be made between competent
supervision in CPE, sensitivity or T-group training, and group therapy. He
points out that because the goals are different for each, so also is the methodology
different. (Unfortunately he does not spell these distinctions out.) Wise is blunt:
"To confuse or not to understand the differences between these three types of
group process is to become inadequate or incompetent in each of them" (171).
He is also insistent that students in CPE need supervision and not therapy, and
he specifically focuses his concern regarding this distinction on supervisor's
(mis)conduct of group work.

During the next few years the situation was to become even more
confusing. Within two months of the Wise editorial, a major presentation was
made at the first national meeting of the "new" organization of clinical educators
(ACPE) which focused on the question, What has sensitivity training to
contribute to the enterprise of clinical pastoral education? The presentation
was made by seminary professor David John Wieand, from Bethany Theological
Seminary in Oak Brook, Illinois, where the leadership training component of
sensitivity training (known as T-groups) had been integrated into the curriculum.
"[We] are engaged in training men in pastoral care, much of which is counseling,"
Wieand explained. "It is my conviction that counseling and group process are
closely related" (1968, 17).

Wieand's presentation gave the history of the development of sensitivity training and sorted out three different foci of T-groups: personal growth, leadership skills, and organizational effectiveness. He listed the goals and methods conducive to group learning, shared tips on leading a group, and explained phases of group development. Wieand then explained the modified T-group structure called the colloquia (for undergraduates) and the advanced pastoral training seminar (for pastors) offered at Bethany. He concluded with the hope that his presentation "might have something to contribute to the designs and methods now employed in clinical pastoral education" (29).

For some supervisors this might have been the first time they had heard a comprehensive presentation on the concepts behind T-groups or sensitivity training, certainly at one of their own national meetings. Such terms as *unfreezing* (when a group member decompensates and decides to change), *cognitive maps* (models for understanding human behavior), *transfer of learning* (application of learning to the "back home situation"), and the difference between the *clinical model* (therapy for "normals") and the *action research model* (data collection and analysis by "professionals") were outlined by Wieand. On the other hand, these same supervisors may have wondered how this approach to group work compared to past approaches as described by Leslie, Bruder, Howard and others in the CPE tradition. They also might have wondered why Wieand seemed to assume they had no experience in small-group work.

Perhaps Wieand had read the recent Wise editorial, since he is careful to make the following point:

> ...the aim of the trainer should be to develop a permissive atmosphere in which trust can grow, and defenses be reduced. In this way the individual will be able to expose his behavior to analysis by himself and the group. There is sufficient anxiety inherent in the beginning of a new group and the T-group format that more harm than help can occur through fostering anxiety at this stage. The authority-dependency problem can be handled in other ways....(24)

As someone who had first attended a T-group training session in 1955 and also had some perspective on the field of pastoral psychology, Wieand includes in his presentation the important observation that, "As practitioners from Freudian and non-directive schools of psychology joined the group dynamics laboratory, the interpreting models became less sociological and Lewinian and more psychoanalytic and Rogerian" (19). It would have been helpful if Wieand had developed this somewhat offhand but significant–and complicated–remark.

The following year *The Journal of Pastoral Care* ran a major article on yet another approach to group work based on William Glasser's Reality Therapy. Written by a chaplain working with delinquent boys at the Kentucky Reception Center in Louisville, the article outlined the basic tenets of reality therapy: taking responsibility, determining right from wrong, and facing reality. There was little interest in underlying dynamics or unconscious material in this approach. Major components of the experience were feeling loved by the group, focusing on behavior change, dealing with the present, focusing on strengths rather than shortcomings, accepting no excuses, and never giving up: "The concept of forgiveness is strongly inherent in such a group, even though they are repeatedly let down" (Burck 1968, 22). The writer, in contrast to Glasser, maintains that knowledge of the "psychodynamic meaning of what takes place in groups" is essential for the leader even though it is never shared. The writer faults Glasser on several counts including his apparent obliviousness to the concept of sin.

The next year *The Journal of Pastoral Care* published an article written by Ward Knights, a chaplain supervisor who was running a clinical training program in a general hospital in New Hampshire. He was experimenting with gestalt techniques based on the work of psychoanalyst Frederick S. Perls. The article explains that the major emphasis in gestalt therapy is to become aware of the ever-changing, dynamic relationship between the individual person (figure) and context or group (ground) through specific actions in the here-and-now (called "acting out"). It is not so much the *why* but rather the *what* and *how* which matters in trying to understand human behavior and relationships. After sharing the principles of gestalt psychology with his students, Knights received group agreement to try this approach during their summer unit of training. A total of eighteen "experiments" (exercises or guided experiences) were performed in one-and-a-half-hour sessions. For example, in order to understand the idea of introjection, the students each ate an apple: "They were to begin eating the apple and observe as closely as possible exactly how they did this and to report on everything they were aware of as they ate it" (1970, 197). One student spent a great deal of time preparing the apple. Another gulped it down and got indigestion. Others shared bites with members of the group and so on. "Following this beginning the group naturally moved into a consideration of how things were taken in in other areas of their lives" (197).

The author prefaces his article with a particular plea to those doing clinical training: "Basically, it is my belief that within the clinical pastoral education movement there is a rich store of experience that has been too little shared, especially in relation to the CPE group experience" (193). And he ends with a warning that "it is my firm conviction that the area of group experience in CPE is greatly in need of exploration, and unless we press forward in this area we may indeed become stagnant and hollow" (198).

By the early 1970s the impact of clinical pastoral education (and its small-group experience) on theological education was increasingly acknowledged. In *Professional Education for Ministry*, Edward Thornton notes:

> The part clinical pastoral education plays in provoking crisis of purpose within a traditionally oriented seminary is substantial...[students] press for change from didactic to experiential styles of teaching, from abstract and grand generalizations to the concrete and particular cases; from mass groupings and the lecture method to small groups with individualized supervision of the learning process (1970, 231).

In some seminaries these changes were quite dramatic. James Ashbrook, professor of psychology and theology at Colgate Rochester Divinity School (CRDS), details efforts to use the small group "as an instrument to connect individual dynamics with institutional behaviors" at his school (1970). The faculty had set up mandatory small-group experiences throughout the three-year curriculum to create "some coherent interface" between personal growth ("the Freudian self-actualizers") and organizational change ("the Lewinian organizational-improvers"). Groups were conducted with a combination of T-group skills and psychodynamic understandings.

The first-year small groups focused on increasing student self-awareness, especially in relationship to the student's experience of the school's curriculum. The second-year small groups focused on the relationship between personal identity and professional responsibility (vocation). The third year, which was optional, consisted of two intensive fifty-minute group process sessions back-to-back, plus an additional didactic section each week. "Since students chose to take part [in the third year]," Ashbrook comments, "the leader assumed a more active role in focusing, confronting and exploring individual and group dynamics" (185). Ashbrook concludes:

> By sharpening with students a sense of the dynamics of
> the school as whole, by encouraging them to participate
> in the ongoing events of the school, by sensitizing them
> to one another, by developing their participatory skills
> through an awareness of the complexities of person and
> structure, the groups have had the effect of enabling
> students to be more effective collaborators in the whole
> institutional process. It is impossible to identify what
> change would have come without [the small groups]
> because they have been so integral to the ongoing
> dynamics of change. (191-2).

Though the specific contribution of CPE to these developments at CRDS is not specified by Ashbrook, no doubt student small-group experiences in CPE supplemented such efforts to respond to student unrest and implement curricular change in the seminaries.

Ministers trained through clinical pastoral education were experimenting with small-group experiences in their lives and ministries as well. A frank article in *Pastoral Psychology* describes the experience of five ministers (three of whom had done CPE in the same center) and their wives who met for eight sessions in a "leaderless group." Using a series of tapes they underwent various exercises together, accompanied by debriefings as directed by the voice on the tape. The author explains that the leaderless group was part of a number of variations which were developing at the time: "verbal groups, marathon groups, body-contact exercises, problem-solving situations, nude groups..." (Fitzgerald 1970, 21).

This particular leaderless group experienced some initial resistance (ignoring the tape), some mild enthusiasm at midpoint, and eventually hurtful confrontation and disillusionment, so much so that at the last session the hostess ended up going to her room in tears. The author concedes that the tapes were not intended for a couples group, nor were the specified ten sessions supposed to be telescoped into eight. In addition, the agreed-upon group norm of "minimal refreshments" was changed when meetings were held at one of the members' homes who was a wine maker. Finally, Fitzgerald notes that the "general avoidance of authority problems" led to the final debacle: "So much had broken loose in the final few minutes, and [in retrospect] we kicked our psychic tails for being impotent to change the course of events" (27). His assessment includes comments on the effects of "cheap grace" (Bonhoeffer), the importance of the leadership function in a group (Freud), and the deeper issues of authority (Bion).

One year later *The Journal of Pastoral Care* gives evidence of experimentation with sensitivity training within CPE itself. In the second week of a twelve-week program, "after considerable discussion," three CPE students agreed to participate with five mental health administrators, a chaplain supervisor, a staff psychologist, and two trainers in a week-long lab experience at Larned State Hospital. The design included "unstructured encounter group time" plus "exercises" and didactic sessions. This was apparently a live-in situation since the article specifies that there was "free time" for the group to socialize together in the evenings.

Learning conditions included focus on self-awareness and here-and-now orientation. Methods included feedback and unfreezing—"a graceless term that implies that a period of unlearning or being 'shook up'...must take place before learning can be initiated" (Keeley, Burgin and Kenney 1971, 189). The account indicates considerable anxiety and anger throughout the experience, but also new awareness of self and how people learn. One aspect of this experiment was especially noteworthy to the CPE students who participated:

> The supervisor's ability to risk himself as a peer in a
> time-bounded portion of the [CPE] quarter aided in the
> identification process of seeing a leader serve as a model
> flexible enough to continue learning and include them
> in the process (194).

The article indicates that this program would continue to include the sensitivity lab experience in future CPE training (but perhaps change the timing to mid-unit) in order "to help students become more aware of interpersonal relationships and group dynamics" (195). It is not clear whether there was any ongoing unstructured group time within the CPE program itself in addition to this training experience.

As the 1960s began with the spread of small groups in the church, so do they end with the same theme now writ large in the culture. With the publication of Thomas Oden's *The Intensive Group Experience* (1972), an excess of secular books on group growth (or "group grope," as some would have it), the involvement of Carl Rogers in the movement, and new "radical experiments" in group togetherness at places like Esalen, it was definitely time for those in the field of pastoral counseling and clinical education to take stock. In an editorial entitled "The Plus and Minus of Encounter Groups," the readers of *The Journal of Pastoral Care* are warned that growth and therapy are different, many leaders of groups cannot handle psychodynamic issues, people are too often manipulated through group pressure, and "privacy is invaded, defenses ripped down, and people hurt..." (Stewart 1972, 146). The author points out that a nine to fifteen percent emotional "casualty rate" among group attendees is "irresponsible," standards for trainers are nonexistent, and "the primitivism of some groups, with emphasis on orgiastic thrill seeking [i.e., sex] is not humanistic." The author then compares himself with Paul who remonstrated with the Corinthian church for eating and drinking too much during what should have been the sacred occasion of the Lord's Supper (147).

The editorial is followed by an article on "The Use of Encounter Groups in the Church" written by a highly reputable author, Arthur L. Foster, Ph.D., professor of Theology and Personality at Chicago Theological Seminary and Director of the Center for Theology and the Study of Man (begun by Carl Rogers). Foster's article begins clearly enough:

> While it has obviously been affected by learnings from
> T-groups and group therapy, the encounter mode should
> not be confused with them. The encounter group usually
> consists of normal well-functioning persons whose aim
> is personal growth (Foster 1972, 148).

The author then explains that encounter-group work now utilizes "inventions" from gestalt psychology, bioenergetics, psychosynthesis, psychodrama, sensory awareness, nonverbal communication, meditation, personal journal writing, and yoga. He encourages the use of the "encounter style" in a variety of local church endeavors: theological education for laity, leadership training, inter-generational groups, married couples groups, coffee house staffs, and retreats.

Foster seems most excited about what he calls his "house-church process and concept" which is "a translation into categories of the church and ministry of many of the learnings from encounter groups and the human potential movement" (152). The house-church process involves a "face-to-face group" of from twelve to twenty people who meet initially for a fifteen to eighteen hour session, and then continue with follow-up meetings over a longer period of time. There are six stages: building a faith-trust community, experiencing self-disclosure and personal growth, celebrating belonging, theologizing about the experience, engaging in mission to the world, and evaluating the ongoing house-church process. Faced with what he calls the "dehumanization, rootlessness, and fragmentation of the present age," Foster becomes expansive:

> So far as I can see, there is not a single theological or
> biblical doctrine that is not in some way illumined and
> made more available by the experiencing and reflection
> of the house-church process (153).

Despite the warnings of the editor about the excesses of the encounter-group movement, Foster's article reflects broad acceptance and potentially indiscriminate application of small-group work in the religious field.

This impression is further corroborated by several articles in *Pastoral Psychology*. In "The Small Group Religion" the author, a Catholic layman, encourages "churchmen" (sic) to look to "groupers" for innovative ways to heal estrangement and alienation in a "post-religious" age. The author contends that the intensive group experience and religious faith meet in areas like confession, repentance, forgiveness, and the transcendent. Group activity is like liturgy, the jargon like the Latin High Mass, the symbolic gestures of holding and lifting which are among the "sacred canons" of group conduct, all bring about "'wholly' community in a couple of hours" (Spehn 1972, 57). The author concludes:

> Christianity originated with a group of twelve adults
> engaged in 'learning, growth, and change' during a three-
> year-long, sometimes very intensive, group experience.
> True, the dynamics of the group and the leadership of
> an expert Facilitator didn't seem entirely growth-
> producing for one group member whose dramatic
> eleventh-hour dropping out is well known. But this was
> long ago–religion and group dynamics have both evolved
> much since then. And only the future will show whether
> or not organized religion and the as yet disorganized
> intensive group movement will be wise enough to learn
> from each other (58).

One of the more responsible and influential proponents of small-group work among pastoral counselors, clinical educators, and Protestant ministers at this time was O. Hobart Mowrer, a research psychologist with a particular interest in the moral and social nature of persons. He was concerned that the small-group experience in the church should not focus on the intrapsychic dynamics (neurosis) of the members, but rather on their interrelatedness (identity). This was Mowrer's way of distinguishing between the therapy group in the mental health setting and the interpersonal encounter group. Mowrer saw the small-group experience, whether professionally led or peer-led (such as Alcoholic Anonymous), as reconnecting or reconciling alienated human beings with one another and potentially with the larger church community. In fact, Mowrer claimed the small group movement to be a "revolution in religion" (1972).

By the early 1970s unstructured group work in clinical pastoral education was being strongly influenced by the growing popularity of small-group experiences and different psychologies within the human potential movement of the secular culture and the church. It is evident from a search of the pastoral care literature that responses of supervisors to this phenomenon and its impact on their own professional practice and competence were varied and often creative. Given that supervisors were known for their openness to experience and the degree to which they valued individual autonomy, it was assumed that these qualities could carry them forward in the future:

> It is not to be expected that there will be, or should be uniformity in the kind of group experience offered....Many different kinds of persons have become supervisors of CPE. The methods used successfully by one may be very inappropriate when used by another....The important thing, then, is that the individual supervisor find the approach to his students that works best for him, that he become competent in its use, and that he himself be open to new and more effective ways of functioning (Knights 1972, 191-2).

Knights concludes this "Brief Communication" in the *Journal* with an oblique reference to a larger problem: "In our search for more effective ways of fulfilling the goals of CPE there is another concern which we will have to face in the ACPE. That is the concern in relation to the 'nature' of our process of education and its evaluation" (192). Exactly what Knights is referring to here is not clear, but evidently all is not well from his point of view.

SUMMARY

As the human potential movement reached its peak during this ten-year period, there was a rising popularity of small-group experiences in the liberal churches and within certain quarters of theological education and seminary life as well as throughout the culture. In fact, the year 1968 was described as "the year of the group" by the *New York Times*. A review of the literature reveals the popular spread and application of psychoanalytic concepts to "small group counseling" in the church, the impact of sensitivity training on seminary education, the openness to experimentation in group work in clinical pastoral education, and increasing concern about competence and appropriateness directed at supervisors running training programs. The lack of any further articulation of group theory or group experiences generic to clinical pastoral education is also noteworthy and in clear contrast to the previous decade.

As wave upon wave of the human potential movement crested, one wonders whether clinical pastoral educators sensed themselves to be in danger of being swept out to sea. Were they all as open to trying new approaches in their group work as the literature might suggest? Or did the majority distance themselves to avoid being influenced by the rapidly psychologized and psychologizing popular culture? How were CPE supervisors dealing with the increasingly sensitive issue of education versus therapy in their group work and training programs? What about the questions being raised regarding their own competence? Was the growing trend toward national organization and professionalism causing them to close ranks on their actual practice?

It had been twenty years since chaplain supervisor Robert Leslie first articulated the varied dynamics inherent in the small-group experience. It had been over ten years since Ernest Bruder made his keynote address highlighting the exciting educational and theological dimensions of clinical pastoral education and the small-group experience. It had also been ten years since Judson Howard first wrote about the "peculiar" approach to group work at Boston State Hospital and encouraged research among his graduate students. The subsequent literature not only lacked such comprehensive scope and excitement about the evolution of group work in CPE, but also gave no indication of any awareness of this rich historical legacy. In view of the new organizational developments within the ACPE and aspirations of greater professionalism among chaplain supervisors by the early 1970s, the situation certainly presented a growing challenge for those who would seek to become clinical educators and competent group leaders in the future.

PART TWO: LATER DEVELOPMENTS (1972-1992)

At the end of 1971 the research committees of the Association for Clinical Pastoral Education, Protestant Hospital Association (College of Chaplains), American Association of Pastoral Counselors, and the Association of Mental Health Chaplains decided to coordinate their respective research efforts. They formed a Joint Council in Pastoral Care and Counseling, established a national clearinghouse on research, and began publishing the *Pastoral Care and Counseling Abstracts.*[2] Over the next twenty years the *Abstracts* became a significant source of interdisciplinary communication, listing in fifty-plus categories material scanned from over 100 national and international journals and seventeen other professional abstracts and indexes.

It comes as something of a shock to discover no listing in these same twenty years of any research-based article on the unstructured group experience in clinical pastoral education. Research articles about CPE which are listed in the *Abstracts* focus mainly on the nature of pastoral supervision, personal (student) growth in CPE, the identity issues of the supervisor, and the intrapsychic process of the student. Articles about group work included focus on groups in churches, leadership styles in counseling groups, the effects of prayer on a group, comparative benefits of group therapy, experiences in a minister's peer support group, and leading patient support groups. Despite this lack of published research on group work in CPE, the pastoral care literature does document some diverse and creative developments during the next twenty years.

In 1973 *The Journal of Pastoral Care* turned to a German source, *Dynamische Psychiatrie*, to print a translation of a fascinating article entitled "Some Specifics about Psychoanalytic Group Work with Theologians." The author, a professor of pastoral theology, delves into the usefulness of ministers being together in a psychoanalytically oriented T-group where they can work through their transferences to mother church, their oedipal conflicts with ecclesiastical authorities, their sibling rivalries with group members, and their ambivalence about their role in asking, "When am I a human being? When am I a representative of the church?" (Stollberg 1973, 80). The author has discovered that common defenses among clergy include extreme theological orthodoxy, the anal taboo (high valuing of money, order, and duty), the generation problem (commitment to being guardians of tradition), and "a striking tendency to teach others." The group experience can be helpful in the following ways:

> The analytical group, through the transference situation, takes over largely those functions that until then had been wishfully projected among other things on the

---

[2] Now entitled *Abstracts of Research in Pastoral Care and Counseling* and published by the Commission on Research in Pastoral Care and Counseling of the Congress on Ministry in Specialized Settings (COMISS).

church, the church board, and theology; the group thus relativizes the aggressively, libidinously charged professional situation, the objective problem of which can now be seen all the more soberly and free of anxiety (81).

Though not specifically based on a CPE training group, this article certainly pointed to dynamics pertinent to the clinical training experience, especially when the unstructured peer group is viewed through the lens of the psychoanalytic tradition.

The next year a lengthy article entitled "The 24-Hour Marathon" appeared in the *Journal*. It was co-authored by James Gebhart and Gorden Criswell, both of whom were CPE supervisors and pastoral counselors, and contained material which had been presented at the 1974 annual meeting of the AAPC. Between 1969 and 1973 these two men had run over thirty marathon groups involving a total of 400 participants, most of whom were clients from their counseling practices. A typical group consisted of twelve persons and two leaders who met for twenty-four hours of nonstop "treatment," sometimes in a hotel room, but more often in a retreat setting. Gebhart and Criswell were convinced that resistance to change could be overcome and demons exorcized through "induced" individual regression in a safe small-group environment. Based on gestalt principles such as going with the flow, focusing on the here-and-now, and watching the figure/ground interplay, the authors dismissed any distinction between growth and therapy as "arbitrary and obsolete" (1974, 223).

The most unique element in their design was something called "the nest." After initial introductions and individual contracting for work to be done, the leaders would go to a small corner of the room, throw pillows on the floor, and invite participants to assemble:

> [The nest] is, of course, deliberately designed to bring participants into physical contact with one another....A participant will find himself fanny to fanny, shoulder to shoulder, with his legs overlappping legs across from him. Unless he chooses to fold his hands across his chest, he will find his hands and arms in contact with other hands, arms, legs, or feet (232).

Despite initial anxiety and laughter, according to the authors, "in a short time...all the members relax and begin to enjoy a true group experience" (232).

The article reflects not only a high degree of comfort with the confrontative techniques of the encounter group approach, but also a depth of knowledge about the psychoanalytic tradition. Indeed, the authors compare the twenty-four hour experience to classical psychoanalysis itself in its "movement from the recognition of resistance to relinquishing crippling defenses to a new personality integration" (224, ftnt. 2). They are also aware of the pitfalls of participants with strong transferences or tendencies toward psychoses working in the intimate, sometimes chaotic and intense environment of the marathon experience. They stress the importance of co-leadership and seeking a balance between a "leader-created group" and a "group-created group."[3] All in all, their presentation shares with professional colleagues therapeutic work which is both creative and risky, based on their deep commitment to helping clients "get unstuck" through the "self-actualization potential of groups" (221).

Unfortunately this article is followed in this issue of the *Journal* by an annotated bibliography, compiled by Robert Leslie, on the topic of small-group work in the church. This editorial arrangement confirms the growing confusion between therapeutic groups in the mental health setting, pastoral counseling groups in the church, encounter groups in the popular culture, and process groups in clinical pastoral education. Specifically connecting therapeutic group work conducted by two professionals with the general growth of small groups in the church was inaccurate at best and increasingly problematic at worst.

One event occurred at this time which would directly affect future group work in clinical pastoral education. With the increasing enrollment of women in seminaries beginning in the early 1970s, women students were also entering CPE. At the national ACPE conference in 1974, Christine Hollingsworth and Imogene Bennett from the Southeast Region called a meeting for women students and supervisors to discuss concerns about women and clinical training. A follow-up memorandum sent to the Executive Committee made a number of recommendations including that "where a woman applies for CPE, the center provide a peer group experience for women students consisting of at least one other woman peer" (Hall 1992, 180). It also called for at least one woman on all regional and national certification committees reviewing women supervisory candidates. Though the ACPE as a whole would begin to be more sensitive to women's issues, the effect of women on the small group process in CPE (and vice versa) has yet to be studied in any depth.

---

[3] In a comment that might be aimed at CPE, they write: "The so-called 'non-structured group' does not exist. The 'completely open' group is someone's brainchild with many hidden agendas" (Gebhart and Criswell 1974, 230).

In 1975 the celebration of the fiftieth anniversary of the founding of clinical education became the occasion for historical reflection and theological critique. At the request of the History Committee of the ACPE, physician and historian Robert Powell gave the keynote address at the annual meeting and wrote a monograph entitled *Fifty Years of Learning*. Powell took the occasion not only to review the history of the movement but also to express dissatisfaction with the loss of the "Boisen tradition," especially regarding the theological, social, and pastoral dimensions of the clinical training enterprise. Powell was not alone.[4]

For years Seward Hiltner had expressed his longstanding disappointment that clinical pastoral education had become primarily functional (pragmatic and experiential) rather than theological in nature. An interesting piece which both summarizes Hiltner's views and gives perspective was published in this anniversary year by the *Journal*. Originally written for publication in a German journal, "Fifty Years of CPE" contains the following observation by Hiltner which is of particular interest to the present inquiry:

> The great change that has come in programs since the early days has been the use of the peer group for fostering educational purposes...the nature of the interaction among group members contains a potential, under wise leadership, for stimulating both personal growth and professional maturing that was not fully realized in the early years of the movement. For the most part, the CPE groups, because of the competence of the supervisors, have not fallen victim to the faddisms about small groups now so prominent in the U.S.A. The movement frowns on groups designed directly for therapy rather than educational purposes (1975, 94).

Though some may question the basis for Hiltner's judgment that recent "fads" had not compromised supervisory competence, his noting of the peer group as a later development and distinctive educational resource in CPE is important, especially given Hiltner's in-depth perspective and prominent position in the clinical training movement.

---

[4] See especially J. W. Hammett's "A Second Drink at the Well" in *The Journal of Pastoral Care* (June 1975).

Another aspect of the fiftieth anniversary celebration was the commissioning by the ACPE Research Committee and Executive Board of John Florell, Director of Research at the Virginia Institute of Pastoral Care, to do an analysis of the ACPE membership, their training, education, methods of service and other characteristics. Among the 3,000 members, there was a 45 percent return rate on the questionnaire. Approximately half of the respondents were CPE supervisors or those in the process of certification.

Despite the great diversity of facilities where CPE was being offered in 1975 (general hospitals, state mental institutions, parishes, prisons, pastoral counseling centers, seminaries, mental health clinics), the survey reported that "there is little reported difference in the kinds of services offered or used from one facility to another" (Florell 1975, 223). This high degree of uniformity reflected a decided tilt toward individual, therapeutic work. Indeed, the study showed that two-thirds of the respondents, in addition to their supervisory credentials, "were licensed or accredited to do some sort of therapy with counselees." Eighty-five percent of the membership rated individual supervision as one of the top four methods used in clinical pastoral education (226).[5] Florell noted that

> the trend in direct services is toward individualized personal relationships, rather than being group or liturgically oriented...more time [was] spent in services such as individual counseling as opposed to group work like family, small group, group counseling or corporate worship....Individual supervision was also the most frequently used method of supervision by certified supervisors. This does not deny the concept of group learning as an important element in the CPE learning process, but does show that individual elements were more popular than group elements (222).

Fifty years after the birth of clinical training a strong tradition was certainly in place, a tradition which emphasized experiential learning in the context of a one-on-one relationship with one's supervisor and one's patients (or clients or parishioners or residents). The peer group appears as a steady background or contextual element within this one-on-one educational process. Despite Reuel Howe's original challenge in the early 1950s and Seward Hiltner's observation

---

[5] The other three were structured seminars, unstructured seminars and group supervision.

in 1975, the development and articulation of interpersonal process-group work as a specific educational resource and method for student learning in clinical pastoral education may have been an interest, but it was not yet a priority. This would remain true for the next twenty years as well. Thus Charles Hall can conclude in his recent historical account that "during most of the history of CPE, the focus was on ministry to individuals and learning from individual living human documents" (1992, 164).

While CPE supervisors seldom wrote about the specifics of group dynamics in their own chaplaincy training programs, every so often an article appeared explicating some parallel group work in their institutions. "Education for Interdisciplinary Teamwork" by Larry VandeCreek and Jerry Royer is one such article. It describes the formation of an experimental, interdisciplinary student team of physician, pharmacist, nurse, and chaplain. Initial needs to belong and create a group "culture," subsequent struggles for leadership (especially between the student doctor and student chaplain), ongoing efforts to both work and play, the formation of various alliances, anger at the preceptors, and the eventual growth of trust and interdependency in their task (taking care of patients) are all noted. Reflecting the mood of the times in clinical education, the article concludes that it was primarily due to dynamic individual supervision (mainly with the chaplaincy student) that a depth of learning through the team experience was achieved (183-4).

In one year-long CPE residency program at the University of Chicago Hospital, a creative use of the peer group involved doing a research project together. The supervisors, Jim Gibbons and David Myler, discovered that doing research in this way intensified issues of peer group leadership and group identity and had "a positive impact on group spirit and cohesiveness due to the total group investment in the project" (Gibbons and Myler 1978, 44). It also increased professional self-esteem as the students won recognition both in and outside their hospital. Interestingly, because the supervisor participated in the project as a co-worker, the students experienced the supervisor's behavior and personality in new ways: "The quality of peer participation invokes increased supervisory assertiveness at times, or increased humility, as the project may lead into areas where the supervisor has no competence" (42-3). The success of this effort in doing peer- group-based research in this Chicago program continues to the present day.

Only two articles appeared in *The Journal of Pastoral Care* between 1975 and 1980 which contain any relevance to group work in CPE. The first was by a pastor and psychotherapist whose experience co-leading a therapy group in a mental health center totally changed his perspective on his "expert" role as pastor in the church (Higgins 1976). He realized that good group leadership, like good pastoral leadership, involves maintaining and enhancing group life but not necessarily any direct healing of individual members. The latter is the work of the group, not the work of the leader of the group. Even if a patient is suicidal or a church board member is suddenly beset with a personal crisis, trusting the group (or the board) to respond appropriately and helpfully is the key to healthy group functioning. The author notes:

> When the group leader abandons the group-leader position and attempts to do individual psychotherapy within the context of the group, the group begins to deteriorate and the individuals in the group stop healing each other and look to the leader for healing and therapy. The same is true within the church. When the pastor offers himself/herself as the healing tool instead of allowing the community of believers to be the healing process then the community breaks down and everyone looks for the pastor's healing and vies for the pastor's attention (49).

Though the skills involved in maintaining group functioning in this way are not explicated in any detail, it is clear that the author has learned a great deal about group leadership which could be of interest to those doing group work in CPE.

The other article was written by CPE supervisor Duane Parker and was entitled "Student-Directed CPE." This article was inspired by the work of educator Malcolm Knowles, a proponent of self-directed adult learning whose ideas were becoming popular in CPE circles. Parker's model was clearly an educational rather than a therapeutic approach in which the group becomes a work group along with the supervisor in order to solve certain basic questions: What is our role in the hospital? How are people admitted? What is supervision? What can we learn from patients? (1978, 163). Each group deals with these questions in a different way. Parker eschews the CPE supervisor as an authority figure who keeps his personality hidden behind a special store of knowledge and skill. There is no mention of an interpersonal process group as such in this model, nor any indication that the CPE experience involves dealing with deeper psychological issues either among individual students or in the group. Parker's article reflects the growing interest in supervision as education and here-and-now problem solving in ministry.

In addition to a growing educational thrust, a fresh breeze from yet another discipline was beginning to blow through the CPE and pastoral care circles. The first stirrings appeared in a workshop presentation at the 1977 ACPE National Conference entitled "The Use of Family Therapy as Preparation for Ministry within CPE and the Seminary Context." Led by a seminary professor and a chaplain supervisor, the workshop leaders explored ways in which understanding family systems can help students understand their vocational choice, their professional functioning, their personal growth, and their theological position. The leaders viewed systems thinking and the "new" field of family therapy as having "potential for the most significant impact on pastoral care since Carl Rogers and client-centered therapy." Among the areas of impact would be the "interaction within a clinical learning group" (Anderson and Fitzgerald 1977, 53). Though none of these ideas is developed to any extent in the workshop report, it does give a hint of things to come.

It is several years later before another article appears in the literature which deals, albeit tangentially, with unstructured group work in CPE. In a piece entitled "Clinical Pastoral Education--Exploring Covenants With God," chaplain supervisor Dennis Kenny attempts to correct the psychological emphasis in CPE by reestablishing some theological categories. Verbatims are called "pastoral call reports," supervisory conferences are "pastoral consultations," and the process group is changed to "covenant group" (1980, 109). In addition to changes in terminology, Kenny works with individual students trying to unearth the assumptions in their personal relationship with God which effect their relations with others and give shape to their learning goals in clinical training. Though Kenny does not delve into the group process, he does indicate his general approach:

> In covenant group I have sought to make the focus ministry to each other. The attempt has been to frame our interactions in our theological vocabulary with words like sin, forgiveness, reconciliation, grace, redemption, confession, absolution, etc. (109).

By allowing theological and pastoral (rather than psychological or educational) categories to be uppermost in the training experience, Kenny has tried to take seriously the concerns of Seward Hiltner and recover the spirit of clinical training in the Boisen tradition.

The next mention of group work in CPE is found in a *Journal* article which I wrote in 1980 in an effort to present a coherent theory of education during my own supervisory certification process. Entitled "Position Paper on CPE Supervision and Learning," six major modalities of learning in CPE are outlined: contextual, behaviorial, experiential, relational, developmental, and integrative. Under the relational heading the peer group is described:

> [The CPE peer group] serves as a vital support system as well as a locus for learning. It is a place where old behaviors can be observed, new behaviors attempted, and learning from peers and supervisor directly experienced and assimilated. Issues of trust, intimacy, confidentiality, honest and direct expression of feelings...are actively present....In addition, key areas pertaining to authority issues, anxiety and ambivalence will surface, especially during "open" seminars where usual norms of relating and expected leadership functions are suspended. How thoroughly a group works through these issues will determine to what extent the group can own its own process (Hemenway 1982, 199).

Footnotes to this section include references to the Tavistock Institute and to the psychodynamic approach of Irvin Yalom. The section concludes:

> The supervisor is responsible to participate in enabling the group to become a stimulus for its own learning; the group is not a context for supervisory "brilliance" or individual or group therapy. This latter can be identified when an issue between two students or a student and the supervisor constantly reappears and seems unable to be resolved, or when a student consistently blocks the here-and-now process of the group, or when a person's outside material becomes intrusive (199).

Here there is an understanding of the unstructured group process as distinct from individual supervision and therapy, yet focused on individual change and growth. Efforts to draw the line between student learning and therapeutic issues continue to be a theme as well.

At the 1982 annual convention George Fitchett, CPE supervisor at Rush-Presbyterian-St.Luke's Hospital in Chicago, presented a major paper on his "coherent theory." Fitchett's paper focused on the paradoxical nature of CPE and was influenced by his exposure to the double-bind theory and paradoxical interventions in the family systems field (Fitchett 1982). While accurately lauded as a remarkable effort to clear out the theoretical underbrush and reclaim the best of the CPE tradition (especially the work of Thomas Klink), Fitchett's effort was also criticized in its tendency to lose raw experience to the charms of pristine theory. Even more limiting was his exclusive focus on the individual and student-supervisory relationship. In an effort to dramatize a broader perspective, responder Grover Criswell tells a well-known Hasidic story:

After stumbling around for awhile, [they] come upon a man who has been lost there even longer. They all jump up and down and get excited.....Finally someone who can tell them how to get out of here, a man with answers. With a humility, echoing the best of CPE supervision, the wise old man [sic] responds that he doesn't know the way out. He, too, lives with the anxiety of not knowing. He does know where some thickets are. He has been lost in them. He does know where some bushes are that scratch and wound. He has the scars. "Maybe," he invites them, "if we journey together we can find our way, but at the very least, we will have each other" (1982, 118).

Though Criswell does not point this out explicitly, it is clear by implication (once again) that the group experience continues to be fundamental to both the theological and psychological situation in the learning of ministry through clinical pastoral education. Criswell's story might also serve as an apt metaphor for the general lack of clarity about group work in CPE. Though we may be somewhat lost, at least "we have each other."

Though there are relatively few articles published over the next ten years which focus directly on group work in CPE, those articles which made their way into print reflect growing originality and sophistication in supervisory practice. In 1987 *The Journal of Pastoral Care* published an article entitled "Families and Groups: Their Nature and Function from a Systems Perspective" written by Daniel DeArment, a CPE supervisor at Presbyterian Hospital in Philadelphia who was also trained in family therapy. The first half of the article reviewed recent books relevant to work with families in the church, while the second half of the article explored the differences between groups and families from the author's point of view.

DeArment notes that families are basically ontological (they simply are) while groups are teleological (they are only brought together by a task or goal). Individuals try to separate from families; on the other hand, individuals try to get included into groups. Thus, the primary dynamic in family life is intimacy, while the primary dynamic in group life is power. Despite this distinction, DeArment recognizes that families "undergo power struggles" (especially with adolescents) while groups "work hard on intimacy issues" (especially in CPE). DeArment concludes that the church or synagogue in order to become a community of faith must mix both these constructs–family and group, intimacy and power, love and justice. Thus, the rabbi or local pastor needs to be ready to deal with the complications of both these dynamics together (1987, 115-17).

The next issue of the *Journal* contains three articles relating to group work. The first article by Edward Madera and Barrie Peterson focuses on self-help groups in the church. It presents an excellent summary of the interface between these groups and the work of pastoral care. This article not only reflects the tremendous spread of Alcoholics Anonymous (AA) and its methods into the broader culture, but also signals a clear move away from some of the past excesses of encounter groups and sensitivity training experiences of the 1960s and 1970s (Madara and Peterson 1987).

This article is followed by the most comprehensive theoretical presentation of group work in CPE to appear in the literature. Summarizing his doctoral work, Graeme Gibbons, a chaplain supervisor from Australia, presents a model of small-group process work based on "Seasons of a Group's Life." He outlines three major structure-building seasons plus "structure-changing transition phases" which include "inter-season life" and "intra-structure life." Following R. B. Lacoursiere's *The Life Cycle of Groups* (1980), Gibbons outlines group tasks for each season and "proposes some of the essential leadership functions which need to be marshalled together from among its total membership if it is to realize its full potential as a group" (1987, 241). For example, during Early Life, these shared leadership functions include caring, directing, and negotiating. In Mid-Life these include integration, conciliation and imagination. In Late Life, the leadership tasks involve evaluating, celebrating and dispersing (242-3).

Gibbons emphasizes the importance of early group development if the CPE group is to reach its full potential. This is dependent upon the group leader stating at the outset the three-fold purpose (or task) of the group:

1. to provide as a project team and group a pastoral care service to the institution they are serving;
2. to learn as it works by studying the group's approach to providing pastoral care; and
3. to study the life of the group as the group evolves and develops in the here-and-now of its life (245).

In addition to describing various behaviors of group members at each stage, Gibbons deals with such group phenomena as inclusion of individual members, finding consensus, establishing boundaries (confidentiality), dealing with conflicts, identification, use of metaphor, and expressing loss and sadness when the group disperses. Among his original contributions is the concept of the transitional phases during which the leader must use the functions of analysis and strategy in order to help students deal with feelings of anxiety (dependency) and dissatisfaction (fight/flight) and consequent projections and scapegoating–psychoanalytic group concepts based on the work of Wilfred Bion. Identifying estrangement and disruption in interpersonal relationships as a "common enemy" to CPE groups (part of a transitional phase which can get stuck), Gibbons offers his own model of reconciliation based on the work of process theologian Daniel Day Williams. Of particular interest is Gibbons's insight that expectancy, hope, and optimism come through dyadic relationships (Bion) which, as he points out, is precisely the function of the individual student relationship with the supervisor and/or the effect of the presence of a co-leader in the CPE group. Gibbons's work is a thorough and substantial contribution to the theory of group work in CPE.

In this same issue of the *Journal* is an article by CPE supervisor Benjamin Bogia entitled "Group Supervision Versus Group Psychotherapy: Similarities and Differences For Clinical Pastoral Education." Bogia is responding to the longstanding dilemma in CPE of "the increasing interest in learning how to use skills and knowledge gained from psychotherapy for the benefit of CPE groups, while at the same time maintaining an educational focus" (1987, 252). Though Bogia does not really deal in any depth with group dynamics in this article, he does try to make clear that CPE is different from therapy because it focuses on clinical material and the educational/professional (rather than personal) growth of the individual student. The key to this difference is how the transference is handled. Bogia quotes an earlier presentation at a national ACPE conference by CPE supervisor (and psychoanalyst) Stuart Plummer:

> Supervision within CPE makes use of transference and countertransference to inform the supervisor. But transference is managed and diluted rather than ripened and intensified. To put it rather overly succinctly, in supervision the primary focus is clinical material and secondarily the student's reactions and responses. In psychotherapy the primary focus is the patient and his/her inner life and fantasies (Plummer 1983, 25).

In dealing with the dynamics of the group situation Bogia is basically using a psychotherapeutic model of individual supervision which he is applying to the group process experience. Throughout he is at pains to both hold on to the individual therapeutic dimension and keep it in perspective:

> There are, of course, times in an educational approach when a limited amount of personal "therapeutic" work must be done, but it is ideally always done for the sake of professional learning and growth, not for the resolution of personal life issues (Bogia 1987, 257).

The article is typical of the extent to which CPE supervisors continue to be ambivalent about letting go of the familiar psychotherapeutic model of working with individual students and their lack of awareness of any alternative conceptual model for working with the process group.

The idea that the small group situation in CPE could evolve into a team or group ministry first finds its way into print in a 1988 article written by CPE supervisor David Duncombe. This innovative approach, which involved a clinical training program on the campus of the University of San Francisco where team ministry was the norm, had certain built-in advantages:

> In team ministry we could observe one another in action and could give either immediate feedback or bring our observations back to group sessions. Since I was a member of the team, this allowed the supervisor to play the role of participant-observer (51).

Duncombe discovered that the group's involvement in public social justice efforts as a team permeated all parts of the program. Thus, unstructured group time often included personal feelings of the members about their team involvement in the ministry, and the verbatim seminars tended to focus on group interventions rather than one-on-one interactions. Duncombe notes that the biggest challenge was learning to work together. He concludes: "Supervision is at its best when it is interactive, not only conversationally, but participatively" (51).

The most recent article related to group work in CPE appeared in *The Journal of Pastoral Care* in 1990. This is an account by a male CPE supervisor and a female pastoral counselor (with licensure in marriage and family therapy) who applied family systems theory based on the work of Murray Bowen to their co-supervision of two different CPE units of training. Genograms were used to help each student surface family of origin dynamics, while in the more intensive interpersonal group work ("the family matrix") the development of sibling relationships and the taking on of family "roles" were examined. There is a welcome balance in this article between focusing on insights about individual students' efforts to "differentiate" and do more effective ministry, and the highlighting of dynamics within the group and the pastoral care department based on systems theory. The summer training unit was especially successful. When the CPE program ended–

> [The students] arranged for a group picture with everyone dressed "hillbilly," sitting on the front porch of the house where group meetings were held. We were designated as Ma and Pa sending the "kids" out to make their own way (Burton and Weinrich 1990, 338).

A sign that group work in CPE may be attracting more attention and interest is confirmed in the 1990 issue of *Journal of Supervision and Training in Ministry* in which there are three pertinent references. In a piece entitled "In Praise of Manipulation," CPE supervisor Dean Williams reflects on learning the art of supervision in the 1960s. He specifically remembers how the manipulative techniques of Fritz Perls helped him learn some dramatic interventions, especially about how to use group pressure and dynamics to overcome student resistance. Williams is forthright about the excesses of the past:

> Some of my early supervisors had manipulated our socks off by refusing to answer direct questions in an attempt to raise anxiety and force students into making choices for themselves. They used long silences in the group...and "attacked" candidates in certification committees to see how they would respond and whether or not they could handle conflict (214).

Williams now engages student cooperation and input into what he considers to be the more manipulative aspects of supervision, letting students know that "they have the power to stop the process at any time–not unlike the 'kill switch' some dentists give to their patients while doing heavy drilling" (216).

A second article is entitled "Ethics in CPE: A Consumer's Report" and is written by John Weston, an administrator of a health care center. Weston, who has done extensive CPE and supervisory training, explores the ethical dimensions of five aspects of the CPE experience: health care policy, patient care, interpersonal relationships, group dynamics, and the supervisory relationship. Weston's concerns about the interpersonal dimension focus on responsible versus irresponsible student behavior; his focus on group dynamics raises up concerns in the field of social ethics about scapegoating and "the tyrannies of the majority" (1990, 180). Weston is convinced that discussion of ethical issues in the CPE process is continually derailed in favor of the language of personal feelings and history. In this way the opportunity for practical moral thinking about relational and social obligations is dissipated in favor of expressing individual needs and emotions. He voices an important challenge for the future, especially in what he terms to be the forte of CPE–its group work:

> Rich with ethically interesting occasions, by rights CPE should be a seed-ground of ethical reflection and ethical training....What a shame it would be to allow CPE to continue to ignore this underexplored territory! (181-2).

The third article explains a four-week unit of training sponsored by the Department of Practical Theology at Vrije Universiteit, Amsterdam, which involves the students in doing pastoral care among local church members. This approach to CPE is quite directive and structured, and includes a one-and-a-half hour interpersonal group session every day. During the first half-hour group members talk about whatever they choose while the supervisor observes. The next hour is spent processing the implications concerning what went on in the first half hour. The author explains that the division of group time becomes less strict as the weeks progress and the students learn more about processing their feelings and giving feedback and evaluation among themselves. Supervisors meet with individual students for one-half hour weekly, and boundaries between students and supervisor are strict:

> The supervisor is not a member of the group. The supervisor will see the group only during official time, and not even during meals. We find that this distance forces the group to solve most problems internally, and the supervisor's normal social and private family life is preserved (Stange 1990, 93).

In 1992 ACPE Executive Director Duane Parker wrote an editorial for the *ACPE News* entitled "A Question of Paradigm." Through the lens of his own study of liberation theology Parker wondered aloud whether CPE supervisors need to look at group (social) rather than individual suffering in order to understand "the possibilities for transformation" in today's world. He sees that while CPE supervisors are busy helping individual students form their pastoral identity and feel better about themselves, the larger systems of family, church, health care, and culture are increasingly in crisis. He reports that at a recent meeting one supervisor commented, "Isn't it time that we discontinue individual supervision and use group supervision as our primary teaching modality?" Parker comments:

> Interesting question! At each International Congress, at least one German supervisor asks, "Are you still doing individual supervision in the U.S.?" Apparently most German supervisors do group supervision, not individual supervision. What would happen to a CPE program if it offered group supervision and if the supervisor and students were in covenant to discuss all aspects of learning in the group? (6).

This approach might also have advantages from the student's point of view. Indeed, in a following issue of the *ACPE News* one CPE student from Washington, D.C. reports a very positive experience in which group supervision was used in both the pastoral and personal integration group (process group) and the clinical presentations (Reed 1992). In this program individual supervision was offered only on request.[6] "The focus was community. The model was Jesus and Jesus' ministry in the midst of community....It was our responsibility as adults and pastors to look and care for our needs" (7). The student reports the growth of greater trusting and risking than she had known in previous CPE training. In the process the supervisor became

> a sojourner with me in my journey....[The group] became that community traveling down the road to Emmaus....We conversed with each other about things in our lives: our pastoral life history, our theology of pastoral care, our patient, family and staff ministry, our

---

[6] Some supervisors report that after their final certification they felt free to take this approach to individual supervision, but the practice is undocumented.

gifts and our growing edges....I had a team of pastoral caregivers in my midst that I had overlooked....We became pastors to one another, and we supervised one another....I realized that there was very little taken to individual supervision that could not be taken to group supervision. This was a very affirming and empowering realization (6-7).

Correspondence with Cameron Byrd, CPE supervisor of this program, confirms its value. He writes: "I am now pretty firm in pursuing this direction and will probably adopt it as the way I do business....I want it to influence our center to move in what I consider 'a more excellent way'."

Summary

The literature survey for the twenty years between 1972 and 1992 reveals a remarkable range of material which reflects a steady evolution regarding interpersonal group work in clinical pastoral education–despite the lack of any substantial research efforts or articulation of a clear theoretical base. The survey began with two somewhat excessive group examples occurring outside of CPE itself: the heavily psychotherapeutic model of a German clergy group (Stollberg 1973) and the excitement of risk and healing engendered by the American-born marathon group experience (Gebhart and Criswell 1974). By 1975, as the fiftieth anniversary of clinical training is celebrated, there is clearly a nation-wide "CPE tradition" which includes the interpersonal process group experience as a necessary contextual element for the more familiar and valued focus of individual supervision (Florell 1975). Openness to tension and critique is also part of this tradition. Questions about the loss of Boisen's original vision (Powell 1975b) and the submergence of the theological to the psychological (Hiltner 1975) serve as quarter-century markers and challenges. By this time the increasing presence of women in training groups is beginning to be recognized. One article, though not written by a CPE supervisor, clearly states that working to change or heal people individually within a group context undermines healthy group functioning (Higgins 1976).

New developments include the application of group work to team ministry in the hospital setting (Vandecreek and Royer 1975) and to research in CPE (Gibbons and Myler 1978). A beginning effort to reshape CPE and group work based on methodology from the field of education is noted (Parker 1978) as well as an effort to refocus CPE in theological rather than psychological terms

(Kenny 1980). The impact of systems thinking and family therapy initially expressed at a national conference (Anderson and Fitzgerald 1977) is later developed by practicing supervisors: one notes the differences between a group and a family (DeArment 1987) and another notes and applies the similarities in a CPE training program (Burck and Weinrich 1990). Systems thinking also begins to influence the search for a coherent theory of education in CPE (Fitchett 1982).

There is evidence that the group excesses of the 1960s have been replaced in the general culture with the more circumspect approach of a wide range of self-help groups (Madara and Peterson 1987). Differences between therapy and education continue to haunt CPE practitioners. While one CPE supervisor-turned-analyst is able to draw this line clearly for himself (Plummer 1983), another remains more ambivalent and thus more typical of CPE supervisors in general (Bogia 1987). The exciting impact of team ministry on a CPE program and its supervisor holds promise for the future (Duncombe 1988), as does a similar change in supervisory stance within a more traditional program in a medical center (Reed 1992). A report from a program in Amsterdam highlights a highly-structured approach to CPE and group work (Stange 1990), while on the American side cogent issues are being raised about the ethical nature of CPE, including the group experience. It is not surprising that at the present time major questions are beginning to be raised publicly about the balance between individual and group work in CPE (Parker 1992). Further, it interesting to note that the most comprehensive theory of group work in CPE in the literature during this twenty-year period has been presented by a CPE supervisor from Australia (Gibbons 1987) who based many of his ideas on the psychoanalytic work of Wilfred Bion.

It is fair to conclude that, in general, CPE supervisors have been lax about developing and articulating theoretical material relevant to their group work, or to subject themselves to the rigors of research in group dynamics. For the most part they are not cognizant of the history of group work in CPE nor are they particularly aware of suitable theoreticians to guide them in their practice. Since the group itself is a vital, if not *the* vital, component of the CPE experience, the task of understanding and utilizing the group more effectively emerges as a critical need today. In fact, knowledgeable and competent group process work may well be key to both the present and future of clinical pastoral education if its continuing contribution to theological education and training is to endure.

GROUP WORK
OUTSIDE CPE

PART ONE: HISTORICAL DEVELOPMENTS

T he early history of group psychotherapy grows out of initial developments in the field of group psychology.[1] One of the earliest proponents in this field was Gustave Le Bon, a French social psychologist. His book entitled *The Crowd: A Study of the Popular Mind* (1897) explores the loss of individuality which occurs when a person joins a group and comes under the sway of a charismatic leader. Le Bon viewed the "group mind" as having many primitive and impulse-ridden characteristics similar to a child. Le Bon was especially concerned with the suggestibility and disorganized nature of large groups. His work was no doubt influenced by some of the political developments in Europe at the turn of the century.

Interest in group psychology was further stimulated by the onset of World War I because physicians and psychologists were called upon to deal with the loss of individual identity and the problem of morale among soldiers. In 1916 Wilfred Trotter, an English neurosurgeon working among the troops, published a paper on the herd instinct in peace and war. He compared the multicellular and evolutionary structure of higher organisms with the instinct of humans to group together and develop multi-functional skills for the sake of survival. His work was much more positive regarding group phenomenon than the earlier approach of Le Bon.

American psychologist William McDougall sought to bring these differing points of view together in *The Group Mind* (1920). McDougall viewed the disorganized group, previously described by Le Bon, as fickle, emotional,

---

[1] Articles by E. James Anthony (1971) and Mark F. Ettin (1988) were especially helpful in writing this section.

93

suggestible, violent, and wild. On the other hand, the organized group uses its inherent emotionality for higher, more disciplined achievements. McDougall pointed out that five conditions need to be met to assure that a group becomes organized: group continuity, a system of group relationships, the stimulus of intergroup rivalries, the development of traditions, and the differentiation of functions within the group.

In 1921 Sigmund Freud published *Group Psychology and the Analysis of the Ego*. Freud distinguished between transient and permanent groups, heterogeneous and homogeneous groups, natural and artificial groups. He thought the most important distinguishing factor was between leadered and leaderless groups. Further, the type of leadership determined group life. The more dominant a leader the more regressive (less "real") the group becomes. When a group unexpectedly loses its leader, contagion of affect (anxiety) and panic will follow. Freud explored the psychological mechanism of identification which underlies group life, the development of group cohesiveness, and the projection of narcissism which can make a group seem special and transform the leader into an ego ideal for its members.

Freud thought that a group comes together not out of some herd instinct but rather as a primal horde drawn to a leader (strong male) to satisfy each member's libidinal drives. In this he was following Darwin's ideas as well as developing his own theory about the Oedipus complex. Freud noted that the psychological reasons for a member joining a group are fundamentally different from the psychological reasons for a person leading a group. This makes the situation psychologically and emotionally complex. Freud also thought that in a well-organized group individual neurosis is protected against and eventually disappears

Though none of Freud's immediate followers moved exclusively into the field of group psychotherapy, there were several who incorporated into their psychological theories a greater awareness of the social and interpersonal situation of the individual. Alfred Adler (1870-1937) thought that instead of instinctual biological drives determining individual destiny, there was an inner nature of the self shaped by both subjective values and social (interpersonal) interaction. Aggression rather than sexuality was the organizing principle of the personality. Breaking with Freud as early as 1911, Adler is considered the founder of the "new social psychology." Adler thought group treatment "made sense," and used to invite groups of patients into his home to experience a better social environment (Adler 1956).

Probably the most innovative contribution to the new field of social psychology was made by American-born Harry Stack Sullivan (1892-1949).

Creator of an interpersonal theory of psychiatry, Sullivan believed that the *self system* is a creation of responses to anxiety which the person experiences in the interpersonal context, especially during the protracted period of helplessness in infancy. Parataxic distortions, or the tendency to misrepresent one's perceptions of others, can be corrected by the consensual validation experienced in an interactive context (group). Sullivan developed the concept of the therapist as a participant observer within the treatment situation which he called the "psychiatric interview." Known for his highly empathic abilities, much of Sullivan's work focused on the latency stage of development when genuine interpersonal relationships are first formed.

The first psychiatrist to actually conduct psychoanalytically-oriented groups in a hospital setting was Louis Wender. Working in the mid-1930s, Wender realized that the group situation increased patient motivation to work through transferences toward both the therapist and other patients. Using the already established "class method," Wender lectured to his groups on the dynamics of human behavior and the significance of dreams, and then held general discussions. Like others working at the time, he had no particular knowledge of group dynamics. Later work by Alexander Wolf, an American psychoanalyst, became a prototype for the application of psychoanalytic principles in the group situation. In his classic manuscript "The Psychoanalysis of Groups," Wolf presented his views of the group as containing sets of "interlocking psychoanalytic structures" which make up the "group ego" and offer support to each individual's psychoanalytic work. Wolf thought that because of the formation of the group ego, it is possible to go deeper in the analytic work than in the individual situation. In addition, experienced group members can act as ancillary therapists. Wolf saw treatment occurring in a series of stages, and he often programmed certain set therapeutic tasks for the group with these in mind. He also initiated the use of alternate sessions in which the group would meet without the therapist in attendance.

Another influential person on the American scene in the 1930s was Samuel R. Slavson. In contrast to some of the previous leaders, Slavson always emphasized the autonomy of the individual intrapsychic process over the group process. Though he could be dogmatic at times, Slavson did some creative work with children in groups and also began "activity group" psychotherapy for adults. Not only did Slavson lead in efforts to organize group work (he founded the American Group Psychotherapy Association in 1942), he also made sure that group psychotherapy stayed within the field of applied psychoanalysis. This both protected and isolated the field of group psychology from the influence of more creative developments.

Probably the most colorful and creative of the early founders of group work is J. L. Moreno. He first met Freud in 1912 while working at the Psychiatric Clinic at the University of Vienna. After an evening lecture, Moreno reports saying:

> Well, Dr. Freud, I start where you leave off. You meet people in the artificial setting of your office. I meet them on the street and in their homes, in their natural surroundings. You analyze their dreams. I try to give them the courage to dream again. I teach people how to play God (1972, 460).

Moreno began working with people (including prostitutes) in groups beginning in 1913 through a street Theatre of Spontaneity. He emigrated to the United States in 1925 and became a tireless organizer and writer on behalf of group psychotherapy. In 1931 he first coined the term *group therapy* and edited a journal called *Impromptu* which in 1949 would become *Group Psychotherapy*.

Moreno believed that group and action methods comprise a veritable psychiatric revolution. More of an actor than a therapist, Moreno thought that by acting out life's tragedies, the protagonist, the director, and the audience could experience together a catharsis of feelings which would bring about absolution and healing for everyone. His methods included psychodrama (reenacting the actual situation), sociodrama (enactment of a concrete societal problem), and role playing. Moreno has had a wide influence. His sociometric method of measuring interactions between individuals in a group setting has become a useful research tool. His use of dramatic games as warm-up exercises became popular in sensitivity training. His emphasis on here-and-now action and existential experience has been adopted by gestalt therapists and encounter groups.

If World War I elicited growing interest in group psychology, World War II gave birth to group psychotherapy. Not only did the war cause many leading psychoanalysts from Europe to emigrate to Britain and the United States, resulting in a rapid growth in the cross-fertilization of ideas, it also generated the need for new treatment modalities. In England, one of the largest Army centers for psychiatric casualties was located at Northfield. Treating the patients as if they were responsible civilians, the analysts in the Northfield Experiment created discussion groups and a therapeutic milieu in which the group itself became instrumental in the treatment of its individual members. Unfortunately, the Army was not supportive of this radical approach to those with war psychoses and discontinued support of the effort after six months. However, in response to deepening excitement about the Northfield Experiment in the psychiatric community, analytic practitioners began in earnest to discuss the implications of their ideas about leaderless groups and the analytic approach to understanding group behavior. Two leaders involved in this effort were Wilfred Bion and S. H. Foulkes.

Wilfred Bion (1906-1976) was a British psychoanalyst who was influenced by the British object relations school and particularly Melanie Klein's theory of projective identification. Though Bion did not consider himself to be a group psychotherapist, he was a psychoanalyst who was deeply interested in group psychology, especially leaderless groups. In his position as director of group psychotherapy at the Tavistock Clinic in London (1945-1953), Bion would make a unique and substantive contribution to both the theoretical and practical aspects of group work within the psychoanalytic tradition (see chapters 6 and 7).

Building on the work of Le Bon and McDougall, Bion viewed a group as working at both a manifest and a latent level. Without a leader to help organize and focus its task (manifest level), the group's unconscious and irrational fears and fantasies take over (latent level). Thus, within any group there are actually two groups: a working group and a *basic assumptions* (BA) group. The latter will do anything to meet the group's primary emotional needs for a leader when these needs are not being met on the manifest level. Ba groups communicate nonverbally, intuitively, and by contagion of affect. They are of three types—dependency, fight/flight, and pairing. Though individuals contain all three inclinations, each have certain leanings or *valences* which they prefer. According to Bion, there are actual social institutions or cultures in which the needs of the basic assumptions groups have been realized: the dependency group in the church, fight/flight in the army, and pairing among the aristocracy.

S. H. Foulkes (1898-1976) was not only a creative and inspiring practitioner of group work himself, but he was also an innovator in terms of theory. Foulkes was interested in how illness occurs in a person. In the analytic group situation (usually of two to three years' duration), this is explored within the group matrix (small group) with the help of a conductor (the therapist). Because the group matrix is related to the patient's larger network (family, other patients, community), the patient's symptoms and illness are considered to be part of an interdependent social field of interaction. As illness abates, this change can cause crisis and disequilibrium in the larger network. Though Foulkes focused primarily on the group analytic situation (giving his attention to transference, resistances, defenses in the here-and-now in the group), his awareness of the patient's total network was noteworthy and reflected the influence of one of the emerging leaders in the field of social psychology and group relations–Kurt Lewin.

Kurt Lewin (1890-1947), variously regarded as a social psychologist, personality theorist, and creative experimentalist, is considered to be the founder of group dynamics and "action research." He began his career as a professor of psychology at the University of Berlin, but being a Jew in Germany, he was forced to emigrate in 1932. Initially influenced by the "wholism" within German gestalt psychology, Lewin later developed his own field theory of the personality. Lewin thought that human behavior is largely shaped by the psychological need for "life space," which is determined by the permeable boundary between the individual and the groups to which one belongs (family, nation, race). Lewin explained human behavior through such dynamic concepts as psychical energy, tension, equilibrium and disequilibrium, need, valence, and vector (or force).

Lewin first used the term *group dynamics* in an article published in 1939. He was referring not only to the positive and negative tensions within a group as members vie for adequate life space, but also to the ways a group can change individual behavior. His approach was ahistorical since he was interested primarily in how people communicate (process) rather than what they communicate (content) or why they communicate (analysis). Lewin was primarily interested in helping groups serve more socially responsible roles in society.

In 1946 Lewin was asked to help the Connecticut State Inter-Racial Commission in its efforts to increase understanding of and compliance with the Fair Employment Practices Act. On the first evening of a two-week predesigned workshop, a feedback session was planned for the total staff concerning the group work done during the day. Research observers in each group had recorded behavioral interactions and sequences among group members. Several of the trainees asked to attend the feedback session with unexpected results:

> The open discussion of their own behavior and its observed consequences had an electric effect both on the participants and on the training leaders.... Immediately participants began to join observers and training leaders in trying to analyze and interpret behavioral events....Before many evenings had passed, all participants...were attending these sessions. Many [sessions] continued for as long as three hours. Participants reported that they were deriving important

understandings of their own behavior and of the behavior
of their groups (Benne 1964, 82-3).

Out of this unexpected experience, was born the Basic Skills Training
Group (BST) in which a process observer was present to feed back data about
group interactions. The following summer the BST was built into a three-week
workshop held at Gould Academy in Bethel, Maine. The site, a virtual "cultural
island," was chosen because of Lewin's conviction that "change was more likely
if the usual situational forces which acted to resist change could be left behind"
(Lubin and Eddy 1972, 822). Within a year the BST groups evolved into training
or T-groups and the National Training Laboratory Institute (NTL) was
established (under the aegis of the National Education Association) at the Bethel
site. Unfortunately Lewin's early death in 1947 precluded his knowing the
wide-ranging ramifications of his contributions about leadership and learning
in the small group context.

It is important to note that the theories of Wilfred Bion had a major impact
on the T-group theorists during the 1950s. One historian notes that "conceivably,
a therapy group at Dr. Bion's at Tavistock, in London, might not differ very
much from a T-group at Bethel" (Bennis 1964, 273). At that time it was with
growing excitement that the Americans awaited publication of Bion's latest
articles from abroad and began to work with his ideas around the determination
of a work group, the formation of a group culture, and how the valence of
individuals contributed to the underlying emotional components of the small
group experience.

However, as T-groups increasingly came under the influence of sensitivity
training and the encounter-group movement in the United States during the
1960s, Bion's emphases on learning about and working with the unconscious
group process as a whole were lost. Instead, NTL group work began to focus
on interpersonal relationships, the here-and-now group experience, and
individual (therapeutic) change. In this assimilation process NTL's original
agenda of understanding group dynamics as fundamental to organizational
development and social change was also obscured. These shifts were reinforced
by the increasing tendency in the NTL work to abandon the use of sociological
and Lewinian terms of reference in favor of therapeutic and Rogerian concepts
in the training (Benne 1964, 91-2). An example of this phenomenon is seen in
the growing unwillingness at NTL to distinguish between role development
(education) and personality change (therapy) in group work. "Attention by the
trainer to one, to the exclusion of the other," one of the experts declared, " will
limit the richness of the group experience."

One of the reasons T-group work, and later sensitivity training, became so influential in the United States was the focus from the beginning at NTL on developing theories about group dynamics and publishing research efforts. Significant ideas were developed linking group change and personal growth (Gibb 1964), delineating stages of group life (Bennis 1964), outlining the psychodynamic principles underlying the T-group process (Whitman 1964), and explicating "process analysis" known as T-grouping (Shepard 1964). As the NTL approach broadened into "human relations training," it joined the human potential movement of the 1970s and made a major and lasting impact on the wider culture. Requests for two-week training workshops poured in from church and denominational executive offices, industrial organizations, oil companies, and public school systems, as well as colleges and universities.

Behind all these developments was the extraordinary blossoming of humanistic psychology during the late 1950s and early 1960s in the United States. In large part these developments were a reaction against "organizational man" and what was increasingly experienced as the impersonal nature of post-war American industrial, technocratic society. In smaller part this was also a reaction against the previous pervasiveness and disciplined strictures of the psychoanalytic tradition itself. One historian comments: "They [proponents of the 'new' psychology] concluded that it was those higher capacities, rather than unconscious conflicts or habits, that most deeply defined the self" (Holifield 1983, 310). Abraham Maslow, Karen Horney, and Rollo May were among those who accented the human potential for growth, fulfillment, and creativity. Modern experiences of meaninglessness and nonbeing in an increasingly secular culture also found resonance in the growing philosophical interest in existentialism (Camus, Sartre, Kierkegaard, Victor Frankl), phenomenology (Husserl, Heidegger), "in-depth" theology (Paul Tillich), and mysticism (Martin Buber). The creative popularization of psychoanalytic ideas added to the array of therapeutic opportunities for healing and growth.

In 1950 Frederick Perls, who was a trained psychoanalyst and had been one of Theodore Reich's patients, published his treatise on gestalt therapy. Combined with Perls's charismatic self- presentation and pragmatic approach to solving intrapsychic problems, gestalt therapy had a huge impact on the general culture with its emphasis on emotional spontaneity, enhanced self awareness and increased physical expression. The flavor of Perls's approach is immediately captured in the "Gestalt Prayer":

> I do my thing, and you do your thing. I am not in this
> world to live up to your expectations. And you are not

in this world to live up to mine. You are you, and I am I,
and if by chance we find each other, it's beautiful. If
not, it can't be helped (Perls 1969, frontispiece).

By 1965 Perls's workshops at the Esalen Institute at Big Sur in California were taking in over $1 million a year and had spawned nearly one hundred "growth centers" around the country.

In 1966 Eric Berne, psychotherapist and popular author of *Games People Play*, published his *Principles of Group Treatment* in which he applied his games theory and transactional approach (based on psychoanalytic theory) to a group treatment modality. Berne's ideas were cogent and accessible to a wide variety of people in the helping professions. Thomas Harris's *I'm Ok–You're Okay*, published in 1967, assured the wide influence of transactional analysis (TA) at that time and for the next two decades. One author comments that by the late 1960s in clergy circles, the Bernean terms for the three ego states–parent, adult, child–"became almost as familiar as Father, Son, and Holy Ghost" (Hulme 1973). When psychologist William Schutz published *Joy: Expanding Human Awareness* in 1967, it too was an instant bestseller. It was Schutz, more than anyone else, who transformed the sensitivity training approach into a freewheeling encounter-group movement, encouraging weekend marathons among strangers which involved physical contact games and group fantasies– all intended as emotional shortcuts to psychotherapeutic change.

So it was that by the early 1970s the small-group experience had become an exciting, extremely diverse, and somewhat distrusted ingredient in American popular culture. News reporter Jane Howard, on leave from her job at *Life* magazine, researched material for her book *Please Touch: A Guided Tour of the Human Potential Movement* by attending all sorts of groups: marathon weekends, nude fests, drug rehabilitation seminars, interracial groups, an advanced personal growth labs, nonverbal sensitivity training sessions, and so on. Even Carl Rogers had joined the effort, establishing himself as a strong proponent of humanistic psychology at his Center for the Studies of the Person in La Jolla, California. Rogers now claimed without reservation that the person-centered small-group experience is "the most rapidly spreading social invention of the century, and probably the most potent" (1970, 1).

By the early 1970s it was possible to distinguish between sixteen different types of groups. The following is a condensed version of Hyman Spotnitz's article, "Comparison of Different Types of Group Psychotherapy" (1971). Such a listing gives immediate evidence of the richness and diversity of the group phenomenon at that time.

1. Analytic Group Psychotherapy (Freudian)
Based on the individual psychoanalytic approach (Freud, Wender, Wolf, Slavson) conducted in a long-term group setting. The goal is characterological change and psychosexual maturation. Resistance and transference are worked through by dreams and free association. There is little interest in interpersonal functioning. Ego strength and tolerance for regression needs to be assessed before entry into the group.

2. Analytic Group Psychotherapy (neo-Freudian)
The Adlerian approach posits members as social beings whose behavior is directed toward a unity (dynamic, somatic, psychological, social) of the personality. The atmosphere is based on social equality and helpfulness. Efforts are made to change maladaptive behavior and to increase self-confidence. Includes the Sullivanian approach which notes the creation of an interpersonal group culture, focuses on feelings of anxiety and loneliness, and pays attention to nonverbal behavior in order to become more socially effective. The primary focus is on the individual in the group context.

3. Psychotherapy Through the Group Process
Based on Bion, Foulkes and Ezriel, and developed by Whitaker and Lieberman (1964), it focuses on the development of a "group focal conflict" which arouses anxiety regarding individual intrapsychic conflicts from childhood. This anxiety is defended against by stereotypical individual and group behavior. The group offers a corrective emotional experience in an effort to change individual maladaptive behavior. Insight and catharsis may happen but they are not central. Treatment occurs through the group process, the therapist is relatively inactive, commenting only on the group dynamics.

4. Existential or Experiential Groups
Based on Binswanger (1942) and Thomas Hora (1959), this approach emphasizes authentic group participation under conditions of openness, receptivity, and responsiveness. Unconscious material is not explored and little attention is paid to alleviating symptoms. Rather, focus is on the here-and-now being in the world. There is a high respect for integrity and freedom (ability to choose) and concern with experiences of anxiety, loneliness, and meaningless (human values). Psychodynamic and

sociodynamic approach is broadened to include phenomenology and ontology.

5. Group Psychotherapy (Adaptational Approach)
Conducted at a support level for psychiatric in- and out-patients. No effort made to remove unconscious conflicts. Emphasis is on anxiety experienced in the group situation as a defense against intimacy. Therapist is an authority figure, keeps control of sessions, encourages ventilation of hostile feelings. Goals are to improve reality testing, socialization, and motivation for further therapy. Under stress patients will regress. Not considered a method for personality maturation.

6. Psychodrama
Begun by J.L. Moreno in 1920s, this approach uses acting out as a method for catharsis and reality testing. It is especially effective with psychomotor disturbances as well as marital and family conflict. Goals are to structure internal and external experience, and secondarily, to increase spontaneity. Tends to foreclose on freely-chosen behavior. Tends to meet narcissistic need gratification rather than focus on emotional maturation.

7. Transactional Group Therapy
Founded by Eric Berne, focuses on loosening up resistances and transference through transactional "games" and "scripts." Unconscious material worked with but not stressed. Patient learns to control his energy and move between different ego states (adult, parent, child). There is high value on personal authenticity in the group situation. Patients are picked at random. The playful and accessible character of this approach tends to obscure its seriousness.

8. Person-Centered Psychotherapy
Introduced by Carl Rogers, this is a nondirective, nondiagnostic, and nonclinical method. Therapist conveys empathy, acceptance, and understanding to enhance self-esteem, ability to cope with stress, and capacity for self-direction. There are no interpretations, no dealing with transference, no process comments, no planned "exercises." Can lead to some functional improvement but not necessarily ability to deal with deeper problems. Particularly appealing to people who feel resentful about past authority figures.

9. Behavioral Group Therapy
Characterized by short-term approach with specific goals, desensitization, and assertiveness training (Lazarus). It is effective with sexual disorders and maladaptive habits. Therapist is didactic and sympathetic–using role playing, psychodrama, group feedback, modeling, and reinforcement. Underlying anxiety and impulses are not dealt with. Tends to further inhibition and repression for the sake of coping.

10. Gestalt Group Therapy
An experiential approach founded by Fritz Perls. The goal is to stay with here-and-now feelings and physiological responses. Uses flexible games and rules, and is more interested in the "what" and the "how" than the "why." Goal is to integrate disowned parts of self under direction of the therapist and through the motivation of the group presence. Work primarily done with individuals on a "hot seat." Helpful for people with a "low drive" to learn.

11. Reality Therapy Groups
This approach, founded by William Glasser in the mid-1950s, rejects concept of mental illness and other analytic categories. It focuses on individual responsibility and behavior in a group context, using educational and problem-solving approach. It emphasizes personal involvement, development of a plan of action, and relationship with "real" group members and therapist. Goal is emergence of a "success identity." Particularly effective with juvenile offenders.

12. Rational/Emotive Group Therapy
The goal of this educational approach, founded by Albert Ellis in the late 1960s, is symptom removal and acceptance of reality. Therapist takes active role in uncovering irrational thinking (Belief System) and anxiety aroused by Activating Events which lie behind self-defeating feelings. Uses homework assignments to bring about change. Goal is to take responsibility for one's emotional life, and become more tolerant and rational.

13. Sensitivity Training Groups
This short-term (1-2 weeks) approach evolved from NTL and T-groups and was initially used in community and industry. Individual learning

derived from interpersonal group process. Diffuse boundary between education and therapy; techniques are not standardized and depend on training of the leader. Role play, nonverbal techniques and body contact are used. Valuable in developing leadership skills. Participants need to be well defended (i.e., "normal"). Goal is to promote personal growth, greater authenticity and self awareness.

14. Marathon Group Therapy

Developed out of sensitivity training groups by George Bach and Frederick Stoller. Group pressure is exploited to generate psychological intimacy via single 24-hour or weekend experience. This approach is supplemental to individual therapy. Therapist sets tone and models patient role, looks for rapid change, honesty and authenticity, eschews psychological language. Goal is new behaviors to deal with old problems, but overpowering of defenses can be countertherapeutic.

15. Encounter Groups

An umbrella term used to include sensitivity training, gestalt, marathon, person-centered groups. Group is time-limited and requires minimal screening for membership. Goal is personal and interpersonal growth, valuing honesty and reciprocity. Leader as facilitator and model. Group experience meets intimacy needs and craving for self-discovery. More immediate gratification than T-group (educational) or psychoanalytic approach (therapy). Emphasis is on interpersonal more than group process (Egan 1973). Influential in group psychotherapy field since 1970s (Yalom 1985).

16. Self-Help Groups

Successor in late 1980s to encounter groups, but actually begun in 1935 (AA). Employs some encounter techniques with high degree of honesty and reciprocity expected. Membership based on specific problem area (alcohol, divorce, loss of child). Groups are member-run and generally leaderless. Norms include nonintrusiveness, anonymity, and story-telling with an emphasis on self-healing and change. Combines didactic and discussion approach in a supportive and comforting atmosphere.

PART TWO: CURRENT CONSIDERATIONS
DEVELOPMENTS AFTER 1970

During the next twenty years the field of small-group work would struggle to plumb the riches, avoid the excesses, and sort out the confusions of the previous twenty years. One of the earliest and most succinct presentations was offered by Malcolm and Hulda Knowles in *Introduction to Group Dynamics* (1972). The Knowles managed to make sense of the then-current array of groups, suggested clear stages of group development, and outlined ten properties of functional groups: background of the members, participation patterns, clarity of communication, degree of cohesion, atmosphere, ethical standards, sociometric patterns of relationships, structure and organization, procedures and rules, and goals (Knowles and Knowles 1972, 39-50). Though the authors emphasize that to understand groups one must start with the individual, they also incorporated the work of Bion, Lewin, and the NTL in an effort to avoid the pitfalls of doing psychotherapeutic work in a learning group context.

In 1973 Gerard Egan published *Face to Face: The Small-Group Experience and Interpersonal Growth* in which he also makes an effort to establish operational and behavioral norms which would assure that a small-group experience is a laboratory for learning interpersonal skills rather than a therapeutic free-for-all. Basing his theoretical approach on Abraham Maslow's *Toward a Psychology of Being* (1968), he writes:

> A great deal of human energy and money has been poured into the task of moving people from a state of "mental illness" to "mental health," but not nearly enough energy has been spent on the task of moving the mentally healthy in the direction of self-actualization (1973, 1).

Enthusiasm for "normals" to achieve personal growth and greater self-actualization through a meaningful small-group experience continued to be fueled by antipathy toward a technocratic establishment which favored repression and "the psychopathology of the normal." In step with the times, Egan espouses "unfreezing" techniques which break through defenses (maintenance activities) in order to make life less bland and more self- enhancing, value-driven, and emotionally involving.

Pastoral theologians tended to view the burgeoning small-group movement as a coalescence of the medical (that is, psychoanalytic) tradition, social science research, and the revivalistic practice of small-group healing and devotion within the church (Holified 1983, 316). Not surprisingly, Thomas Oden, a professor of pastoral theology at Drew University, heralded "the new pietism" in *The Intensive Group Experience* (1972). Oden drew parallels between Hasidic Judaism and Protestant pietism of the eighteenth century and boldly proclaimed, "The movement spawned by Moreno, Lewin and Rogers, Perls, Maslow, and Benne could not have occurred without the available models of societal interaction derived from the Judeo-Christian tradition" (87). Others might just as sincerely have claimed the egalitarian values of American democracy, progressivism, and pragmatism as the fertile soil for such a humanistic blossoming.

Another example of the confluence of forces within pastoral theology is reflected in a volume of essays in honor of Paul Johnson (1898-1974), longtime professor of psychology of religion at Boston University (Strunk 1973). Johnson's concept of *dynamic interpersonalism* was an effort to move away from the individualistic Rogerian approach to a more interpersonal and dynamic understanding of human nature and the pastoral task. Influenced by Pratt, Moreno, Sullivan, Frankl, and Buber, Johnson believed that "the community of interacting persons is sustained by the creative power and love of God" (Schilling 1973, 47). One author noted, "In this perspective interpersonal psychology may be aptly described as psychotheology. It is inseparable from a theology of relationship in which the I of psychology meets the Thou of theology" (Schilling 1973, 47).

More than anyone else, it was existential group psychotherapist Irvin Yalom who led efforts to establish an "eclectic mainstream" within the field of group psychotherapy. First publishing his influential *The Theory and Practice of Group Psychotherapy* in 1970, Yalom sought to articulate the core or curative factors which bring about "a corrective emotional experience" for individuals in any group, regardless of its particular "trappings" or "front" or "type." Basing his approach on an outpatient psychotherapy group, Yalom's humanistic, self-actualizing emphasis–though cognizant of a distinct group process with its underlying anxieties and conflicts–focuses primarily on individual therapeutic change experienced here-and-now in a cohesive group setting.

Initially trained in the Sullivanian tradition, Yalom's focus on interpersonal dynamics as key to a cohesive group found ready grounding in the encounter-group movement. So it is not surprising to learn that in the early 1970s Yalom and two colleagues initiated a huge research project which attempted to find out exactly what goes on in encounter groups. Out of this effort came data about group characteristics, leadership styles, how people learn, the hazards of the group experience, and the social implications of the encounter-group movement. This material was published in an influential volume entitled *Encounter Groups: First Facts* (Lieberman, Yalom, and Miles 1973). Interestingly, in his most recent revision of *The Theory and Practice of Group Psychotherapy* (1985) Yalom hesitates to even include his 1975 chapter entitled "Group Therapy and the Encounter Group." In an effort to distance himself, he comments:

> My previous edition of this book contained a heady forty-two-page chapter on encounter groups studded with extravagant predictions, my own and others, about the soaring, perdurable destiny of the entire encounter-group movement. Today, a decade later, as I poke around in the ashes of that movement, I consider deleting this chapter entirely (1985, 486).

Nevertheless, Yalom is quick to claim that his understanding of contemporary group psychotherapy grows largely out of his experience in the encounter-group movement in the 1970s (1985, 488). Though Yalom has been highly influential among CPE supervisors seeking a basis for their group work in the past twenty years, his contribution is limited because it leans so heavily toward the individualistic and therapeutic bias of the 1970s.

A second development which occurred in the early 1970s was an effort by those in the field of group psychotherapy to find a firmer and more modern theoretical footing. In 1971 the American Group Psychotherapy Association (AGPA) appointed a special committee to explore the relationship between General System Theory (GST) and group psychotherapy. This was an effort to bring to the field a scientific and theoretical framework which would (hopefully) both clarify and improve the practice of group psychotherapy. After ten years of work, the committee published its results in *Living Groups: Group Psychotherapy and General System Theory* edited by James Durkin (1981).

Based on the theoretical work of Ludwig von Bertalanffy, an eminent biologist, GST grows out of two propositions: 1) that a system is more than the aggregate of its parts; and 2) to understand a system one should focus on the relationship or interactions between its various parts. Bertalanffy stressed that every system (from a cell to a society) is organic or living, expressive of certain values or beliefs, and arranged in hierarchies which form their own interacting continuum (or synergy). In formulating these ideas, Bertalanffy was distinguishing his approach from what he considered to be problems with the mechanistic approach of cybernetic theory, the negative feedback system of communication theorists, and the pathologizing of the psychoanalytic tradition.

Several key concepts caught the particular attention of group therapists (Durkin 1981, 7-23). First, underneath the diversity of content among all forms of life, there are identical structures and organized processes. This principle is called *isomorphism*. Through observing behavior, it provided a way to bridge the conceptual gap between individual therapy and group work. Second, all organisms selectively open and close their boundaries to the rest of the environment. This is a self-regulating and self-transforming metabolic process called "flux equilibrium" which involves a "boundarying" process facilitated by the therapist. Third, all living systems (no matter how dysfunctional they have become) retain the potential to become open, active, and autonomous again. That is, living systems are always engaged in an open exchange of matter/energy with their environments in an "unprogrammed but non-random goal-directed process called equifinality" (Durkin 1981, 17). The concept of equifinality provided an inherently optimistic and goal-driven framework for group work.

One of the chief merits of GST was that therapists could adapt and apply previous conceptual understandings from psychoanalytic theory, transactional analysis, studies of leadership styles, and member role functions (T-groups) under the rubric of this broader framework. A second strength was its positive focus on growth and change rather than a deficit focus on conflict or pathology. One of the weaknesses of the GST application to the field of group psychotherapy is that it seems to have grown initially more out of a quest for theoretical credibility by professionals working in the field than out of the excitement of practical experience and experimentation.

On balance it can be concluded that general systems theory, while somewhat complicated and esoteric at first blush, has provided a creative theoretical base from which to begin to think systemically about the group experience. A leading proponent and practitioner is Yvonne Agazarian whose initial efforts to integrate GST with psychodynamic theory (Bion) and Lewin's field theory are presented in *The Visible and Invisible Group* (1981). Agazarian is continuing to make a major contribution which connects systems thinking to the group-as-a-whole approach.

By 1984 group psychotherapy was considered to be part of the mainstream of therapeutic theory and professional practice with over 5,000 subscribers to *The International Journal of Group Psychotherapy*. Despite this success, there were fewer and fewer clinicians who actually claimed group therapy as their primary identity (Liff 1984). In addition, the field of group work itself continued to be influenced by an astonishing variety of psychological theories and organizational interests. The 1994 annual meeting of the American Group Psychotherapy Association (AGPA) lists seven different levels of leadership certification, twenty-two special interest sections, over 125 workshops along with ten plenary presentations, plus a special study track dealing with the theme of rage and abuse from the point of view of transactional analysis, communication theory, group psychotherapy, psychodrama, and family/marital relationships. Some have gone so far as to call the field "polymorphously diverse" in its bewildering pursuit of psychological ideas and therapeutic approaches (Dies 1992, 1-2).

In the last twenty years the Association for Specialists in Group Work, a subdivision of the American Counseling Association, has joined the AGPA in making a contribution to establishing standards, ethical practice, and ongoing research into group methods, particularly in the educational field. Its publication *The Journal for Specialists in Group Work* now focuses primarily on "group counseling"–an umbrella term intended to encompass the entire field of group work. Gerald Corey's *Theory and Practice of Group Counseling* (1990) is the most recent example of a comprehensive presentation under this rubric. Corey pays particular attention to such issues as the multicultural and contextual issues of group life, the ethical practices of group leaders, and the working through of group themes. Another new contribution, *Focal Group Psychotherapy* by Matthew McKay and Kim Paleg (1992), focuses on various types of treatment groups–for agoraphobia, shyness, eating disorders, survivors of incest, and domestic violence perpetrators. Thus it is that the diversity and richness of this field continues to be both its greatest asset and its greatest liability, the potential source of both creativity and confusion to practitioners, theorists, and participants alike.

STAGES OF GROUP DEVELOPMENT

Most people who work with interpersonal groups are aware that each group goes through specific stages of development. Typically there is a four-part sequence (Hunter 1990, 481-2; Corey 1990). The first stage is one of orientation or encounter in which needs for safety, inclusion, and acceptance are in the forefront. The second stage involves dealing with issues of dominance and control. This stage can be difficult, with patterns of scapegoating, resistance to authority, and rigidity of roles becoming increasingly evident. When this is successfully worked through, the group moves to the third stage, which is one of cohesiveness and group productivity. This stage brings a new round of self-disclosure, a deepening of intimacy, higher morale, and clearer success in the group work. The final stage is one of consolidation and separation in which members try to make sense of the overall experience and anticipate the end of the group life. Those who work with groups from a psychoanalytic perspective tend to think of these stages as cyclical, while those who work from an educational or training perspective view the stages as successive and time-bound.

Discerning and naming the stages of group life has been a popular way to try and understand what is happening in groups. Malcolm and Hulda Knowles (1972) outlined eight different theorists' efforts to delineate such stages. They reference research done in the mid-1960s by B. W. Tuchman which provided a five-part schema: forming (testing and dependency), storming (tension and conflict), norming (developing cohesion), performing (functional and role relating) and adjourning (or mourning). These continue to be a source of reference in the field. The most comprehensive recent summary of stages of group development is found in Napier and Gershenfeld's textbook *Groups: Theory and Experience* (1985). Finally, popular psychiatrist and author Scott Peck entered the realm of group work in 1987 with *A Different Drum*. Coming up through the ranks of human relations training labs, marathons, and church groups in the late 1960s, Peck brings this experience together with some of Wilfred Bion's ideas and his own observations about the dynamics and work of small groups. His suggestive stages move from "pseudocommunity" through "chaos" to "emptiness" and finally "real community" (Peck 1987).

The most in-depth effort to link stages of group development with the dynamics of human development as understood from the object relations perspective has been done by Roy Lacoursiere, a psychiatrist at the Menninger Clinic. In *The Life Cycle of Groups* (1980), Lacoursiere outlines five general group stages: orientation, dissatisfaction, resolution, production, and termination. He gives particular attention to the resolution stage, which involves group members achieving a rapproachment between their expectations (fantasies) about the group and themselves, and the realities of the group. It is easy to get stuck at this transition stage (noted by repetitive efforts to test and act out), especially if the task is difficult (such as expression of negative feelings toward other members) or if membership in the group has not been voluntary. In this latter situation, a negative orientation stage blends into the dissatisfaction stage. Lacoursiere emphasizes the importance of morale and is upbeat about task accomplishment despite these hazards:

Even a training group that spends much time or even
most of its time in the orientation and dissatisfaction
stages is learning about groups in general and their group
in particular through this experience. In other words,
they are constantly working on their task (36).

GROUPS AND FAMILIES

There has always been some theoretical and practical interplay between
work with groups and work with families. In a sense our first group *is* the
family. All the major volumes on group work have included articles on family
therapy (Gazda 1968a, 1968b; Kaplan and Sadock 1971; Sager and Kaplan
1972). And comprehensive texts on family therapy include major sections on
the influence of group work (see Nichols and Schwartz 1991).

As noted previously, the early theories of analytic group work (Freud,
Burrow, Wolf, Slavson) were based on an individual's projection of unconscious
intrapsychic material from experiences in the family of origin onto individual
members of the group. This early work in the analytic group method needs to
be distinguished from later efforts to discover a group process or "group analytic"
unique onto itself.

Later, as experiential and existential approaches to group work became
popular (including sensitivity training, psychodrama and gestalt therapy), these
developments influenced work being done in the family field, particularly that
by Carl Whitaker and Virginia Satir in their active, direct, and intuitive therapeutic
approach. Finally, recent work (Agazarian 1992) has been done on making
theoretical connections between the general system theory used to understand
some group work and the communications theory which informs some family
work. In addition, both the group and family fields share origins in the
psychoanalytic tradition. So it is not surprising that from the beginning there
has been considerable theoretical and practical give-and-take between the two
fields–and that this continues to the present day.

When Freud wrote his monograph on group psychology in 1921, he was
careful to distinguish between the natural grouping of a family and the artificial
gathering of a group of strangers. What exactly are these differences? First,
the family has a collective history and a group of strangers does not. Second,
the family situation is often stressful while the group usually offers safety,
support, and even sympathy. In groups the individual members tend to have
more equal status as peers than do members of the family. Groups can be a
laboratory for change in which there is opportunity for more behavioral flexibility

and experimentation than in the roles and rigid patterns usually operative in the family. Groups can give feedback and encourage reality testing, whereas perceptions made in the family context are often hopelessly distorted in order to maintain family equilibrium. Finally, transference and countertransference can sometimes be more easily worked through with substitute figures who are group leaders than they can be worked through with one's real parents.

All in all it is no wonder that "the family haunts the group" (Yalom 1985, 91) and, indeed, at certain times the group becomes a family. To what extent should this material be the focus for group work? Psychoanalytic practitioners who choose to do individual therapeutic work in a group context would say that the family dynamics each person brings to the group and acts out within the group is precisely the focus. Group-as-a-whole practitioners would eschew family of origin material in favor of beginning with uniquely group-generated phenomena. Eclectic group psychotherapists, so heavily influenced by the centrality of the interpersonal group process, would also tend to veer away from this historic material and stay in the here-and-now.

Co-Leadership

As the use of treatment groups in the mental hospital grew, so did the practice of using two therapists in group therapy sessions. Initially this development was an inexpensive way to train psychiatric residents about both patient pathology and group work. A senior psychiatrist was the active leader while the psychiatric trainee took a more passive role. In this training situation, there was no particular noting of changes in dynamics or opportunities for therapeutic intervention specifically due to the presence of the two leaders in the group. However, the pattern of co-leadership continues to the present day in state hospitals where someone from an adjunctive field (nurse, chaplain, recreational therapist) will co-lead the group with a psychiatric resident.

The use of co-therapists was tried by Alfred Adler and Rudolph Dreikurs in their work with families coming into the child guidance clinic. They noticed that two therapists, especially a male-female team, generated more intense family dynamics and sometimes hastened the therapy. Though J.L. Moreno in his psychodrama groups seldom worked with a co-therapist, he would often train someone from the group to be an auxiliary "alter ego" for the patient. This person would, in fact, act in a collegial capacity with Moreno (albeit in a role). In the early T-groups run by the National Training Laboratory, it was quickly discovered that co-facilitators could avoid some of the pitfalls of solo leadership.

In fact, the role of "research observer" was actually an early example of a type of group co-leadership. In general it is probably fair to say that the field of group therapy and group dynamics inadvertently stumbled on the discovery that co-leaders can offer something different and special to the situation (Rosenbaum 1971, 502.).

It is now evident that the co-therapy model has a number of advantages. For example, if the unconscious group process becomes intense, co-therapists can protect and check with each other about what is happening. It allows one therapist to challenge individual defenses while another supports, one to risk and move closer while the other remains a group ballast. The presence of two therapists tends to stimulate a group, thus allowing it to move more quickly in its therapeutic work. If it is a male-female team, this will tend to evoke greater sexual projections around intimacy in heterosexual relationships. If there are strong negative transference or splitting in a group, these will usually involve only one of the therapists, so that the other can remain more neutral and process-oriented to help work through this important material. Working as a co-therapist can be risky, especially if the two people have not developed a high level of trust and professional respect. It is all too easy to end up engaging in power struggles for the affection of the group members, or allowing group members to pit the therapists against each other in other ways. Clear goals and awareness of differing styles (symmetrical versus complementary) are prerequisites to successful co-leadership.

Co-therapy has received more attention and development in the field of family therapy than in the field of group therapy. One of the most flamboyant and brilliant family practitioners, Carl Whitaker, prefers to always work with a co-therapist. His highly intense and existential style necessitates the presence of another person to keep track of the powerful transferential reactions of family members. Among those in the strategic school, observation teams behind mirrors are used as co-consultants to help the therapist (or co-therapists) plan effective tactical interventions. This approach was helpful in preventing the therapist from becoming co-opted into the family emotional process. Structural therapist Salvador Minuchin tends to employ a member of the family as pseudo co-therapist (for example, coerce a parent into disciplining a child) in an effort to reestablish functional hierarchies in the family. His method (though not his rationale) is reminiscent of Moreno's work. Like the field of group therapy, those in family work make considerable use of co-leadership as a method to train new practitioners. However, there has been relatively little research or focused theoretical work done on this rich and varied aspect of work with groups.

WOMEN AND GROUPS

As group members, women tend to bring a mixture of highly developed social skills, natural empathy, and relational sensitivity into a group setting.[2] On an interpersonal level their contribution usually enriches and deepens the group experience. However, as the group life develops it becomes clear that at a deeper level women often struggle with issues of lack of trust, need for nurturance, low self esteem, lack of self- direction, anger, and loss of power. In a mixed-gender, psychoanalytically-oriented group, these issues are worked through by way of the transference and projections, with particular attention given to sexual and aggressive impulses (Alonso 1987). In a more relationally-oriented therapeutic approach, the preference is for a same-sex group with the focus on validation, empowerment, development of self-empathy, and mutuality (Fedele and Harrington 1990).

Because of the recent developments within psychoanalytic theory based on object relations, there is increasing awareness of the central importance of the relationship with the mother (rather than the father, the husband, the son, or the culture) in therapeutic group work. This development has confronted the female leader of a group with several unique challenges. First, it is expected that both male and female group members will be thrown back unconsciously into the pre-oedipal relationship with the mother. This involves feelings of both fearing the withdrawal of her love (bad mother) and/or idealizing her presence (good mother). Greater regression (than with a male leader) is also to be expected in this situation.

Second, overt or covert comparisons between male and female group leaders are inevitable. A competent female leader will tend to receive negative projections from group members (too aloof and powerful), while a competent male leader will receive positive projections (knowledgeable and authoritative). If a female leader compensates for this expected response by being more self-disclosing and available in her effort to appear less competent, the group will tend to become anxiety-ridden and feel even more out of control (Haines 1988). It is important to be aware that a woman leader probably needs to provide more structure (boundaries, objective feedback, direction) in an unstructured group in order to reduce anxiety and regression. To further cope with this situation,

---

[2] "This is not to imply that women are more sensitive or empathic than men, only that culture rewards those skills more routinely in women than in men, and thus women are more often comfortable with those skills than are men" (Alonso 1987, 155).

the group may unconsciously choose the strongest male member to be her co-leader.[3]

A third concern is that women members of a female-led group will tend to either compete with or criticize the female leader. This response is based on unconscious ambivalence about seeing a woman exercise authority and thus play a stereo-typical male role in a group. In an all-woman's group these feelings can result in group collusion regarding what they perceive as the leader's apparent incompetence, which is actually only their own unconscious projected self-devaluation (McWilliams and Stein 1987). This phenomenon is particularly difficult, if not heart-rending, among groups of Black women with Black women leaders all of whom have an unusually high degree of internalized oppression (Gainor 1992). Finally, some theorists point out that as a group becomes a stable source of nurturance and self-worth, both male and female members will eventually have to struggle with issues of separation and autonomy from the group (symbolic mother), a struggle reminiscent of early childhood. All these issues are beginning to receive attention as women continue to take roles of significant leadership and authority in small groups and large.

SUMMARY

In the psychotherapeutic community, group therapy has always played second fiddle to the individual approach to treatment. Group work originally began as an inexpensive method of doing individual therapy in a group setting, particularly in mental hospitals. In its early approach, group dynamics were primarily understood from an individually-oriented psychoanalytic point of view adapted to the group situation. As experience and interest in group work grew, the unconscious dynamics of the group-as-a-whole became apparent to practitioners and theorists alike, as did the social and interactive value of well-functioning groups within schools and industry.

A mixture of psychoanalytic theory, interpersonal psychology, social psychology, and field theory combined in the early 1950s with the creation of the National Training Laboratory in the United States. In the convergence of these several approaches, distinctions between therapeutic change, personal growth, social action and individual learning in a group context became increasingly blurred. The blossoming in the 1960s of humanistic psychology with its widespread encounter-group movement rapidly transformed this slow

---

[3] These last two observations have been my own experience in leading CPE groups.

process of evolution which had been occurring for fifty years in the field of group work. Suddenly group experiences were for everyone and anyone who wanted personal growth, self-enhancement, and the opportunity to achieve one's full potential.

In the past twenty years the field of group therapy has attempted to recover its balance in several ways. First, it has continued to develop the psychotherapeutic dimensions of group treatment for psychiatric outpatients, combining these with the best of the interpersonal and interactive techniques learned from the encounter-group movement. Second, it has tried to lay claim to the theoretical base of general system theory in order to modernize and legitimize the field of group work itself and set it apart from the purely psychoanalytic treatment model. Third, it has sought to set standards for competent and ethical practice by group leaders, and increase the exchange of ideas in the profession through ongoing publication and research.

The problem of classification continues to elude solutions. On the occasion of the fiftieth anniversary of AGPA in 1992, the editor of *The International Journal* tried to "sift through the confusion" by sending out a questionnaire to 500 clinicians asking them to identify their theoretical orientation. Though the majority of the 111 responses identified either highly individualized eclectic or general multiple-treatment models, the more specific responses clustered into ten different, but sometimes overlapping, orientations: psychodynamic and psychoanalytic; group-as-a-whole and systems; TA and Gestalt; interpersonal and interactional; cognitive and behavioral; object relations; group analysis; psychodrama; existential and humanistic; and self psychology (Dies 1992, 3). In an effort to make sense of this array of data, the editor ended up proposing a simple schema of basically three types of groups: action-oriented, interpersonal, and psychodynamic.

In the meantime, not only has a burgeoning of self-help groups inundated the popular culture, but also a new sister field of family systems and family therapy has taken center stage. A recent scanning of *The International Journal of Group Psychotherapy* reveals a "polymorphously diverse" situation: efforts to apply self psychology and object relations theory to group work, efforts to meet the needs of specific patient populations, and efforts to incorporate ideas from family systems into group therapy practice–to name but a few themes. The general impression is that the field of group work, while filled with creativity and enthusiastic proponents, continues to remain largely adjunctive, contextual, and reactive to both the psychotherapeutic and the educational enterprise.

In 1921 Freud wrote that it was the task of a theoretical group psychology to answer three questions:

> What, then, is a group? How does it acquire the capacity for exercising such a decisive influence over the mental life of the individual? And what is the nature of the mental change which it forces upon the individual? (4).

Today those of us who work with groups in clinical pastoral education are still trying to find answers to these intriguing questions, and many more.

THE PRESENT SITUATION IN CPE

PART ONE: APPROACH TO RESEARCH

This chapter delineates the results of my efforts to discover the current theory (or theories) and practice (or practices) of interpersonal process-group work in clinical pastoral education. The chapter begins by explicating the two main approaches to research which are now being used in the pastoral care and education field. It then establishes that the approach of this study is grounded in qualitative research methods, pointing out how this phenomenological approach to research is congruent with the theological assumptions within CPE and the modern pastoral care movement.

The chapter then gives the background for, and summarizes the results of, my survey reading of one hundred theoretical position papers which were written between 1988 and 1992 by candidates seeking supervisory credentials in the Association for Clinical Pastoral Education. The third section reports my experience of viewing fifteen videotapes of interpersonal group sessions conducted by CPE supervisors between July 1992 and March 1993. Salient themes and learnings from the papers, the videos, and the visits with supervisors are summarized in each section and at the end of the chapter.

In recent years research efforts in the field of pastoral care and counseling, as well as in other aspects of ministry, have been on the increase. This increase is partly due to the emphasis on practical application in Doctor of Ministry programs. It is also due to efforts by some to respond to perceived (and real) pressures for more empirical research in the field of pastoral care and education in order to prove credibility and effectiveness as a profession.

Research efforts divide along two lines–quantitative (deductive) versus qualitative (inductive) approaches. A major leap forward for the application of empirical or quantitative research methods in the field of pastoral care occurred in 1988 with the publication of Larry VandeCreek's *A Research Primer for Pastoral Care and Counseling*. VandeCreek views the lack of empirical research as a sign that those of us in the field of pastoral care and counseling are not "pulling our weight as a profession in this scientific age" (2). His critique is harsh:

> We have been unable to put the capstone in place. That is, we have not built an empirical research tradition which tests our observations and theories....That, I believe, makes us morally culpable. As members of our respective organizations we have been too ready to make a living on existing, borrowed insights and practice patterns, and not ready enough to test our own insights. Consequently, we can legitimately be seen in the scientific world as a "do nothing" profession which has failed to make a contribution to knowledge in a scientific age (2-3).

VandeCreek focuses on helping chaplains and clinical educators use scientific research methods. Formulating an hypothesis, establishing criteria, and creating a reliable research instrument which will produce hard data are central to the empirical approach. Knowing the basics of statistical analysis, conducting a focused literature search, designing an effective questionnaire, and acquiring adequate writing skills are essential. In addition to his book and his own research efforts, VandeCreek has led in the creation of a network of CPE supervisors and chaplains doing research, the publication of a quarterly newsletter, the planning of workshops on research at national ACPE meetings, and the publication of a number of articles.

Though the quantitative, scientific approach of empirical research has been influential, it has not come easily or naturally to those in the field of pastoral care and theological education. Not only are research monies hard to come by, but there are also considerable methodological problems. In 1989 the *Journal of Supervision and Training in Ministry* published an article entitled "The Doctorate of Ministry as an Exercise in Practical Theology: Qualitative Research with Living Human Documents" by Bonnie Miller-McLemore and William Myers. The authors specifically challenged the appropriateness of empirical criteria. Distinguishing between research *about* ministry and research which *enhances the practice of* ministry, the authors advocated focusing on the latter. They point particularly to "the lived moment"–or "the incarnational dimension of ministry"–out of which grows the subject for research. This subject is more appropriately explored by a qualitative rather than a quantitative approach by the student (18).

Miller-McLemore and Myers note that the tools of the qualitative approach to research are quite different from the quantitative approach–and more appropriate to study of the living human document within the ministry field. Instead of discrete pieces of objective information based on a limited set of questions designed to prove cause and effect, the qualitative researcher looks for correlations, convergences, and contextual elements within descriptive material from which new insights, methods, and trends can be garnered. Such "soft" data is gathered through open-ended interviews, direct observation, and examination of an array of written and historic documents. In contrast to the quantitative approach, Miller-McLemore and Myers point out that qualitative research is holistic rather than discrete; it is responsive to influences from the research process itself rather than limited by a predetermined research content and expectations. It also assumes a certain degree of involvement by the researcher as meaning-maker and interpreter. At first glance, the quantitative versus qualitative argument may seem to depend on the goal of the researcher. If the researcher wants to document that a chaplain's visit to a patient has some (hopefully positive) effect which can be measured, the more controlled quantitative approach would seem promising–especially in an environment such as a medical setting which understands and values the empirical assumptions of scientific positivism. On the other hand, if the researcher wants to understand the subtleties and paradoxes of human experience in a specific context of ministry, he or she might prefer to gather descriptive details, listen to individual stories, and work with (rather than against) the inevitable inconsistencies and variables of the research situation. Rather than manipulating the testing environment to achieve constancy, a qualitative approach notices the vagaries of human experience, counting these among the factors central to the evolving research process itself.

The field of clinical pastoral education has straddled these two worlds from its very beginnings. While Boisen was basically interested in research into the human condition and its subjective meaning, Cabot pushed to develop the chaplain as an effective professional clinician in an objective interdisciplinary situation. While Boisen pushed into his own madness in order to wrest its redemptive meaning for the entire human condition, Cabot pushed to make religion the spiritual handmaiden and clinical tool of medicine (Lawrence 1992). So it is not surprising that CPE Supervisors are often caught in the middle, thinking of themselves, on the one hand, primarily as educators, mentors, and even prophets for the next generation of ecclesial leaders, yet being expected, on the other hand, to deliver a specific product (pastoral care services) to institutions many of which exemplify a highly technical, scientific, and demanding environment.

The philosophical basis for choosing qualitative research as the method of choice for this inquiry is its grounding in phenomenology. It was William James in his *Varieties of Religious Experience* who first applied the phenomenological approach to the field of religion. James's effort to get behind religious symbols and concepts and discover the origin of religious experience in human consciousness deeply influenced the founders of clinical pastoral education. Whether one focuses on Anton Boisen's living human documents, the parables of Jesus, the details of the case study method, the here-and-now situation of hospital patients, or the personal histories of a group of CPE students–the intent of the phenomenologist (or the qualitative researcher, chaplain, or clinical educator) is to get as close as possible to the so-called facticity of existence in order to understand subjectively what is going on. In doing so, the researcher grounded in phenomenology is able to grasp both the facticity of the situation *and* its "surplus of meaning" (Moore 1991, 94).

Not only does phenomenology provide a firm philosophical base for research efforts in the qualitative tradition, it also coheres with that which has become foundational for modern pastoral care and clinical pastoral education in the liberal Protestant tradition–the belief in a divine/human encounter which takes place specifically in the world of human experience and lies within human grasp (perception). Whether or not such perceptions are named as experiences of an ultimate reality glimpsed in the history of Israel, the mysterious essence of Jesus the Christ, the ongoing work of the Holy Spirit, or the divine presence made manifest through a particular moment in ministry, the point is that from a phenomenological point of view these religious experiences can be uniquely discerned and understood. For these reasons phenomenology provides philosophical thrust and vigor to the Christian doctrine of an incarnate, loving God uniquely and constantly, albeit always mysteriously, involved in the web and fullness of human history and experience.

One of the keys to success in using the phenomenological approach is the method of "bracketing" by the researcher. This method requires the observer or listener to suspend his or her preconceptions, judgments, and speculations about what is going on in order to fully apprehend the experience itself. Pastoral theologian John Patton notes that what is being sought here is not knowledge about things but direct experience of things (1990, 30). This is further achieved through the effective use of empathy which is the capacity to "feel into" an experience and thus illuminate its interior terrain or "inscape" (34). Through bracketing, an experience is initially allowed to speak for itself in all its reality and facticity. Through empathy, one becomes aware of what is being perceived and engages with its surplus of meaning in imaginative and creative ways. Because working phenomenologically is a process of first becoming aware and then being affected by one's awareness, it is an interpersonal and interactive process rather than exclusively individualistic and subjective (Patton 1990, 39). It assumes that truth is both unique to the individual and able to be shared and experienced by others. It is an I-Thou rather than an I-It relationship (Buber 1958).

The strengths of the qualitative approach to research are several. The method allows direct observation of human activity in its natural setting. The researcher enters that setting in a dynamic subject-to-subject, rather than a more static subject-to-object, manner. Living texts or situations speak for themselves rather than needing to fit into a preconceived hypothesis. The method requires the researcher "to adjust and adapt skillfully to concrete conditions of daily life" (Jorgensen 1989, 8) and be open to being affected by the research process itself. In fact, he or she must be able to enter into the field in such a way that "through participation, the researcher is able to observe and experience the meanings and interactions of people from the role of the insider" (Jorgensen 1989, 21).

Thus, the approach to research in this inquiry employs the ten basic strategies outlined in Michael Patton's seminal work *Qualitative Evaluation and Research Methods* (1980): it is naturalistic (does not manipulate the setting), inductive (immersed in details in order to discover important categories), holistic (assumes the whole phenomenon is greater than the sum of its parts), employs in-depth questions to get at the "thickness" of experience, uses the researcher's personal contact and insight, pays attention to process (and assumes change is constant), is sensitive to context, employs empathic neutrality and builds in a certain amount of design flexibility (Patton 1980, 40). Finally, "the researcher is the instrument" (Patton 1980, 14). That is, he or she depends upon being able to take an insider position, gaining access to that which is hidden, listening and perceiving while bracketing preconceptions, and trusting the process of inquiry and the people involved. In these many ways, diverse and sometimes disparate data can eventually be organized into patterns and trends which make sense and are illuminating.

PART TWO: SURVEY OF POSITION PAPERS
THE BACKGROUND

This section begins by outlining the current standards regarding group work in CPE. It then explores the general development of supervisory certification procedures by the Association for Clinical Pastoral Education, especially noting references to group work. Finally, it documents the emergence of position papers as a requirement in the certification process, including articulation of a theory for group work within the educational theory paper. The section seeks to highlight both the problems and the achievements within the ACPE certification process in general and in relationship to the position papers in particular.

The 1993 *Standards* for accreditation of educational programs by the Association for Clinical Pastoral Education require each CPE program to have "a small group of at least three peers in a common learning experience" (122.8). Ongoing program objectives reflect the use of didactic sessions, group supervision, and interpersonal group work as central to CPE educational methodology. In the current *Standards* the process group is described as:

> Participation of Basic student(s) or Basic and Advanced student(s)[1] in a peer group which is large enough to enable the student to experience a variety of relationships and small enough to provide time for each student to enter into a creative interpersonal process for learning (123.14).

The significance of the small-group experience is further reflected in specific objectives for student learning at the basic level: 1) "To learn to utilize the support, confrontation, and clarification of the peer group for the integration of personal attributes and pastoral functioning"; and 2) "To utilize individual and group supervision for personal and professional growth and for developing the capacity to evaluate one's ministry" (123.23, 123.24). Within the supervisory training component, supervisors-to-be must show "competence in CPE Group Supervision," which means developing "the ability to facilitate the development

---

[1] The distinction between two levels of training in CPE developed in the 1950s. The subjective nature of this distinction, along with unclear programmatic differentiation of these two levels, led to the decision by ACPE to abandon these levels, effective in January of 1996. Currently there are only two types of training – clinical pastoral education and supervisory CPE.

of group interpersonal interaction as a pastoral concern" and developing "the ability to lead a small group of student peers, enabling the students to use their response to the program as a learning experience"(125.2221, 125.2222). Thus, woven into the small-group experience are expectations for growth in personal and professional development, interpersonal skills, self-reflective learning, and program evaluation under the direction of a trained and certified supervisor.

The certification of CPE supervisors began as a somewhat informal process which later came to be tightly controlled by each organization—initially the Institute for Pastoral Care (IPC) and the Council for Clinical Training (CCT). Aspirants worked as assistants to a certified supervisor, conducting one or two units of training under the watchful eye of a more experienced mentor. By the time the person met with a review committee consisting of other supervisors, many within this relatively small circle knew about the person's work and assumed his (sic) competence. The person was then accepted into the ranks and celebrated accordingly.

Though the process had become slightly more standardized by the time Charles Hall was certified in the early 1950s, his description, complete with theological reflection, gives a detailed account of the ways things were:

> I was certified by the Council in 1953. It took place in an upper room at a retreat center on Lake Geneva, Wisconsin, a few minutes after midnight. This was one of the first years that the committee required written work from the candidate. It did not seem as if the committee members had read my material. Fred Kuether asked one question about my personal psychotherapy. My training supervisor, Thomas Klink, was asked about my work. After hearing from Klink, one committee member said, "Klink thinks he is a good supervisor, I move we certify him." It was unanimous and I was handed the open bottle of spirits (bourbon) from which they had been drinking. Offering me a drink was a symbol that I was accepted as one of them. This experience of sharing the "cup," as strange as it may sound to an outsider, was like a "Holy Communion" for me. It was a sacred symbol of acceptance (Hall 1992, 96).

After the ACPE was formed in 1967, the joint Certification and Accreditation Committee not only presented the acid test of whether supervisors from each organization (IPC and CCT) could trust one another and work together, it also quickly became the most powerful group in ACPE because it controlled the development of centers *and* the certification of new supervisors. The joining together of these two aspects in order to assure national standardization was certainly a strong asset for the fledgling organization. However, by the mid-1970s, the Association was ready to separate these two functions. This change brought about further development of distinct standards for each and represented a new level of achievement for the organization as a whole.

It took a number of years for supervisory training to evolve from an exclusively "up close and personal" mentoring process into a more professionally-based educational experience at the graduate level. The first major step occurred in the mid-1970s when a new emphasis on educational theory and its clinical application was added to the previously established certification expectations. Among required materials was a paper conceptualizing a coherent theory of education based on various learning and personality theories as well as theological insights. Other requirements included a second paper demonstrating through clinical illustrations how the supervisor's theoretical understanding and self-understanding inform his or her practice of supervision, as well as a personal history paper, student evaluations, two-page summaries of work with students, and an outline of the curriculum. It is notable that there was no explicit request to mention group work in any of this material; it was simply assumed that this aspect of CPE supervision would be presented for review.

Throughout the 1970s and well into the 1980s the supervisory certification process as a whole remained largely mysterious and increasingly frustrating: curriculum elements were unclear, training depended on the individual expertise of the supervisor in each center, differences between regions were becoming more noticeable, and lack of clarity about the distinction between therapy and education in CPE persisted. To make matters more difficult, the highly subjective nature of the committee process itself (both regionally and nationally) promoted an uncomfortable and anxious undercurrent in the organization as a whole and among training supervisors and their trainees in particular.

In 1978 a Special Study Committee was convened to establish a "design for the eighties" for the Association for Clinical Pastoral Education. In its final proposals four general goals for reform and future development were outlined: encourage the ACPE to help unify the national pastoral care movement, establish a more dynamic and representative form of government for itself, establish a new philosophy of membership, and suggest a new approach to certification

(*Special Study Committee Report* 1978-1980, i). These goals determined the agenda for ACPE for the next ten years.

Based on the *Special Study Committee Report*, a series of study documents were issued between 1980-1984 which prepared the way for approval by the General Assembly (the ACPE governing body) of a new set of certification standards. These represented the most far-reaching changes in both substance and methods for supervisory training and certification in CPE since its founding in the 1920s. The standards included creating three levels of certification: Supervisory Candidate (similar to the old supervisor-in-training category), Associate Supervisor (instead of Acting Supervisor) and CPE Supervisor (instead of Full Supervisor). In an effort to increase the national success rate for final certification, the biggest hurdle was to be positioned between the Candidacy and Associate levels. To assure standardization this examination was to be done by a face-to-face interview with subcommittees of the National Commission instead of regional certification committees (ACPE Standards Committee Study Document 1984, 11-15).

Primary among the hopes for the new standards was the achievement of clearer integration of the tension between experiential (clinical) and theoretical (conceptual) learning. To this end the process required writing theoretical papers and taking an objective exam *before* applying for certification at the Associate level. The position papers (on theology, personality, and educational methodology) were to be read by three anonymous readers and deemed satisfactory by at least two. It was not long before an outcry was heard. The entire process had become too lengthy, too costly, too demanding on the training supervisor and the center, too focused on the theoretical, and too dependent on a small but powerful national committee.

In an effort to give expression to the confusion and controversy generated by some of these changes, Executive Director Duane Parker printed a "Certification Pursuit Game" in the February-March 1985 issue of the *ACPE News*. Sample questions included:

1. The number of years it takes to become an ACPE certified supervisor in the new process is: a) 1 year b) 2 years c) Forever d) It depends e) God only knows.

3. The new term for supervisors entering the certification process is: a) Supervisor in Training b) Course Assistant c) Supervisory Candidate) A confused person

9. An objective exam will be part of the certification process with the goal being to determine a candidate's a) understanding of life b) lack of understanding of life c) desire to understand life d) basic and elementary knowledge of personality, theology and supervision e) intelligence level (ACPE Certification Pursuit Game 1985, 11-17).

This written game was a spoof on the objective exam which, along with the position papers, was rapidly becoming the target for increasing anger and resistance among supervisory education students and supervisors.

During a meeting of the nine Regional Directors in March 1988, concern was expressed about the new certification process and the notable decrease in CPE supervisory education students since 1984. Among the many questions raised in their report, it was noted that:

> Position papers are viewed as a real barrier to certification. Moreover, their evaluation by anonymous readers feels like a violation of the face-to-face relationship emphasized in all levels of CPE (Regional Directors' Consultation 1988).

Problems with inconsistencies among the readers, lack of timely dispersal of the papers, and a high rejection rate continued. One year later the Certification Commission Chair wrote Commission members: "There is nothing in the new process that has caused as much consternation among students, training supervisors and readers as the position papers!" (Morgan 1989, 2). Questions of uniformity and criteria remained unanswered.

Probably the most helpful thing the Commission did was to publish a certification manual in 1989. The manual clearly stated that it would take a combination of pastoral, conceptual and supervisory competence for successful certification. There were seven bottom-line requirements: passing the exam,[2] a positive evaluation of position papers, *a theory of group process*, self-knowledge sufficient to the task of supervision, use of self as a primary teaching/learning resource, theological reflection as it relates to the practice of supervision, supervised supervision of students (*Certification Manual* 1989, 4; italics added).

---

[2] This was quickly changed to simply "taking the exam" and eventually used as a diagnostic tool in the training of supervisory education students. Due to prohibitive costs to update it, the exam requirement was dropped altogether in 1992.

The position papers themselves were to demonstrate the *why* (theory) of supervision while the *how* was to be demonstrated through papers submitted to the Commission itself about actual work with students.

The Educational Theory Paper was to include a theory of group process. The student was to show "what educational theory guides goals and decision making in supervisory practice with individuals *and with groups*, what is the Candidate's understanding of how persons learn, and how does the Candidate's educational theory impinge upon evaluation of students and their work?" (*Certification Manual* 1989, 4; italics added). By placing group process within the Educational Theory Paper, rather than the Personality Theory Paper, the Commission seemed to be signaling that group work was primarily an educational, rather than a therapeutic, endeavor.

There was one final gasp on the long road to establishing and accepting the new certification process in ACPE. In response to continued expressions of concern and dissatisfaction, a Presidential Task Force was appointed in 1990 to study the new process. Taking a detailed survey of training supervisors, centers accredited to do supervisory education, and the trainees themselves, the Task Force discovered a surprising degree of acceptance and effectiveness–despite the persistence of complaints. Positive indicators included improvement in the overall final certification percentage, evidence of theoretical and clinical competence of newly certified supervisors, new centers being developed, and jobs being filled. The survey confirmed the growth of supervisory training in "mega centers" (employing two or more supervisors) and clusters of centers. The importance of the peer group experience for supervisory students was noted. The certification interview process at Associate and final levels was being experienced as less subjective. Regional differences did not seem to be affecting standards of training as much. A majority of task force members agreed that theoretical grounding through the position papers had the potential for becoming a valuable part of the process.

THE PAPERS

In an effort to discover current theoretical approaches to process-group work in CPE, I decided to read the Educational Theory Papers which had been written by supervisory candidates and passed[3] by the readers between 1988 and 1992 as part of the certification process. In May 1992 I received permission

---

[3] According to the *Certification Manual*, papers were to be judged as superior, good, adequate, inadequate, or unacceptable. Over time these distinctions have not proven to be very important.

from the Certification Commission to do this work with the understanding that I would adhere to the ACPE standards of complete anonymity of the writers and readers.

The only previously published survey reading of certification papers is found in George Fitchett's article, "A Coherent Theory of Education Relevant for CPE." In his own search for a coherent theory, Fitchett reviewed forty-five papers written for the purpose of certification between 1963 and 1982. Some of these papers were submitted for publication in the *Journal of Supervision and Training in Ministry*, of which Fitchett was the editor. Others were in his own files and those of his department members who had served on regional certification committees through the years. Still others were written by supervisory education students at his training center. The papers ranged in length from one page to thirty-five double-spaced pages. Fitchett notes at least two factors which might be considered limiting in this current survey as well. First, it is impossible to know to what degree the material students write for certification may be influenced by their own projections regarding the expectations of others for a suitable theory. Second, "it may be a distortion if we treat the work of our youngest members as representative of the mature wisdom of our field" (Fitchett 1982, 77). A third problem is the uncertain relationship between articulating a theory and actual practice. Nevertheless, there is much to learn from this type of material.

Fitchett's work serves as an appropriate and interesting backdrop to the current survey. While he discovers quite a wide range of both favorite and new authors in the fields of theology, personality theory, and educational methodology, he notes only Irvin Yalom in terms of group work, adding this comment: "We appear to read little else regarding group therapy [sic] aside from him" (79). Based on his reading of papers, Fitchett comes to three general conclusions about those of us in clinical pastoral education: we are both "traditional and innovative"; we are both "eclectic and pragmatic"; and "we appear to be uncritical regarding our sources. We select what fits and appear to disregard the rest" (80-1). These same conclusions are corroborated by this current survey.

A total of one hundred papers written between 1988 and 1992 were read for this research. At the time I was working with the papers, sixty of the one hundred writers had been certified at the Associate level since their papers had been read and passed. Forty of the writers had not yet appeared before the Commission for certification. Attached to the papers were comments from various sets of readers, depending on how many times the papers had been reviewed. Among the one hundred papers, 45 percent had passed on the first try, 39 percent had passed on the second writing, 11 percent had passed on the third, 4 percent on the fourth, and 1 percent on the sixth try. These statistics represent some improvement in the pass/fail ratio from seventeen months prior (Galloway 1991).

Determining the actual group theory within each Educational Theory Paper was not an easy task. Forty of the approved one hundred papers contained no explicit theory at all. In these papers, if the peer group was mentioned, it was only as a background curriculum or contextual element within which individual student learning and/or the student-supervisory relationship was to take place. Among the sixty writers who did articulate a theory, general approaches divided as follows: nineteen papers (or 32 percent) focused on Yalom and a primarily therapeutic (i.e., individual healing) approach to group work; eighteen papers (or 30 percent) outlined the development of interpersonal and communication skills (feedback, honesty, dealing with anger) as the primary focus for individual learning in the group; ten papers (or 16 percent) focused on Wilfred Bion (and A.K. Rice) or object relations to understand the group process itself; seven papers (or 12 percent) used family systems (mainly Murray Bowen); two papers simply used a creative metaphor to describe their group work; and two (.03 percent) explained the interpersonal group experience by explicating the stages of group development.

The question arises as to how aware the readers (mainly CPE supervisors) were of the relative strengths and weaknesses of these theory papers regarding the group process requirement. Among the one hundred papers (and perhaps as many readers between 1988 and 1992),[4] there were a total of thirty-one reader comments regarding group theory. The overwhelming majority of papers which passed with no mention of group theory (40 percent) received no comment from the readers about this omission. Among the thirty-one reader comments, two were positive, one was mixed, and twenty-eight were either critical or expressed concern that group theory was not referenced. Though there is some evidence that reader comments regarding group theory have increased in the last two years, it is obvious that focus on this aspect of CPE is minimal among both student writers and supervisor readers.

One of the general criteria for writing and evaluating the position papers is that the supervisory candidate demonstrate a "critical purchase" on the

---

[4] There is actually a pool of readers from each region, many of whom have read several sets of papers over time. In the last two years readers have shared written or verbal comments with one another and then written one report.

material, that he or she be able to show an understanding of the assumptions and implications of a particular theoretical model or approach and be able to apply this approach to CPE supervision. As I read the papers, I determined that at least fifteen (25 percent) of the sixty papers demonstrated some degree of critical purchase on group theory material. These fifteen writers took group work seriously in the CPE experience, named it as a major component in their educational methodology, and articulated both their theory and practice to some extent. They reflect the broad cross-section of approaches and theorists which is characteristic of people in clinical pastoral education.

In general these fifteen papers reflect a mixture of an interpersonal model for group work and the psychoanalytic model. Approximately half the writers express awareness of an unconscious group process which can impede or enhance the educational process. Nearly all the writers stress the importance of individual growth in the group context. Over half the writers begin their theoretical formulation with some mention of stages of group development. Most point to the importance of understanding one's self/behavior in relationship (in the group) as foundational for ministry. Only one writer among the fifteen had actually participated as a member in a year-long psychotherapeutic group. That writer received special commendation from the readers for understanding "the centrality of the group experience" to the CPE process of learning. One writer made a special point of distinguishing between a masculine model of group leadership (provides structure and expertise) and a feminine model (provides participation, personal growth, and empowerment). One author expressed surprise in discovering that 25 percent of the total time, and 85 percent of the educational time, in CPE is spent in group activities. One writer begins the CPE program by sharing his or her group theory with the students. Another author begins the program with an overnight retreat and models self-revelation as a group norm by sharing his or her own story on that occasion. Several writers mention using the Johari Window and the Myers-Briggs Type Indicator as tools for helping students understand their group experience.

It is admittedly difficult to adequately digest and accurately summarize this amount of material. One way a sense of the essence or spirit of the papers can best be captured is by sharing some of the dynamic metaphors used by various writers to describe either CPE itself, the nature of supervision, or the group experience. The ease with which these metaphors either contain or point toward theological understandings is particularly noteworthy.

* The supervisor is often thought of as a midwife who is trying to bring the group (or the individual) to birth.

* The group is a community of faith walking on the Emmaus Road, telling stories and making discoveries.

* Working with students is like a dance complete with its own music and rhythm.

* Students bring the threads of their lives into CPE and weave a new tapestry. The unraveling and reweaving which occurs in the action-reflection model of learning reflects the work of creation and redemption.

* The supervisor is a sower in the "field of CPE, the learning contract is a fence, and the peer group is a tool for cultivation, but finally the miracle of growth is a mystery."

* The group is an orchestra and the supervisor is a conductor. During the CPE experience, as the group practices and matures, they learn how to make music together.

* The three aspects of supervision (administrative, therapeutic and relational) are like three fishing poles each of which catch different "fish" at different times.

* The "liturgy of the group" provides a holding space, not only to deepen pastoral capabilities but also to receive "absolution" through inclusion and acceptance.

* There is the Wells Fargo model of supervision in which the supervisor sits beside the novice driver of the stage coach going through the badlands, identifying rough spots and Indians and bandits along the way but never taking over the driving.

* "Each group is like making a suit. The cloth has to be cut according to both the grain [sic] of the cloth as well as the size of the person. No two suits are alike."

* CPE is education for liberation and thus it is like Israel in the wilderness. As Moses was taught to share his burden as leader of the people, so will CPE supervisors teach the students how to share the burdens of the group.

* Supervision is an art like baking bread and the peer group is one ingredient. "God makes use of the ingredients and guides us as participants in the process." The supervisor moderates the temperature of the group, intervening "when the group threatens to scald students," thus maintaining a safe environment for learning.

A number of general conclusions and concerns can be drawn from this survey of one hundred educational theory papers. First, it is clear that in general insufficient attention has been paid by supervisory trainees in CPE to the development and articulation of a group theory. Second, by extension this inattention is also true for the trainees' training supervisors. Third, there is evidence that readers of position papers are not uniform in their interest in or expectations of group theory or in pressing writers to develop a group theory–despite long-standing clarity regarding this requirement in ACPE *Standards* and currently in the *Certification Manual*. Fourth, among those who articulated a theory, there is an incredible range of creative "takes" on the subject. Each student seems to start from the ground up, whether theoretically or experientially, and this kind of effort is apparently expected and valued. Fifth, there continues to be a strong focus on individual learning within the group context and only mild interest in understanding and using group dynamics or the group-as-a-whole process. Sixth, there is continuing tension between interpersonal and intrapsychic approaches to psychology, and this tension shows up in uncertainty about how to approach group work. Seventh, working out authority and leadership issues (transference and countertransference) is accomplished in individual supervision rather than in the group. Eighth, the long-standing tension between CPE as education versus CPE as therapy continues to find expression and cause confusion, especially in the area of group work. Finally, writers who tried to integrate several often disparate theories were less clear than writers who explicated one theory and then applied it to their supervisory practice.

One entirely overlooked issue in the papers is the possible theoretical and practical difference between process-group work in a first unit of CPE training versus additional units of training. While supervisory candidates are to function as supervisors for basic students only, often student groups have a mixture of people working on several levels. In addition, supervisory candidates themselves are much closer to their own group experiences in a CPE residency rather than a first unit. To further complicate the situation, the distinction between basic and advanced CPE has been a source of considerable confusion and misunderstanding in ACPE through the years.

In general, first unit students tend to be more aware of personal growth and identity-in-ministry issues, while those taking additional units concentrate on ministerial functioning, skill development, and integration of the personal and professional aspects of their pastoral identity. While the ACPE *Standards* *(prior to 1996)* noted in some detail the differences between so-called Basic and Advanced program elements and objectives, there was never any clear indication in these *Standards* that the peer group experience would or should be any different. However, as the result of work done on this study, it is my growing conviction that differences between the group experience in a first summer unit and group experience in a year-long residency program must be taken into consideration when formulating an adequate theory *and* practice of group work in clinical pastoral education.

PART THREE: SURVEY OF SUPERVISORY PRACTICE

THE INTERVIEWS AND TAPES

Among the various program elements in clinical pastoral education, the two which are most highly valued by CPE supervisors are the individual student supervisory hour and the interpersonal relations group seminar. Though CPE supervisors sometimes talk about and seek consultation in their work with individual students, it is seldom that an outsider is allowed to directly step onto the "holy ground" of the ongoing small-group experience. As a result, this is an area of the educational program which remains largely private and confidential, and not easily accessible to student critique or peer review.

For the last three years a group of CPE supervisors in Connecticut have been meeting monthly to build collegiality and review their work with students. From time to time a particular supervisor would bring a tape of a recent IPR (interpersonal relations) or "open" process group session and solicit feedback and discussion. (All taping and sharing of tapes was done with student permission.) Out of the experience of both observing and presenting tapes, I realized the value and the need for such sharing. It gave renewed impetus to my conviction that supervision of process-group work in CPE was highly valued by both students and supervisors, but often misunderstood and misapplied.

To conduct the current study I made a request that individual supervisors videotape one session of an interpersonal relations group so that I might view the tape afterwards with the supervisor in order to see and understand his or her group work with students.[5] In order to encourage participation I decided not to distinguish between whether the supervisor was doing a summer unit of training, an extended unit, or a residency program. I initially sent letters of inquiry to twenty-four supervisors explaining that their contribution would be anonymous and that I would share the results of my study with them. Among this group, four supervisors had no equipment available with which to videotape a group session; one supervisor was ill; and one had no CPE students in a program at the time. I ended up viewing a total of fifteen tapes between December 1992 and March 1993. Four of the fifteen tapes were group sessions conducted by two supervisors working together as co-supervisors. The other eleven tapes showed the work of individual supervisors in their student groups.

Each of my visits to view and discuss the fifteen videotapes with specific supervisors was unique. However, I generally tried to conduct a half-hour interview up front, then view the tape with the supervisor(s), and debrief at the end. The entire timeframe was between two-and-one-half and three hours long. During our conversation time I asked the supervisor(s) about his or her group theory, background in group work, relationship of individual supervision to group supervision, and theological reflections on the process group component of clinical pastoral education. I did not prepare the supervisors ahead of time for these questions. I tried to avoid their efforts to receive consultation with or feedback from me, or in any other way render either implicit or explicit judgment on their group work. I took extensive verbatim notes during the interviews and during my viewing of the videotapes themselves. After each visit I wrote up a contact summary sheet for my own use in which I noted the attitude of the supervisor(s), what I learned, what I needed to think about for the next visit, and any theoretical assumptions that needed to be reconsidered or added to the research project.

The overall response to my research topic and request was positive. The supervisors were welcoming of my effort to look at this area of CPE supervisory practice and theory. They too seemed to sense some untapped potential in this element of our training programs. During the process of contacting and interviewing them, most also expressed some anxiety about their own competence in doing process-group work. They expressed eagerness to receive feedback and participate in research which might be helpful to themselves and others in the future.

---

[5] Though the presence of the video camera would affect group dynamics to some extent, I knew my actual presence would have been more disconcerting–to say nothing of the logistics involved.

A total of five female and fourteen male supervisors participated in this study. Five of the supervisors in this survey routinely taped their IPR sessions on a fairly regular basis (several times during each unit of training). The other ten did the videotaping specifically in response to my request. For seven of the ten this was either the first or second time they had *ever* taped the IPR group in their careers as CPE supervisors. Two supervisors either lost or mislaid the tape they wanted to review with me, and substituted with one from a previous summer unit at the last minute.[6]

The interviews revealed a wide array of experience and background knowledge in small-group work among the supervisors. Experiences included T-groups in the 1960s or other contact with groups through the human potential movement and NTL, running koininia groups in the church in the 1970s, attending Tavistock conferences, co-leading groups in the mental health setting, and being part of a psychotherapy group led by a psychiatrist. Theoretical knowledge about group work ranged from reading Wilfred Bion, Irvin Yalom, Fritz Perls, and Kurt Lewin to studying and applying object relations theory, family systems, communications theory, and stages of group development. Two supervisors frankly admitted to having no clear theoretical knowledge for doing process-group work in CPE. One of these employed analytic psychology (Jung) as the basis for doing CPE supervision. I learned that, for many, their own experience as a member of a small group (in CPE, the church, psychotherapy, or a workshop) had been both healing and revelatory at some point. For example, one supervisor's attendance at a Tavistock conference was a "watershed event." This person commented:

> Everything looked different after that. There was a subterranean level of group life which I never knew about before....I have never been so mad in my life....I certainly got in touch with my own dependency needs.

Whether they presently reflected a broad or limited exposure to group work, only two of these supervisors felt they had received adequate training to run process groups during their own CPE supervisory training. Three supervisors now regularly offer a didactic on group process to their student groups. Two programs send their students to at least one weekend Tavistock conference. One program has the students meet regularly with a group psychotherapist for

---

[6] Though this study does not focus on students, there were a total of seventy-five students who participated through the videotapes, thirty-three males and forty-two female students.

a process group time. All of the supervisors expressed an ongoing desire to improve their group leadership skills. During the interviews and viewing of the tape, few explicitly connected their theoretical ideas with their practice. Several specifically mentioned previous negative experiences in CPE in which (male) training supervisors either remained distant in the small group or became aggressive, putting individuals on the hot seat "in order to see what you were made of." Several strongly eschew such intrusive tactics in their current group practice. One compared this potentially abusive approach to his experience as a teenager working in a zoo in which animals were trained by cracking whips and grabbing their ears in order to teach them by hurting them.

All these supervisors placed a strong theological value on the process group experience in CPE. The majority viewed the group as a covenant or faith community on a pilgrimage. One person emphasized the important connection between koininia (group), kerygma (faith) and diakonia (service) of the CPE model of education for ministry. Another made special efforts to create a "holy space" in which people could be together. Others described the group variously as a safe place for students to express anger and experience hospitality, a corrective or transforming experience, an opportunity to accept anxiety and become more trusting, a place to empower individual students and encourage authenticity.

Theological terms such as grace, salvation, reconciliation, and redemption were used to express the meaning of the small-group experience. One supervisor noted, "In group engagement it is a meeting of meetings which replicates what God was trying to do in the incarnation." Another thought of the small group as a loving community of shared pain–in contrast to what is (not) going on in the "real" church. Another noted that group members meet Christ in the experience. Still another said, "The group has a wisdom beyond the individual," and then added, "we don't slip into the Kingdom one by one." The idea of becoming aware of the connectedness to all of creation through the small-group experience was noted by several.

There was general agreement that the leadership role of the CPE supervisor in the process group has several guises–consultant, facilitator, participant-observer, or coach. Several supervisors pointed to the group experience as an educational laboratory, a catechetical opportunity (for teaching and modeling), or a clinical tool. One emphasized that the focus should be on the members' ability to work together rather than their ability to be intimate. Another stressed the importance of being able to handle conflict "because it genuine-izes the group process." Almost all the supervisors emphasized weekly individual supervision as a preparation or rehearsal for group work. Several had a rule that anything about a peer brought up in individual supervision by the student must be brought to the group. One supervisor experienced individual supervision as being "too therapeutic" and had come to rely on the small group process to keep the CPE experience "on track." Another was thinking about abandoning individual supervision altogether.

In working with the notes from the videotaped group sessions, important patterns became evident. For example, each group had a certain way of getting started. Usually this involved a verbal or nonverbal signal from the supervisor(s) followed by a brief period of silence. It usually took from three to five minutes for the group to focus on one person or concern. Most group members participated, but several tapes revealed at least one nonparticipant. In terms of content alone, each group seemed to have a predominant focus: conflict between two people (4 groups), avoidance of conflict between members (1 group), one individual's anger at the church (1 group), group inclusion issues (1 group), sexuality (2 groups), power or lack of power (5 groups); and mortality (1 group). In addition, gender issues were lively in at least half the groups and multicultural issues were present in six groups.[7]

In analyzing the tapes particular attention was given to the types of supervisory interventions and their consequences in the group. (Attention is paid to the students only to the extent that they offer opportunity for supervisory response.) Though all the taped sessions contained a mixture of supervisory approaches, each tape also revealed the eventual establishment of a direction or focus for the group work that particular day. These foci were of four general types with several subcomponents:

Type A EDUCATIONAL FOCUS ON STUDENT–1 tape
 1. Supervisor working with an individual student on professional functioning.
 2. Supervisor helping group members work with an individual student on professional functioning.

Type B THERAPEUTIC FOCUS ON STUDENT–6 tapes
 1. Supervisor working with an individual student on personal or relational issues.
 2. Supervisor helping group members work with an individual student on personal or relational issues.

---

[7] Among the total of the seventy-five students represented in these fifteen groups, nine were non-Caucasian and included Afro-American, Haitian, Nigerian, Caribbean, and Korean.

Type C FOCUS ON SUPERVISOR–4 tapes
1. Supervisor doing group maintenance activities (scheduling, etc.).
2. Supervisor presenting own point of view (preaching, teaching, modeling)
3. Supervisor joining with the group (self revealing), distancing from the group, or asking for care.

Type D FOCUS ON GROUP AS A WHOLE–4 tapes[8]
1. Supervisor commenting on here-and-now group dynamics.
2. Supervisor working with group unconscious material.

In reviewing this material it is easy to pick out points for critique: the tendency to intellectualize, allowing one student to dominate, failure to exercise supervisory authority, inability to make group-as-a-whole comments, little use of the full potential of co-supervision, and avoidance of student anger. However, it is also important to point out the uniqueness of the small process group in CPE and the commitment, by both students and supervisors, to have this educational component be worthwhile, meaningful, and relevant. For the most part, the students in all the groups were well engaged with one another and taking the requisite risks to deal with a potentially anxiety-producing situation in ways which would meet their own needs and contribute to their own learning. The supervisors were exercising appropriate degrees of helpfulness, insight, patience, role modeling, boundary-setting, critique, and caring.

Despite the obvious limitations of this survey and presentation, it is nevertheless important to draw some general conclusions and to voice some concerns. First, it is clear that the majority of these supervisors when working in the context of the interpersonal relations group are most comfortable establishing a primarily therapeutic and personal focus on an individual student and encouraging other students to participate in this effort. (Though the overall approach is gentler, it is nevertheless dynamically similar to the "hot seat" of the past.) The expectation is that a nondefensive and motivated student will gain insight into his or her behavior and feelings and then make changes which will improve self-image and interpersonal relating in ministry. The popularity of this approach to group work in CPE confirms the strong individualistic and

---

[8] Among the four tapes in type D, three were of residency groups involving advanced-level CPE students.

therapeutic bias with which many continue to view the clinical pastoral education experience.

Second, a primarily educational approach with a focus on professional functioning in ministry is basically not within the realm of the interpersonal process group experience in CPE. In fact, several supervisors have gone to great lengths to separate out this material from the IPR time by scheduling specific weekly "ministry event" group supervision seminars to meet this need, or specifying that such ministry review must occur in verbatim seminar or case conference time. Other supervisors make a point of interpreting this material when it comes up in the open seminar as resistance to the group process–especially if it persists beyond the first few weeks of the program.

Third, the supervisors who are able to perceive and comment on the group process itself are easy to identify. It is clear that they are doing something different. This use of metacommunication about the process itself tends to separate them from the student group and, when adhered to consistently, pushes the group to do its own work within a set of group-determined norms. This approach seems to require enough supervisory distance and self confidence to see the group as a whole and enough discipline not to get sucked into individual neediness or pathology. It also requires an ability to self-supervise in relationship to one's own potential countertransference. Supervisors who are able to effectively comment on here-and-now dynamics are usually able to work either directly or indirectly with the unconscious group material. On occasion they do focus on individual students, but only temporarily and always in the context or theme of the larger group dynamic.

Fourth, among these fifteen videotapes at least six revealed a significant degree of supervisory self-focus and/or potential dysfunction of the group process. Different behaviors which became problematic included the repetitive sharing of personally revealing information, persistent and enthusiastic collegial interactions with students, retentive and withdrawn supervisory presence in the group, uncertainty about supervisory authority, unwillingness to exercise supervisory authority, and direct or indirect signalling of the need to be taken care of by the group. In addition, some supervisors seemed to bind their anxiety either through detailed scheduling and other maintenance activities, or in one or two cases through forced casualness. No doubt some of these behaviors were more pronounced due to the fact of the videotaping itself.

Finally, there was very little evidence of the direct application of theoretical material about group process or dynamics by any of these students or supervisors. Though there was establishment of some clear norms (getting in touch with feelings, being direct, and working in the here-and-now), there were few references by either students or supervisor(s) to a larger body of psychological knowledge about the dynamics of self, relationships with others, or group functioning. The lack of clear theoretical grounding for group work was corroborated in the interviews and feedback sessions with some, but not all, of the supervisors.

Obviously this survey of fifteen videotapes presents only a limited view of process-group work in clinical pastoral education. Filtered through the lens of my own perceptions and descriptions, and further limited by time and geography and a host of other variables, this inquiry is a preliminary effort to establish a baseline of information and impressions regarding process-group work in clinical pastoral education. Though this effort lacks the elegance of a carefully controlled research project in the empirical tradition, it does begin to get at the "thickness" and complexity and educational potential of the group experience in CPE. Hopefully it raises some significant questions and areas for future research as well.

In 1990 Bonnie Miller-McLemore and William Myers wrote a follow-up article entitled "Can One Be Faithful While Teaching Research Methods to D.Min. Students?" Basing their discussion on the insights of social theorist Jurgen Habermas, the authors distinguish between three kinds of approaches to research: efforts to control the world (quantitative methods), efforts to understand the world (qualitative methods), and efforts to critically transform the world (correlative methods). These methods reflect three different cognitive fields: the technical (objective), the practical (subjective), and "the emancipatory" (Habermas 1971, 308). Myers and Miller-McLemore write: "In a sense D.Min. research must strive for a certain kind of responsible multi-lingual stance. It must utilize all three of these approaches critically and self-consciously" (25).

The implications of such a three-fold understanding of the purpose of research is pertinent to this inquiry at several levels. First, it confirms the need for the field of clinical pastoral education to bring theory and practice concerning group process work into closer relationship in order to procure knowledge and exercise some technical control over this element within the educational methodology of CPE. It *is* important to know "how it works." Second, it confirms the validity of the highly contextual and subjective nature of both the group process experience itself and the qualitative research approach of this particular inquiry. As Donald Schoen writes:

> [Such studies] choose the swampy lowlands. They
> deliberately involve themselves in messy but crucially

important problems, and when asked to describe their methods of inquiry, they speak of experience, trial and error, intution and muddling through (1983, 43).

Third, the emancipatory aspect of this three-fold approach to research, highlights the potential for change. By being both passionately committed to the usefulness of the group process in CPE *and* standing in an engaged but critical relationship to it, the transformative implications of such research are actualized. Small process-group work may well be the jewel in the back of the crown of the educational methodology upon which clinical pastoral education is based. If so, perhaps now is the time to turn it around, feel its surface contours, discover its deeper characteristics, and polish it for all to see.

6

DEVELOPING AN INTEGRATIVE THEORY

PART ONE: PSYCHOLOGICAL FOUNDATIONS

This chapter establishes the psychological foundations necessary to formulating a theoretical basis for group work in clinical pastoral education. Part One traces the connection between Freudian concepts and object relations theory, demonstrating that the psychoanalytic tradition is fundamental to understanding the individual in the group as well as the group-as-a-whole process. Part Two explicates the ideas of Wilfred Bion about groups, and the impact of his work on later divergent developments in both Britain and the United States. It points to the loss of this psychoanalytic perspective in the small process-group work in CPE and the important emergence of a group-as-a-whole perspective when this tradition is recovered.

In 1902 Sigmund Freud convened what become known as the Wednesday Evening Society.[1] This began with a small group of four people, mostly from nonmedical professions, who had undergone analysis with Freud. They met in order to continue their psychoanalytic education. Freud also hoped this small group, which by 1906 called itself the Vienna Psychoanalytic Society, would help the spread of psychoanalytic ideas into the wider world.

These young men[2] met in Freud's office weekly where "Herr Professor" presided. After a formal case presentation by Freud or one of the participants, names were drawn from an urn to determine which among the gathered was to respond. Each responder was expected to free associate based on Freud's theories about sexuality and the unconscious. It was assumed that the focus would shift back and forth from analysis of the material to analysis of the

---

[1] This introductory section is based on an article by Kanzer (1971).
[2] The first woman to join the group was Lou Andreas Salome in 1912.

145

responder's "psychoneurosis" which would inevitably be projected onto the material. During these meetings Freud would make interpretations and usually have the last word. He also would be a genial host, serving coffee and handing out cigars. After trips abroad he often brought gifts for his "Wednesday evening gentlemen." Many say Freud was at his most available and most human in this small group.

As time went on, there was competition among the "sons" and rebellion toward "the father"–first by Wilhelm Stekel, then Alfred Adler, and finally Carl Jung. These were extremely painful developments which tested the tenets of Freud's theories and resulted in difficult political strains as well as broken personal relationships. After 1910 the norms of the Wednesday Evening Society were changed. The urn was abolished. The group no longer met in Freud's office. Membership was extended to people beyond Freud's chosen circle. Publication of a journal began and leadership during meetings was shared. Rather than being a small group of followers meeting in an intimate personal setting, they became a heterogenous society of professional colleagues with a variety of points of view and agendas. One author comments about "the gentlemen":

> [Freud's] faults could now be discerned, tolerated, and
> understood just like their own. The children had grown
> up. The former students, like former analysands, had
> become sufficiently detached to form new object
> relationships that still left Freud realistically a teacher
> and prophet (Kanzer 1971, 45).

In 1912 and 1913 Freud published a series of four essays collected under the title *Totem and Taboo* in which he applied the Oedipal theory to understanding the beginnings of social organization, morality, and religion. In tracing the evolution of a group from a patriarchal horde into a clan or kinship tribe, Freud used principles from his understanding of the psychological development of the individual, specifically the repressed emotions involved in the father-son relationship and the Oedipal complex. When the sons become jealous of the father's sole possession of the women in the tribe (secured by the incest taboo), the sons kill the father. They then create a totem (or father surrogate) through which they can both atone for their guilt, relive the deed, and protect themselves from repeating it. Often the totem is in the form of a sacred meal. Freud thought that this "myth of the primal father" and the subsequent creation of the kinship group became part of a "collective mind" which was transmitted from one generation to another. A lively and creative sociological application of Freud's theory is found in *Microcosm* by Philip Slater (1966).

Though there is no mention of the Wednesday Evening Society in this series of essays, it is easy to imagine that Freud might have had his own experience in mind as he wrote:

> One day the brothers who had been driven out came together, killed and devoured their father and so made an end of the patriarchal horde....The violent primal father had doubtless been the feared and envied model of each one of the company of brothers, and in the act of devouring him they accomplished their identification with him, and each one of them acquired a portion of his strength (Freud 1950, 142).

These thoughts would lead Freud to understand the development of the ego as a consequence of object identification. They would also lead him to understand the roots of civilization as a consequence of the resolution of the Oedipal complex and the emergence of the super ego.

In 1921 Freud further pursued his efforts to understand the experience of individuals in groups by writing *Group Psychology and the Analysis of the Ego*. Here he sought to respond to the relatively new field of social psychology by applying his evolving libido theory to understanding group phenomena. This brief essay is remarkable for its further elucidation of themes from *Totem and Taboo* and for the richness of its nascent ideas, particularly about narcissism, object relations, and the development of the ego.

Freud maintained that in human development libidinal ties (love energy) are first expressed in object cathexis or attachment to the mother. Later these ties are directed toward working through an identification with the father during the crucial Oedipal period. However, in a group situation which by nature tends to be regressive due to anxiety, identification occurs with other group members while object cathexis is directed toward the leader. Thus, a group is reminiscent of the primal horde in its unconscious evocation of shared irrational emotion and potential expression of repressed hostile and aggressive feelings toward authority. As a way of handling these feelings, the group not only creates a totem but also the illusion that the (idealized) leader loves all members of the group equally. This illusion is institutionalized in artificially structured groups such as the church and the army, as well as in the natural group of the family.

Freud was particularly interested to compare the group's inherent suggestibility and fascination with its leader to the "mysterious power" of the hypnotist. He was referring here to the transference in the relationship with authority which is shaped by early object identifications, especially with the father. Freud made it clear that only a "hero" (poet or genius) could free himself from these powerful feelings and assume leadership himself. Presumably, this was what self analysis did for Freud–though it is difficult to know whether he has himself in mind as he writes. It *is* clear that Freud considered the evolution of individual psychology to be an advancement over the more primitive group psychology.

In this essay on group psychology Freud proposed a number of ideas about the development of the ego. He was particularly interested in how the unconscious drives (both libido and aggression) are satisfied in relation to objects outside the ego. Freud thought that when the ego identifies with an object, it introjects the object and is subsequently enriched by it. However, when the ego surrenders to the object, it is in bondage to it and is depleted by it (Freud 1921, 45). In normal human development, when the narcissistic needs of the infant's ego are inevitably frustrated by the demands and limits of the external world (reality principle), an ego ideal is formed to satisfy these frustrated needs and protect the ego. All too often, however, the cathected object *becomes* the ego ideal (idealization). Then the ego is in danger of losing itself to, and fusing with, the object.

On the other hand, any object which has been cathected or identified with can be lost or die. Then the ego is forced to take its libido back into itself (anti-cathexis) which results in the development of secondary narcissism. In either case, whether through idealization or loss, the love toward others (object cathexis) is dangerous because it limits love of self (narcissism) upon which basic survival of the ego depends. For Freud, the mythic leader of the primal horde *was* the ideal superman–free of any libidinal ties, totally narcissistic and independent: "To objects his ego gave away no more than was barely necessary" (Freud 1959, 55).

This material highlights Freud's determination to maintain his view of the self-contained and instinctually driven nature of the psyche. However, in the process of establishing broad foundations for psychoanalytic thought, he could not help but open up new possibilities as well. This was especially true concerning the give-and-take relationship between the ego and objects in its external world. One author comments:

> Freud never really abandoned his psychobiology. Nevertheless, from about 1915 to 1920 onward, the strong wine of Freud's relentless quest began once more to burst the bottles of old theory (Guntrip 1971, 31).

Over the following three decades, new ideas and leaders in both Britain and the United States would challenge and enlarge the ideas of their founder. Among the most important of these was Scottish psychoanalyst W.R.D. Fairbairn (1889-1963) who, more than anyone else, dared to abandon the biological basis of Freudian drive theory and take seriously the implications of a "pure" object relations model of psychology (St. Clair 1986, 53). Fairbairn, contrary to Freud, maintained that the ego is a dynamic, unitary structure which includes the unconscious. Libidinal energy resides within the ego, causing it to seek relationship with objects outside itself for the sake of its own development. The ego is no longer subservient to mechanistic or biologically determined drives lodged in a separate structure (id). In striving for relationship, the ego determines its own structure from the very moment of birth. Thus there is no such thing as primary narcissism. Relationships are not secondary to reducing tension, but rather primary to ego formation and functioning. The main condition in infancy is not helplessness in the face of the need for drive satisfaction, but rather separation anxiety in the face of the reality of dependence on others (breast and mother). By putting forth these ideas Fairbairn shifted focus from the Oedipal struggle during the phallic period of development to the earliest years of life during the oral stage of development. Now the relationship with the mother, rather than with the father, was of central importance. In the process, Fairbairn not only broke with Freud's lifelong effort to base psychoanalytic thought in scientific positivism, but he also significantly altered Freud's interior mapping of the mind.

Instead of the three-part structure (super ego, id, ego) in which an essentially weak ego is buffeted by uncontrollable libidinal energies and ongoing conflicts between the id and the super ego, Fairbairn proposed a model in which the ego takes center stage. In an "endopsychic structure of the mind," the ego is shaped by its own efforts to respond to its earliest relational needs. Recognizing that the object (mother) is a source of *both* frustration *and* excitement, the ego by using aggression splits and introjects these parts (experiences) of the object, attaching (cathecting) part of itself to each of these aspects. This psychological maneuver both protects the "good" aspects and controls the "bad." A *libidinal ego* (based on the exciting aspects of the object) and an *antilibidinal ego* sometimes called "the internal saboteur" (based on the rejecting aspects of the object) are repressed. The first contains feelings of longing and craving for the exciting object while the second contains feelings of anger and sadness toward the rejecting object. The *central ego*, based on the "good enough" aspects of the internalized "ideal" object, remains conscious and is projected onto outside objects in order to continue to experience them as satisfying. As the person matures, the central ego "suffuses the entire personality" (Scharff and Scharff 1992, 27) All three parts of the ego remain in dynamic relationship: "It is as if there are now a multiplicity of egos at war with one another" (St. Clair 1986, 55).

Fairbairn's focus on the internalization of "bad" objects was consistent with his interest in psychopathology and especially what he called "the schizoid problem"–the tendency of the infant to withdraw from all relationships in order to protect the good objects from his or her devouring love and in order to protect the ego from further weakening by giving away more libido. British psychoanalyst Harry Guntrip (1901-1975), following these ideas, thought that there was a further split in response to the now-repressed internal object world, thus creating a lost or *regressed ego*, "a part of the infantile libidinal ego in which the infant found his world so intolerable that the sensitive heart of him fled into himself" (Guntrip 171, 152). Those experiencing such feelings of "ego weakness" are concerned not so much with how to be in relationship with others but whether or not one has a self at all. The regressed ego seeks a return to the womb where it can await rebirth in a safer environment later through the therapeutic relationship.[3] Though Guntrip claimed that Fairbairn accepted this revision to his endopsychic structure (1971, 152) there is no direct evidence from Fairbairn himself.

Fairbairn and others working in the area of object relations introduced the idea of *positions* instead of stages of development. A position is the emotional stance from which the infant's ego relates to both internal and external objects. This approach was of particular interest to Melanie Klein (1882-1960), a Viennese psychoanalyst who moved to London in the mid-1920s. Though Klein remained neo-Freudian in her lifelong allegiance to drive theory and the three-part structure of the mind, she was also innovative–not only because she was the first psychoanalyst to work with children, but also because she developed many of her own theoretical ideas about object relations.

---

[3] Greenberg and Mitchell point out that Guntrip's creation of a regressed ego from within the internal world of the infant is not an object relations concept since it is not related to external reality (Greenberg and Mitchell 1983, 214).

Klein thought the internal life of the infant was made up almost entirely of fantasies. These are mental expressions of libidinal (life) and aggressive (death) drives which are primitive, even psychotic in nature. They first occur in relationship to the mother as a defense against the persecutory anxiety caused by maternal deprivation and the inevitable feelings of frustration experienced by the infant. During the initial six months of life, defensive fantasies about "part objects" are primarily projected onto the mother and only secondarily introjected back into the infant. The ego reacts by splitting the part objects, idealizing the "good" (gratifying breast) and denying the "bad" (frustrating breast). During these earliest months of life the infant's ego assumes a *paranoid-schizoid position* to protect the good part objects which have been internalized from its own devouring love.

By four months of age, the infant begins to recognize and introject the mother as a *whole* person. This begins a major psychological task because the internal effort of trying to hold both good and bad aspects of the whole object together creates additional anxiety and even despair. The infant now fears his or her combined love *and* hate will destroy the whole object (mother) along with the infant's own ego which has identified with the object. This development signals the emergence of the *depressive position* in which the infant's awareness of separation from, and possible damage to, the formerly split-off and idealized part object predominates. Feelings of concern for the whole object arouse feelings of guilt and loss. Those who cannot bear these feelings skip over the depressive position and develop manic defenses which can lead to pathology. During this difficult time the infant realizes that objects cannot be so easily destroyed or taken away by wishes or feelings. Eventually the desire for reparation arises–that is, restoration of relationship with the now good/bad whole object. This desire brings about the important achievement of internal object constancy for the infant. In addition, reparative fantasies help resolve the depressive anxiety and strengthen the ego in its relationship with reality. Throughout the rest of our lives we move dynamically between these two positions in dealing with our emotional reactions to external reality.

Among Klein's many new ideas was the concept of *projective identification*. This is a psychological maneuver in which the infant splits off the bad parts, projects them onto the object, and then unconsciously inducts the object into behaving like the bad projected parts. It involves a reciprocal process inside the self and between the self and the external object. Its purpose is to externalize the infant's internal struggle over badness in order to feel better about one's self *and* to feel empathic toward the object.

It is as if one individual forces another to play a role in the enactment of that person's internal drama–one involving early object relations. The target of the manipulation is induced to engage in an *identification* with a disowned aspect of the person doing the *projection*-- hence the term projective identification."(Cashdan 1988, 56).

Klein's concept of projective identification is noteworthy both for its interactive implications and its manipulative power in interpersonal relationships. It marks a new way to understand the psychoanalytic concepts of transference and countertransference.

These ideas caught the attention of many, including British psychoanalyst Wilfred R. Bion (1897-1976). Bion would be the first since Freud to put forth some radically new ideas about the psychological dynamics of the group situation based on the work of Melanie Klein. Bion was born of English parents but grew up in India where his father was a civil engineer. His parents were active Christians and through them he became familiar with religious concepts and practices. When he was eight years old, Bion was sent off to a private school in England where he initially found the regimen "barbaric." After his graduation Bion joined the war effort in 1915 and became a decorated war hero as one of only two survivors of his regiment. Bion went on to study history at Queen's College, Oxford. He never returned to India. Bion was a large man, somewhat quiet and shy, whose excellence in swimming and rugby assured him peer acceptance and respect.

Black-haired, swarthy, deep-chested and muscular, he commanded respect in the School House common-room, where his laconic and gloomy voiced pronouncements, so often counterpointed by a mischievous grin and a sardonic chuckle, were unchallengeable (Anon 1992, 386).

After teaching briefly, Bion went to medical school where he was attracted to new ideas about "dynamic psychology" and group work. From 1933 on he was affiliated with the Tavistock Clinic in London. After being involved in the (in)famous Northfield Experiment during World War II, Bion served as director of group psychotherapy at Tavistock between 1948 and 1957. The ideas which were generated during these years were shared at annual meetings of the British

Psychoanalytic Society and were eventually published in a collection entitled *Experiences in Groups* (1960). This volume has since been called "the shortest and most influential text in psychoanalytic group psychotherapy" (Pines 1992, xiii).

Bion's personal life was marred by the death of his wife three days after the birth of their only child in 1943. Bion remarried in 1951 and had two more children. Bion began a training analysis with his colleague John Rickman and later completed a personal analysis with Melanie Klein. From 1960 on Bion focused on individual psychoanalytic thought and practice. Though it is not clear why he left group work, in the mid-1950s he once commented to a friend: "Why does it always have to be me who has to bear the brunt? I feel as though I have been on the front lines unrelieved for ten years. I do not want to stay there another ten years" (Trist 1992, 3).

Bion's later writings are somewhat obtuse, involving the application of theories of knowledge and scientific thought to psychoanalytic method. In the latter part of his life he lived in Los Angeles, lectured in Brazil, and planned to retire in England. Upon discovering he was terminally ill, Bion is said to have commented with characteristic brusqueness: "Life is full of surprises...most of them unpleasant" (Anon. 1992, 389). At the time of his death he had completed the first volume of his autobiography entitled *The Long Week-End*. Unfortunately Bion never returned to the field of group work to develop the early ideas for which he had become so well known.

PART TWO: BION AND BEYOND

In his work with groups Bion was "searching for the equivalent of the psychoanalytic method in the group situation" (Trist 1992, 28). Though the existence of group phenomena apply to any size group, Bion thought an "intelligible field of study" was probably presented by a group of from eight to twelve members. He focused on the group itself, encouraging it to become self-interpretive and self-reflexive regarding its own dynamic process in order to facilitate learning about itself. From the beginning Bion's approach to the experiential group was educational both for himself and the group members, but it was not necessarily psychotherapeutic. In his last article written on the subject of groups, Bion commented:

> There remains the question of what therapeutic value is
> to be attached to the procedure I have tried to describe.

I do not think that the time has come to give a definite
opinion (1961, 190).

Bion was intent on establishing the self-reflexive *modus operandi* as the group
task because, when engaged in, it "reveals something that is not otherwise
visible" (Bion 1961, 134). What it reveals is that the basic function of a group
is to preserve itself, just as the basic function of a clock is to keep time. It also
reveals the presence of unconscious processes designed to maintain this basic
function.

Bion, like Freud, was fascinated with the expectations for leadership which
members bring to a group situation, and how such expectations quickly become
a group problem. By keeping himself equidistant from all group members and
focusing exclusively on the group task, Bion frustrated certain basic relational
needs. One of his colleagues (A.K. Rice) said Bion "could sit further behind
his own face than any other man I know" (Lyth 1981, 662). Though this
"consultative approach" was not particularly therapeutic in and of itself, it did
allow Bion to see what was going on and learn about group behavior:

> At the appointed time members of the group begin to
> arrive; individuals engage each other in conversation for
> a short time, and then...a silence falls on the group. After
> a while desultory conversation breaks out again, and then
> another silence falls. It becomes clear to me that I am,
> in some sense, the focus of attention in the group.
> Furthermore, I am aware of feeling uneasily that I am
> expected to do something....I confide my anxieties to
> the group...there is some indignation that I should
> express such feelings without seeming to appreciate that
> the group is entitled to expect something from me....I
> wonder what the expectations are and what has aroused
> them (Bion 1961, 29-30).

Bion thought that the adult's efforts to make emotional contact with the
complexities of life in a group were as formidable as the infant's efforts to
make contact with the mother's breast. When these efforts succeed the infant
digests or metabolizes the good-enough experiences. (This was later called the
"alpha function" by Bion; "alphabetizing experience" is similar to Freud's
primary process.) When these efforts fail, the person experiences frustration
and anxiety and is left with "undigested foreign bodies in his system." This

psychological situation evokes regression and the appearance of certain psychological formations which are "secondary to an extremely primal scene worked out on a level of part objects" (Bion 1961, 164). This is why the emotional storm which goes on in the psychoanalytic dyad becomes a "veritable blizzard" in a group where there is literally a "crossfire of multilateral projective identifications" (Gosling 1981b, 628). Bion thought these phenomena were connected with the primitive paranoid-schizoid and depressive positions identified by Melanie Klein. In making these observations Bion understood the group experience to activate basically psychotic rather than neurotic mechanisms, the fear of the loss of self rather than the fear of the loss of love. These reactions stem from earliest object relations rather than from a later family dynamic (Oedipal complex).

Like others before him, Bion thought every group has two states of mind—organized and unorganized. These states co-exist but are also distinct. The organized or Work (W) group is characterized by structure and organization, its ability to cooperate and engage in the necessary rational mental activity to accomplish a goal and learn through experience (reality). In many ways it has characteristics similar to those attributed by Freud to the ego. It is an open system concerned with consequences, feedback, taking responsibility, and achieving role flexibility (Turquet 1974, 352).

The unorganized or Basic Assumption (BA) group forms out of a "pool" into which "anonymous contributions are made, and through which the impulses and desires implicit in these contributions are gratified" (Bion 1961, 50). It is a closed system in which leadership is idealized and set roles are established to meet unconscious internal needs. "All coldness is outside, all warmth is inside, with members hiding together like so many babes in the wood" (Turquet 1974, 354). One author comments: "The basic assumption states are the 'heart of darkness' of the group. They have a mysterious, unspoken quality about them" (Schermer 1992, 146). The emergence of this BA group mentality, in which the group itself becomes an internal object, tends to divert or obstruct the Work group—especially when the task is difficult as in the reflexive study of itself. Whether or not the dynamics of the BA group become conscious and are understood, the presence of the BA group always undergirds the emotional life of the Work group. This interrelationship assures the potential effectiveness of the Work group.

In a BA group the group experience suffuses everything and is not limited to a specific place or purpose. There is minimal awareness of time or individual differences and high degree of cohesiveness. Not only do individuals tend to fuse with the BA group and enjoy basking in its security and warmth, but they also tend to lose whatever skills and intelligence they had before joining the group. There is also a particular avoidance (Bion called it "hatred") of learning in a BA group. Interventions by the group leader usually sound like rebukes. Bion notes: "Participation in basic-assumption activity requires no training, experience, or mental development. It is instantaneous, inevitable, and instinctive" (1961, 153). Bion regarded the human being as essentially a political or group animal "at war, both with the group and with those aspects of his personality that constitute his 'groupishness'" (168). Despite his awareness of the strength of these unconscious dynamics, Bion believed that in the long run the Work group "triumphs."

As Bion watched groups struggle with their relationship to leadership in their efforts to survive as a group, he saw three different groupish patterns emerge. In the BA *dependency* group, the members unite in their belief that a wise leader will rescue them from their anxiety. When this does not happen they focus on the weakest member of the group (scapegoat) as a way to get the leader to take power and thus prevent the group from destroying itself. The feelings of guilt and depression are the "cement" which holds the dependent group together. In the BA *fight/flight* group, the members are intent on saving the group from the leader who will not lead and is therefore perceived as a threat to the group's preservation. To ease their subsequent panic, they will look for a substitute leader, preferably someone a bit paranoid, to galvanize them into action. Feelings of anger and hate hold them together. In the BA *pairing* group, members become enthralled with the relationship between two group members and begin to live through the pair in hopes they will bring forth an idea (or leader) who will save the group from its destructiveness and sense of despair. Sexual references are common in this type of group. For a group to stay in a BA pairing mode, it is is essential that a "messiah" be conceived but never born.[4]

There is no overt conflict between the three BA groups, but there is always potential conflict between the BA group and the need for the W group to emerge. Thus, it is up to the leader to constantly remind the group of its learning task (to study itself) and its capacity to work (be reality-based and rational). It is

---

[4] Several theorists have added a fourth BA to Bion's list. Pierre Turquet names a BA *oneness* group in which members surrender themselves to join in union with an omnipotent force and experience a deep sense of wholeness and well being. Jill and David Scharff, in applying Bion's BA concepts to work with family groups, propose a BA *fission/fusion* group in which family members regress to a primitive state of either merging or splintering apart.

extremely easy for the leader to be drawn into a particular BA group and become de-skilled because of the strength of the shared projective identifications (fantasy). Bion wrote:

> I believe ability to shake oneself out of the numbing feelings of reality that is a concomitant of this state [of receiving the projective identifications] is the prime requisite of the analyst in the group" (1961, 149).

To put it another way, the leader must be aware of his or her own countertransference and use it to understand the group process. This is one of the most challenging aspects of being a group leader.

Bion thought that at an institutional level the church represented BA dependency, the army represented BA fight/flight, and the aristocracy represented BA pairing. Meeting the emotional needs of the basic assumptions by institutionalizing them avoids their obstructing the work of the whole society. Interestingly, Bion thought that psychoanalysis as a social institution was another example of BA pairing. One psychologist-writer points out that Bion was particularly able to see in the unstructured group "the fundamental and wired-in (instinctive) aspects of our groupishness" (Schermer 1992, 149). This writer calls the three BA's "biogenetic object relations templates" which motivate the organism (person) "along specific lines much like a hormone" (145). As such they embody the three biological imperatives needed for survival: child-rearing (BA dependency), reproduction (BA pairing), and protection (BA fight/flight).

While individuals fear losing themselves to a BA group, each individual also has a particular readiness or inclination to join one of the BA groups based on his or her projective identifications. Probably influenced by Kurt Lewin's concepts, Bion called this readiness *valency*--"a spontaneous, unconscious function of the gregarious quality in the personality of man" (1961, 170). Valencies come from the earliest splitting and identifications projected and introjected by the ego. Each person has the capacity for all three valencies, but is predisposed toward one and will tend to project this onto the group. When under stress this predisposition is readily apparent in each person's preference: to take care of weaker group members (dependency), to advocate for or against the interests of the organization sponsoring the group (fight/flight), or to talk to group members separately after hours (pairing). It is especially important for the group leader to know what his or her valency is.

If a group seems stuck in one BA mode, it will often get unstuck through the introduction of another BA mode by a subgroup. Some groups stay in one

BA mode for months or years, while others experience all three modes within a single group session. The emergence of different BA groups tends to be cyclical rather than developmental and there is a type of sequential succession that can occur. That is, the pairing group produces a "savior" upon whom group members become dependent but eventually rebel (fight/flight), killing the idealized leader and necessitating emergence of yet another pairing group to keep hope for survival alive (Bion 1965). These ideas reflect the influence of Freud's thought about the primal horde, the Oedipal complex, and the emergence of a kinship group.

Sometimes a BA group becomes its "dual"–or reciprocal. Unfortunately Bion did not develop this concept. An example would be a BA dependency group whose leader refuses to sustain and nourish the group so instead the group sustains and nourishes the leader. It is important to note that when one BA combines with the W group, then the other BAs are suppressed. Research has shown that people inclined toward BA pairing and BA fight seem drawn to one another *and* toward the work of the group, while BA dependency and BA flight join with one another and against the possibility of such group work. A group with a range of valencies will be able to deal more explicitly with a wider range of emotional issues. Thus, individual valency is an important consideration in choosing group members.

Though basic assumptions are not exactly the same as internalized objects, the two concepts have been called "parallel activities with correspondence but not exactly overlapping" (Gosling 1981b, 631). This type of observation highlights what Bion called "binocular vision"–the necessity to study the group from the point of view of the individual (psychology) *and* to study the individual from the point of view of the group (sociology) in a corresponding way. Bion's ability to see the human personality as an open system based on its early object relations made his work appealing to educators and sociologists as well as psychotherapists. Most recently his influence is evident in Larry Hirschhorn's *The Workplace Within: Psychodynamics of Organizational Life* (1993). Hirschhorn explores individual and group social defenses as a way to handle anxiety and aggression when roles and boundaries in the workplace become confused or are violated.

As Bion's thought about objects relations developed, he became increasingly interested in the role of the mother as the earliest "container" for the infant's projections (Bion 1962). Her intrapsychic capacity to receive and respond creatively to these demands depends on her degree of "reverie"–that is, the ways she is able to lovingly hold the child's projections rather than become reactive to them. Bion was interested in how the infant then digests these experiences with the mother and creates a container within him- or herself where violent projections and splitting can eventually reside. Thus, psychosis was not the result of splitting and projecting per se, but of not being able to use these psychological mechanisms because of an absent internal container due to a mother who could not receive the initial material and respond with reverie. Bion understood that, like the psychoanalyst in the therapy room, the leader of a group had a certain containing function as well.

Bion returned briefly to his interest in groups in a book entitled *Attention and Interpretation* (1970). Here he explored more deeply the relationship between the individual, the group, and the establishment (which is the Work group institutionalized through rules, dogma, and structures). This conceptual work no doubt grew out of his previous experience at Tavistock where he served, sometimes simultaneously, as clinical director, group leader, individual psychotherapist, and consultant to the staff. In fact Eric Trist, who was Bion's colleague at the clinic, comments, "We always believed that something unique would emerge from the interpenetration of these levels of experience and professional activity" (1992, 38). Bion was particularly interested in the relationship of the "mystic" (poet, messiah, genius) to the group and the establishment. He concluded that if the group is to remain vital, it needs the help of the institution to try and serve as a container for the ideas and presence of the mystic. There is a sense in this material that Bion was trying to understand his own experience as a "genius" at Tavistock and learn from it.

Bion's ideas spread rapidly. In the United States the Research Center for Group Dynamics (RCGD) was established at the Massachusetts Institute of Technology in 1944-1945 by Kurt Lewin and an active group of researchers. In 1947 it expanded into the National Training Laboratory (NTL) located at Bethel, Maine, where the study of T-groups became the focus. By 1948 a new research journal called *Human Relations* was being jointly published by the RCGD and Tavistock with regular contributions from Bion. In 1949 the first joint group relations conference was held at Gerrards Cross, England, sponsored by the Tavistock Institute and attended by leaders from RCGD (now located at the University of Michigan). By the early 1950s extensive research was begun through the Education Department at the University of Chicago to test and validate Bion's theories. These efforts were published in *Emotional Dynamics and Group Culture* (Stock and Thelen 1958) and summarized in Stock's "A Survey of Research on T-groups" (1964). Herbert Thelen was among those involved in these early developments. He writes:

We were indebted to Bion for his coherent imagery of the group as an organism...[it] all seemed economical and elegant to us. I especially liked the broad evolutionary sweep encompassed in fight/flight (animal stress reflex), dependency (family protectiveness for growing up), and pairing (creation of new relationships and through them, new group capabilities). These dynamics seemed intuitively satisfying and fundamental (1992, 123).

On the other side of the Atlantic, the Tavistock Institute was established as a research arm of the clinic in 1947. This development was undergirded both methodologically and theoretically in its study of "the whole" by Kurt Lewin's work of the 1930s and 1940s as well as by von Bertalanffy's "open systems" approach to organisms and, by extension, human organizations. But it was Bion's application of psychoanalytic ideas to group phenomena (and further study of the unconscious), as well as his interest in the role of the group leader, which actually provided the direction and agenda of the Institute itself (Khaleelee and Miller 1992, 358). Among the leaders were A.K. Rice, a member of Bion's first "civilian" (nonpatient) training group begun in 1945 which had met weekly for two years. In 1957 Rice organized the first official conference to study group relations. It was jointly sponsored by the Tavistock Institute (where Rice was director) and the University of Leicester and included the first British experiment in the "laboratory" or T-group method.

"Group relations conferences" began to occur regularly in both the United States and England–the former sponsored by NTL and the latter by Tavistock/Leicester. Both involved the application of Bion's theories and focused on studying the small group process and intergroup relations in a "cultural island" setting away from the world. Great excitement was generated about the possibilities for change in educational institutions, industrial organizations, and government as a result of employees receiving this type of training. Since it was impossible to experience a group relations conference and not be personally affected, from the beginning there was an awareness of the close interrelationship between training and therapy. It was in response to this concern, as well as other influences, that the Americans and British soon parted ways. The clearest explication of these often misunderstood differences between the T-group and the Tavistock study group is found in an article by Edward Klein and Boris Astrachan (1971).

As NTL evolved in the early 1960s it moved in two interrelated directions in its T-group work: 1) using the group as a supportive milieu for doing individual therapy; and 2) helping the group develop itself into a group culture which would help individuals be more self-actualized (Thelen 1992, 121). Trainers were clinicians from a variety of professions–education, social work, the church, industry–and labs were suitable for a variety of interested registrants. Focus was on lowering anxiety and defenses, establishing group norms, encouraging the growth of interdependency, and increasing self- awareness and authenticity among the individuals through feedback and validation. The trainer was an observer-participant who modelled the behaviors of a good group member, facilitated the growth of group trust through his or her own nonjudgmental and open manner, and encouraged collaborative interactions with him- or herself. Irrational or unconscious aspects of the group experience were minimized in favor of emphasizing the possibility for here-and-now individual change and improved interpersonal skills. Nonverbal behavior was seen as promoting emotional maturation rather than as "acting out."

It is noteworthy that these "democratic" developments at NTL were in many ways consistent with Lewin's original political agenda in response to the growth of fascism in Europe in the 1930s. However, they tended to suppress and hide the psychoanalytic origins of group work in the Bion tradition which had so influenced NTL in the 1940s and early 1950s. These developments also reflected the huge impact of humanistic psychology with its burgeoning of small groups in the United States in the 1960s. In addition to the development of the T-group, there was the eventual merging of the encounter group movement with group psychotherapy, especially through the work of Irvin Yalom in the early 1970s. This three-part amalgam has come to be known generally as the humanistic tradition of group experience and leadership.

In contrast, the Tavistock model for group relations conferences was developed in England, largely by A. Kenneth Rice and his colleague Pierre Turquet. These conferences focused on the group dynamics involved in learning about leadership and authority and were run by psychoanalytically trained consultants. For the first few years psychiatrists were not permitted to be consultants in order to assure that conferences were educational and not therapeutic experiences. Despite these efforts, the line can be unclear:

> where training crosses over into therapy is seldom a
> clearly defined boundary...it is also true that, for those
> whose profession is therapeutic or educational, the

borderline between therapy or education and leadership
or management is obscure (Rice 1965, 161).

Structurally the conferences included a combination of small group, large group, intergroup relations, plenary sessions, and didactic presentations on group dynamics. Over the years the Tavistock Institute's work has been extended through other organizations such as the Grubb Institute of London, Rosehill Institute of Human Relations in Canada, International Foundation for Social Innovation in France, and the Indian Society for Individual and Social Development.

The Tavistock model, based on the application of Bion's ideas, was then (re)introduced to the United States by Morris Parloff and Margaret Rioch of the Washington, D.C., School of Psychiatry (who had attended a Leicester/Tavistock Conference in 1963). The first two-week "Tavi" in the United States was held in June 1965 at Mount Holyoke College (South Hadley, Massachusetts), sponsored jointly by the Washington School of Psychiatry and the Yale Department of Psychiatry. In one of his last appearances having to do with group work, Bion attended a conference held at Amherst College in 1969. Such training conferences in group relations have continued to be held at least annually up to the present time under the sponsorship of the A.K. Rice Institute and usually in conjunction with an educational institution.

Issues of boundary setting, the role of the consultant, the emergence of the mature (Work) group, and "back-home application" in one's professional organization all became staples of the Tavistock experience. The focus was on the study of group dynamics in the here-and-now where there is no stated agenda aside from this group reflexive study task. The consultant/leader remains detached and nondirective, but pays close attention to setting boundaries–especially time, place, and his or her role. By using his or her hierarchial position as stimulus and staying closely focused on the task, consequent responses from the group then become the raw data for study of group and individual behavior. Interest is focused on the unconscious elements underlying the group experience, the shared regression and fantasies (mainly about authority) of the members, and the emergence of basic assumption groups. It was hoped that by the end of the conference group members may have established enough of a Work group (either in the small or large group) to have gained insight into their own transference as well as into how groups function both consciously and unconsciously.

In comparing these two approaches, Klein and Astrachan comment:

> Interestingly, the study group, which was derived from
> individual psychoanalytic theory, focuses on the group,
> while the social psychological theory underlying
> T-groups results in a focus on the individual (1971, 673).

This difference is especially clear in the types of interventions made by the leader. In a T-group the leader is constantly trying to negotiate his or her way into the group in order to present a new insight or pick up a point which has been missed. Thus he or she will say, "I feel that..." or "Would you give me a little feedback about..." In the study group, the leader does not work at getting into the group, nor does he or she care whether members wish to hear what he or she has to say. For example, an intervention might begin with "The group is avoiding their feelings about..." Thus, in the T-group members speak *with* the leader; in a study group they speak *about* or *to* the leader (Klein and Astrachan 1971, 672). In terms of stages of group development, the Tavistock study groups tend to move from initial fear, hostility, and aggression toward warmth and affection, while the T-groups start out with openness and affection and later move toward frustration and hostility.

CONCLUSION

There was a point in time somewhere between 1945 and 1965 when the small-group experience in clinical pastoral education stood at the crossroads between employing an interpersonal and humanistic understanding of group work versus employing a psychoanalytic group-as-a-whole understanding. From the previous literature survey (chapters 2 and 3), it is clear that both approaches were part of the historical foundations of CPE. On the one hand there were the interpersonal and intimate experiences of the earliest student groups, Boisen's quest for healing by joining "the fellowship of the best," Cabot's emphasis on learning pastoral skills, and Leslie's conviction that the human being is essentially a social animal. On the other hand, there was the longstanding interest in Freudian psychology among those in the liberal Protestant tradition and especially CPE, the strong influence of psychoanalysis (and the so-called medical model) on supervisors affiliated with the Council for Clinical Training in the 1940s, and the fascinating development of the "peculiar" approach (based on the early NTL days) of the New England group in the late 1950s. Moving as a strong undercurrent in these waters was group psychotherapy, a form of treatment (if not education) with which CPE practitioners, and especially those in mental hospitals, had been acquainted from the beginning.

Given the fledgling status of CPE–and especially the process group component of its educational programs–it is not surprising to find that as time went on these issues were not articulated nor was their importance clearly understood. Though there were continued concerns about the differences between education and therapy, trying to make this distinction (either in work with individual students or in the small group) did not really get at the root of the problem. Unfortunately, the confusion was compounded since both the psychoanalytic and humanistic approaches contained therapeutic *and* educational elements, albeit quite different from each other.

In retrospect we know that like most of American culture after 1965, CPE supervisors welcomed and assimilated into their small-group work (whether consciously or not) the humanistic psychology tradition with its emphasis on individual change, group cohesiveness, and the democratic style of exercising authority. Further, this approach was certainly congruent with other longstanding emphases in CPE: the love of incarnational theology, the focus on each student's emotional development, concern about teaching effective pastoral (i.e., interpersonal) skills, and general optimism about the human situation and the students' ability to learn. That this approach to group work might have been potentially at odds with a psychoanalytic understanding of the individual (and by extension patient or parishioner) did not seem to trouble CPE practitioners who increasingly depended upon the eclectic work of Irvin Yalom to integrate the two. Nor was it troubling that the actual group-as-a-whole dimension of the training experience had been virtually lost.

There are some who would maintain that process-group work in CPE based on the humanistic tradition is simply one way to talk about the Work group in Bion's terms. When it "works," students increase their self-esteem, interpersonal competence, and trust of a small group environment for learning. Others are more suspicious that this so-called humanistic approach is either group psychotherapy in disguise or has actually perpetuated the wide-scale formation of Bion's basic assumption groups in CPE. This latter could take several forms: a BA dependency group with its self-contained atmosphere and idealized view of the CPE supervisor; a BA fight/flight group which has become resistant to part or all of the CPE experience; or a BA pairing group which looks on during session after session as the supervisor (or a strong student) works dynamically with an individual group member during the majority of the process group time.

From this analysis it should be clear that this inquiry is calling for a renewed effort by CPE supervisors to take a group-as-a-whole approach in supervising the small process group based on the psychoanalytic tradition and subsequent work on group theory in the object relations tradition. Given the facts of the CPE historical heritage, it is my conviction that this is the clearest and most consistent way to redress the balance between the therapeutic and educational intent of the small process group experience in clinical pastoral education. However, this is not an easy task. Margaret Rioch comments:

> This shift in perspective from the individual to the group
> is difficult to make in actual practice although it is often
> given lip service. It is like a *shift to a higher magnitude*,
> which is not easy when the lower order is in itself very
> complex and by no means thoroughly understood. (1975,
> 21; italics added).

Rioch compares this "shift to a higher order of magnitude" in group work to the ability to see an individual or marital relationship in the framework of the larger family system.

It was Wilfred Bion's unique contribution that he was able to see the individual in the larger framework of the group-as-a-whole *and* see that the group-as-a-whole contained its own unique dynamics. Bion (unlike Freud) viewed the personality and the group as an open system in which "personalities of the members of a group are elements of the context of a group, while at the same time a group itself is part of the context of the personalities of its members" (Hopper 1984, 345). A.K. Rice puts it this way:

> The individual is a creature of the group, the group of
> the individual. Each, according to his capacity and
> experience, carries within him the groups of which he
> has been and is a member...(Miller and Rice 1967, 17).

Or, as one participant at a Tavistock conference commented: "When I look for the group, I find myself. When I look for myself, I find the group" (Rioch 1975, 171).

The beginning point in working with groups in this way is to realize that a group is not formed until it has an agreed-upon task–whether that be to study itself in the here-and-now (that is, deal with its own survival) as in the small process group, or to deal with clinical material (as in group supervision), or to absorb and apply ideas (as in didactic group sessions). Secondly, there will always be both conscious and unconscious elements active in group life. Third, working with a self-reflexive study group involves paying particular attention to how the group deals with leadership and authority issues, establishes member roles, understands boundaries, is able to identify basic assumption group patterns and establish itself as a work group. It involves the consultant/leader monitoring amounts of anxiety, degrees of regression and acting out, and generally taking into consideration the influence of individual and group psychotic (irrational) elements which lie just below the surface. It involves individual members becoming aware of their valences, and how identification, splitting, projection, projective identification, and introjection become operative and revealing in the group situation. Finally, it involves seeing each member's personal and interpersonal participation in the light of the larger group-as-a-whole dynamics. It is my conviction that in this way the balance between individual and group *change* (therapeutic value) and individual and group *learning* (educational value) can be most clearly established.

One author comments that "learning about group dynamics can be both exhilarating and horrifying, especially when learning through the vehicle of one's own experience." He continues:

> Doing so requires people to peel back the surface veneers
> of self-presentation and mutually protective etiquettes
> to examine the hidden agendas, covert processes,
> simplifying myths, primitive fantasies, and intense
> anxieties that underlie group life. Unconscious processes
> are exposed as the source of creativity and destruction.
> Participants are confronted with their own beliefs and
> identifications, aggressions, passions, longings, and
> sources of vitality and withdrawal (Krantz 1991, 216).

It is with this awareness of both the exhilarating and horrifying possibilities for those who seriously engage in the small process-group work in CPE that the following case study is shared.

7 | THEORY APPLICATION AND EVALUATION

T he application of my theoretical work specifically began with my supervision of a group of students in a full-time CPE residency program.[1] It was to be their third unit of training at our medical center and took place in the summer of 1993. All four students were well established in their clinical areas and shared the long-term goal of finding professional positions in chaplaincy. The students were Wayne, a thirty-five-year-old United Church of Canada minister; Rose, a fifty-year-old Roman Catholic sister; Brigid, a forty-seven-year-old Roman Catholic sister; and Judy, a thirty-eight-year-old Roman Catholic laywoman. I had previously worked with them as co-supervisor of their initial unit of training in the fall.

I was immediately aware of the small size of the group. Though Bion did not think size made much difference in terms of actual group dynamics, it is generally understood that a very small group (VSG), numbering from three to seven members, tends to be warmer, create stronger boundaries between itself and the outside world, and tolerate subgrouping only intermittently (Gosling 1981a). The physical proximity in a VSG (eye contact, coughing, bodily smells, and posture) initially raises sexual fantasies and anxieties about intimacy. Further, the intense personalization which quickly develops can preclude or tamp down unconscious manifestations such as identification, splitting, projection, and projective identification. This can make it more difficult to actually see what is happening. One writer comments that he often felt like

---

[1] From the beginning the students were aware of their participation in my Doctor of Ministry project and gave permission to record all small process group sessions. Names used in this chapter are pseudonyms.

a bishop or psychotherapist in a confessional, a parent in a family, or an adjudicator involved in intense negotiations when he served as leader of a VSG (Gosling 1981a, 642). Since CPE groups are of the VSG variety, it is unfortunate that there has been very little research done on groups of this size.

During this particular unit of training the clinical focus was on the continued development of pastoral skills in each person's area of ministry specialty. The educational focus was two-fold: to develop the ability to do ongoing peer group supervision of clinical work, and to understand and participate in the dynamics of the small process group (SPG). Initially each student formulated his or her own educational goals. There were two learning slots each week for group sessions for which the students were responsible and rotated leadership. They could present verbatim material, do a teaching seminar, share interdisciplinary team work with other staff, work on theological reflection, or review material connected to their learning goals. Every other week there were ministry review sessions in which ongoing pastoral care cases were verbally presented for group supervision. Supervisory floor visits with each individual student were conducted every other week. Weekly reflection reports were written for the supervisor and it was expected each student would write a final evaluation. All other written work was determined by each student.

As I began work with this group I was aware that during their first two units together these students had developed a significant degree of intimacy and trust with one another and with the other supervisor (male) at our center. I was also aware that during the second unit of training frustration had built up around Brigid, who enjoyed doing ministry but seemed unable to participate emotionally in the CPE process of learning. There was a strong dyadic relationship between Wayne and Judy who shared some personal issues and had become friends during the first weeks of the program in the fall. Rose was the second-year resident who worked outside the hospital as Director of Pastoral Care at a chronic care facility affilated with the hospital. She had done a good job of adjusting to a new group in the fall and was highly developed in processing her own emotional material and using the group for her own learning. Since I had already established relationships with Wayne and Rose (as their previous primary supervisor), my focus initially would be on building a supervisory relationship with Judy and Brigid, for both of whom I was more of an unknown. In terms of future plans, Rose was in the process of job-hunting, while the other three had been accepted as second-year residents at our center and would be staying for an additional year of training. I was in the process of transition, having decided to leave my position as Director of CPE at the end of the summer to complete my doctoral project.

One of the major differences between the CPE process group experience and other types of groups (Tavistock, T-group, and psychotherapeutic group) is that of context (Krantz 1991). CPE students are not strangers or patients who come together for an evening, a week, or a weekend, and then leave. They work and learn together as professionals in ministry for at least three months, and in the case of a residency program at least one full year. In the SPG they are not able to create an isolated cultural island located away from all distractions where they can focus solely on learning about group dynamics. Nor can they create a protected therapeutic space where they can attend to healing their own hurts and receive support. Though these activities are precisely what may go on in the SPG, they do so only in a much larger professional and educational context which creates certain pressures and constraints.

Not only did this particular residency group already have a history and a life together, but by the very nature of the educational program and clinical context it was an "embedded group" (Krantz 1991), surrounded by a number of significant and active influences from which it could not escape–ongoing patient and staff needs, the summer CPE student group, departmental procedures, their own learning expectations, outside therapeutic endeavors,[2] relationships with supervisors and other pastoral care staff, ACPE *Standards*, denominational requirements for endorsement, and so on. These environmental factors are ongoing and have a huge impact on the group, often inhibiting individuality and heightening group cohesion as well as increasing the need to be "good" students and chaplains (Redlich and Astrachan 1975, 246). The CPE supervisor also carries different roles for the student beyond being a consultant or therapist in the group process. These roles include administrator, mentor, colleague, role model, teacher, host/hostess, and evaluator. All of these factors act as significant restrictions and pressures on the dynamics of the small group process, causing relationships to be much more diffuse, varied, and complex than is true of a pure study group or psychotherapy group.

> The denser the environmental web the greater the
> transactional complexity, and the larger the number of
> stakeholders, the greater will be the social constraints
> on an enterprise (Krantz 1991, 224).

Before the unit began I had decided that all learning activities were to be carried out in a group context and that individual supervision would be available

---

[2] Two of the four students were in individual therapy during this unit of training. Therapy is encouraged at our center for those in the full-time CPE residency program.

only by student request during this unit of training. This decision was based on at least four convictions which had crystallized during my work on this study. The convictions were that 1) the dyadic (pairing) relationship between supervisor and individual student has the potential to encourage a therapeutic dimension which increases the likelihood for loss of balance between the therapeutic and the educational experience in CPE; 2) issues with authority can more effectively be dealt with, and utilized for learning, in the group context provided the supervisor has sufficient self confidence, an applicable group theory and competent group skills; 3) doing individual supervision (one hour a week with each student) is not cost effective in a clinical setting which expects the timely delivery of pastoral services to its clients or patients; 4) an individual relationship with the supervisor weakens the student's emotional investment in the CPE group and overall learning experience.

I knew that this unexpected change in structure, combined with my presence as the new supervisor, would cause anxiety and elicit considerable response. In the first open session on Friday morning these changes were ignored as each person spent time catching up with the others and sharing hopes for the training unit itself. I saw this as the students working on their first task, which was to now form a new group in order to begin the unit's work. This was primarily accomplished by affirming shared identifications with one another.

By the second SPG all group members began to give vent to their feelings about my decision. Wayne opened with his feelings of being intimidated by me, his need to please, and his propensity to accept whatever I say. Rose "felt like a guinea pig," had experienced "icy rage" over the weekend, and called me "a clever little devil" during the session. Judy expressed "a little bit of disappointment and a little bit of excitement and a little bit of feeling scared." She also fantasized that the other supervisor would be "snickering" in his knowledge of her trying to deal with this "out-of-control" group situation. Brigid, who initially dissembled into a multitude of vague words and images, was eventually able to be clear about her feelings:

> **BRIGID:** My immediate response was to be angry because the system shifted. I mean it didn't take me but a second to recognize that. For you, Wayne, to just accept whatever from 'the teacher.' I could never do that. I mean I might *publicly* do that but my internal working is *not* to do that....

> **JOAN** *(to Brigid)*: Learning how to let *that* voice speak, to let that little kid out, that it doesn't have to destroy you or anybody else....

BRIGID: Well it doesn't stay in. It comes out sideways. I mean it's a horse that's been tamed somewhat but it still reacts....*(pause, and then to Judy)* I love your button. I want fifty of them (general laughter).

JUDY *(to the group)*: I bought a button in Provincetown which says "It's been lovely but now I think I have to scream!"

BRIGID: I mean it's perfect, absolutely perfect!

By the time the seminar ended the students had agreed that I was being "quietly bad." I was aware that they had had their "scream"; that is, they had formed a BA fight group. Afterwards, two of the four students immediately requested individual supervision. I wondered if this would begin a pattern, but as the unit proceeded it turned out that such requests were infrequent.

The third open seminar focused on Wayne's grief about leaving parish ministry. Themes of trying to find a place in chaplaincy seemed to reflect parallel efforts to find one's place and role in the group as well. Toward the end of the session I confronted Judy directly about her need to control her emotions. The content had to do with her frustration in not being valued as an unordained professional in ministry.

JOAN *(to Judy)*: So what kind of feelings do you live with all the time?

JUDY *(in a small voice)*: Frustration. Anger. *(stronger)* Unappreciated. Unused.

JOAN: Could you say it louder, really loud?

JUDY *(quietly)*: I don't know. *(Several members of the group then encourage her but she retreats.)*

JOAN: What happened to you when I said 'say it louder'?

JUDY: I didn't feel like...I guess I feel like....*(pause)*

JOAN *(loudly)*: I AM A GOOD CHAPLAIN. I CAN DO IT BETTER THAN MOST PEOPLE AND NOBODY EVER RECOGNIZES ME. AND THAT MAKES ME MAD!!!

ROSE *(loudly to Judy)*: I FEEL USED AND ABUSED!

JUDY *(primly)*: I guess I feel resistant to people telling me how to say things and what to do. Being told how to do it...that feels like a priest telling me how to do ministry.

JOAN: No, it's different. See the priest is up here *(pointing)* on a pedestal saying: 'You do it.' This is different. We're here with you *(putting hands in a circle)*. You're not alone with your brothers *[who were abusive to her in her family of origin]*. You have a bunch of sisters and a brother here whom you can trust who want to be with you in ministry.

JUDY *(quietly)*: I guess I don't want to be told what to do and how to do it.

In retrospect this was my rather clumsy effort to move Judy out of what sounded like depression, to try to reframe her projections onto the group and me, and to mobilize her angry energy. In a sense I was trying to move her (and the group) from BA dependency to BA fight/flight–but mainly through interpersonal rather than group-as-a-whole interventions. My efforts were not entirely successful and I realized that in the process I had set up a potentially abusive dynamic with this student, a dynamic I did not want to perpetuate. I would need to supervise Judy on her terms. Before the session ended, the students went on to establish norms around here-and-now feedback, to talk about the extent to which they trusted each other, to stake a claim on their group room, and to discuss the fact that individual goals would also (in a sense) be group goals during this training unit, since all sessions would be group sessions. In effect, a work group was forming.

During the next two weeks the students focused on their ministry efforts, establishing learning goals, and undergoing floor visits with me. I shared the first of two didactic sessions on Bion's group theory, outlining the fundamentals of object relations theory and focusing on BA groups and individual valences. The group seemed intrigued. In subsequent learning slots for group supervision, Judy brought her efforts to do spiritual assessment with intensive care unit patients and Rose presented a didactic session on types of countertransference in working with geriatric patients. In the SPG the students continued to struggle with issues of deeper trust and commitment. At one point I encouraged Wayne and Brigid to sculpt their increasingly blocked relationship–as it was and as each would like it to be. It was a moving moment when Brigid finally lay her head on Wayne's shoulder, relaxed, and cried. At one level she was able to claim her sexual attraction to him; on another level she said she felt like a little girl asking for comfort from the father-priest. As previously set (unconscious) roles in the group became more recognized (conscious), the students seemed to relax with one another and became more flexible and varied in their responses to one another.

One evening Wayne had a terrible emergency on-call period which included the death of a sixteen-year-old girl in an auto accident. As the mother gently washed the body during the final moments of life, Wayne's anguished question "What is fair?" surfaced again. As a gay man committed to AIDS ministry, Wayne lived in the depths of this question with much anger, grief, and fear. Now he described how he and several helicopter nurses who had brought the girl in went to the hospital rooftop after the grueling hours spent in the emergency room. Together they looked at the city and the night and the stars:

WAYNE: We just connected. It was really powerful and nice...a beautiful clear night...seeing the world and how to fit this terrible thing that had happened into a larger framework....

JOAN: This is what worship is about. *(Group becomes quiet).* Do you have more to say?

WAYNE: About the rooftop?

JOAN: No. About yourself.

WAYNE: I was struck that death had touched someone so close to them *(the parents and teen-age friends).* I was struck by their shattering of innocence. They can never go back to the day before. I was trying to be aware of the grief in me, but it was different *(pause).*

JOAN: How was it different?

WAYNE: At some level I have to befriend pain just to be able to go on....At some level I don't think I'm going to be able to escape it.

In his effort to understand and live faithfully into his ministry, Wayne was well aware of the dangers which lurk just below the surface of life and continually color his world. I was aware that doing pastoral work in a hospital setting and dealing daily with the ragged emotional edges of pain, disease, hurt, anger, fear, and grief has a major and continuing impact on both the conscious and unconscious functioning of individuals in CPE and on the process group experience. On an intellectual level, Wayne would deal with his question through a didactic presentation on reframing and second-order change in pastoral care based on the work of pastoral theologian Donald Capps. On an emotional level he would continue to wrestle with things that go bump in the night--as would the group-as-a-whole.

In the fifth week of the unit the anxiety in the group increased considerably when Brigid presented a one-month old verbatim which simply could not be resuscitated. I was silent for most of the session while her peers tried to help her. In the following SGP the group debriefed their feelings about the verbatim session and their awareness of my dissatisfaction as well as their own. This time it was Brigid's ambivalence toward the CPE learning process and the dark side of life (and her ministry) which continued to hover over us. After listening for most of the session, I began to work with the interrelatedness of emotional life (much of which is unconscious) and professional functioning (most of which is conscious). This is an intersection which is fundamental to the action-reflection-action learning situation of CPE students. One of the ways I do this is by actively using myself to surface unacceptable feelings and thus lift the depression and ennui which can so easily pervade this type of pastoral ministry over the long haul.

> **JOAN** *(to Brigid)*: The more ambivalent you feel the harder you work. That's my shot at it right now. The second thing you do is to become more faithful. You feel ambivalent about staying with your patient who is deteriorating and it's for shit. It's really BAD. The strongest part of me wants to run. I say "no,no,no." So now I must stay here for twelve hours and do vigil as compensation for that other side that says "Arghhhh. I hate this."

> **ROSE** *(to Brigid)*: Where are your "I hate this" feelings?

> **BRIGID:** They are felt but inarticulate because they're not acceptable.

JOAN: You don't want a part of your image changed so you don't let anyone else know. It's true for me, too. I don't want other people to know I say fuck and damn and shit when I get mad.

BRIGID: The trouble is I never allowed myself to say those things.

JOAN: I know!

BRIGID: I've said more shits now than ever in my life!

JOAN *(to Wayne)*: When you're up on the floor with AIDS people, do you ever find yourself saying, " I HATE this. I detest this"?

WAYNE: Yeah.

JOAN *(to Judy)*: And when children are dying, do you ever feel like you want to vomit?

JUDY: I've been trying to free the staff to say that because I know they feel that exact same way. So I just say it and that enables them to say it!

JOAN *(to Rose)*: And do you ever look at all those old people and say "fuck old age. Just fuck it because it is for shit."

ROSE: Die first *(before growing old)*. Die first!

JOAN: I mean my niece said to me recently: "Aunt Joan, do you ever get depressed?"

ROSE: Oh Lord yes! *(group laughter)*

JOAN: My niece is seventeen and she's now *getting it.*

ROSE: Just to take and have your heart torn right out when someone is going down.

(Time has now run out and we stir to leave)

BRIGID: Well, I just have to say that I came here this morning thinking it was someone else's turn. I hope I haven't hogged the time and that you each learned something.

JOAN: That's not the point. Maybe they did and maybe they didn't. Maybe we wasted our time. Maybe we wanted to be with you in *your* time.

Strictly speaking, Bion's approach to group work involved the consultant or leader stimulating group members in such a way that they regressed into psychotic-like manifestations (BA groups) in order to make the unconscious available for study either through group behavior and/or group projections onto the leader. My particular style is the opposite of Bion's in that I actively verbalize the unconscious feelings myself. However, in retrospect my use of strong language in the above excerpt (which is quite unusual for me) indicates that I may have become reactive to Brigid's flight (resistance to CPE and difficult ministry) and countered with my own fight (resistance to her resistance!). Was I under the spell and numbing effect of Brigid's projective identification (and my countertransference), having received her repressed angry feelings and now seeking to give them back to her and the group in a slightly different form? Instead of keeping my distance and possibly moving the group toward greater frustration, anger, and even chaos through leadership deprivation, I chose to focus on professional functioning by eliciting through example conscious awareness of unacceptable feelings. Thus the dynamics remain at the interpersonal verbal level as the ego (and work group) stays in charge through supervisory modeling and directing. In this way the small process group in CPE begins to digest repressed feelings in smaller doses, avoiding the regression which might be more apt to take place in a strictly psychotherapeutic group experience by staying in a teaching and learning modality. Again, it is a matter of balance largely determined by supervisory choice, ability, and style:

> Emotionality tends to be nonadaptive, but it builds stress; work tends to be adaptive, because [it is] reality seeking, but it reduces tension with minimum development of further stress. The problem of the group-as-a-whole is to maintain the appropriate blend, balance, or oscillation between these two modes of behaving (Stock and Thelen 1958, 10).

At the midpoint of the unit I realized that so far the quantity of written work (verbatims, case presentations, and critical incidents) from the students had been minimal. I brought this up at the beginning of the next SPG and watched as the anxiety rose and the valences of each student began to be activated. Judy responded immediately and at length, repeating several times that she "did not know what to do" and "needed more help from the group" on her learning goals (BA dependency). Wayne said he felt inadequate and guilty that he was not meeting my expectations (BA dependency). Rose reported that she immediately said to herself, "Oh God here she goes again. Super Parent....I'm not going to bite on that!" (Based on my work with her in the last unit I thought that Rose was probably BA pairing.) Brigid, who already struck me as BA fight/flight, became defensive ("I worked here until 11 pm last night"), and dismissive ("I'm not going to create a monster who doesn't exist"). Wayne responded, "Joan-assic Park. That's what goes through my mind." The loud laughter and high amount of affect in the group indicated something important was being expressed.

The first point to note is that the power and authority invested in the CPE supervisor by students is *the* fact of life upon which group work in the psychoanalytic tradition and object relations is based. The ubiquitous presence of identification, splitting, projection, and projective identification is a constant reminder that the human psyche takes shape amidst an incredibly long period of dependency and that the mental prototypes created as a defense against the earliest feelings of helplessness and anger, as well as all-devouring love, remain active and subject to change throughout our lives. Thus one of the primary tasks as the leader/supervisor of a CPE process group is to receive the projections, including the fantasies, and bear being "used" by the group. This was happening to a degree in the foregoing example.

The extent to which this material remains covert or becomes overt depends on the psychological sophistication and interest of the individual members, the degree of training and self-knowledge of the supervisor, and the learning contract of the group. If it becomes overt, then the degree to which this material is directly experienced, acknowledged, and digested corresponds to the therapeutic dimension of the group, while the degree to which this material is retained by the students as knowledge or theory corresponds to the educational dimension of the group experience. It is probably fair to say that up to now CPE supervisors have depended more on their intuition than anything else in maintaining the critical balance between these two aspects of the SPG experience.

A second leadership task is to establish and keep clear but flexible boundaries between the group and its external environment. The boundary, often called a *membrane* (Foulkes 1964), needs to be semi-permeable in order to assure both the group's safety and its survival:

> On the one hand, *safety* lies in the preservation of [the group's] boundary at all costs and the avoidance of transactions across it; on the other hand, *survival* depends upon the conduct of transactions with the environment and the risk of destruction (Miller and Rice 1967,24).

At a structural level boundary maintenance involves procuring space and keeping time as well as clarifying standards for attendance and evaluation. It involves coming to group agreement around the issue of confidentiality. Boundary maintenance depends upon consistent focusing on the group task by the leader. It also involves teaching group members, or helping group members teach themselves, either by explication or implication how to negotiate effectively concerning the intrusion of outside influences on the group–the beeper, other pastoral staff demands, departmental responsibilities, educational requirements, and personal needs. In these ways the container for doing group work is secured.

At a dynamic level there is a dimension of boundary setting which occurs between the conscious (rational) functioning of the work group and each individual and between the unconscious (feeling and affect) level of functioning of basic assumption group(s) and each individual. In a group with co-supervisors, one will tend to be the rational leader of the work group while the other becomes the emotional leader at the BA group level. Turquet writes:

> The complication for leadership is that, like the psychoanalytic model of the ego, it has to be Janus-like, looking both internally and externally, becoming both participant and observer (1974, 352).

Again it is up to the leader to decide how best to work between this boundary in order to facilitate the group task and to encourage members to begin to assume this leadership task themselves. The ability to participate *and* to observe both internally and externally is key to successful engagement in the reflexive task of an open-agenda study group. In CPE this is sometimes called "activating the observing ego" in order to engage in self-supervision.

The third leadership function involves titrating the amount of anxiety which will enter the group at any one time. In group work based on the psychoanalytic tradition, this function is directly connected with the extent and way in which the leader chooses to exercise his or her authority. At an operational level the CPE supervisor can decrease anxiety by establishing relatively casual and warm relationships with group members, by encouraging group action, shared decision making, and group determination of educational objectives. This type of leadership, which leans toward a participative-democracy style, falls within the humanistic psychology tradition. If the supervisor goes too far in this direction, the group may be in danger of feeling that no one is in charge, finding a substitute leader to meet their dependency needs, and then trying to take care of their disabled former leader.

On the other hand, the supervisor can increase anxiety by moving "behind his or her face," by pointing out objectively and consistently that certain expectations are not negotiable, or by making only group-focused interventions and giving no feedback to individual members. By lowering the degree of personal warmth (sociability) and perceived interpersonal availability, the supervisor establishes himself or herself as more of a hierarchial and strict presence similar to the more distant consultant role in the Tavistock tradition. This leadership approach has the potential to provide a certain amount of stability, safety, and structure. However, if it goes too far in this direction, the group may again regress in the face of its growing anxiety and create a basic assumption group. Because of the small size and many-faceted embeddedness of the CPE group, *and* the often unrecognized and conflicted relationship CPE students have with authority, it takes very little supervisory effort to turn the heat up or down "inside the circle."

During the next several weeks the focus returned to Brigid when she decided to take a chaplaincy job instead of going on in our second-year CPE residency program. As she shared her plans for leaving in August, all the other members came down on her. When I named the possibility of scapegoating (always a tip-off to the potential formation of a BA dependency group) and asked if there were feelings about *my* leaving (displacement), things began to open up. At this point the individual valences of each student again became evident. Brigid (BA fight/flight) said, "Well I was angry that you were leaving and I let you know it when you announced it back in March!" And indeed she had. Wayne (BA dependency) said, "I feel anger and that goes back to when I first heard the news because I had planned a whole second year based on you being here." Judy (BA counter-dependency) responded, "When you, Joan, said in the session today that the three of you [Joan, Rose, and Brigid] are abandoning the two of us [Judy and Wayne, who were staying on] I said to myself, 'Fine! Leave us by ourselves. I don't have enough experience with you to really care.'" And Rose (BA pairing), with whom I had developed a significant relationship over two previous units of training together, said, "If this had happened a year ago I would have been a raging maniac!"

I had begun to make some further theoretical connections between Bion's theories and Fairbairn's endopsychic structure of the mind. I realized that the work group is basically governed by the central ego. The material with which it works comes out of the object representations formed in infancy and its growing ability to stay in contact with reality. On the other hand, BA fight/flight was an expression of the antilibidinal (rejecting) ego. It signals some degree of being stuck in the paranoid position with strong tendencies toward splitting objects into part-objects. In a CPE training center with two supervisors it does not take long for one supervisor to become "good" and the other "bad." In a group large enough to develop subgroups, pro and con sides to any issue are an inevitable occurrence.

The BA pairing valence is created by the libidinal (exciting) ego in which the infant is able to hold together feelings of both love and hate toward the exciting whole object (mother) and thus achieve the depressive position and consequent desires for reparation. This is most often experienced as positive transference from a student toward a supervisor. I was beginning to wonder whether BA dependency might be connected with Guntrip's ideas about the repressed libidinal ego and the schizoid position in which the person feels an overwhelming weakness and hiddenness at the very core of his or her being. If this is the case, then BA dependency (either group or individual), unlike the other two basic assumptions, is less defensive and more developmental in nature, moving as it does between dependence, independence, and interdependence (Agazarian 1989). Because so many CPE groups–including this one–lean toward BA dependency, it seemed important to work some of these ideas through.

At about this time a female applicant for my position came into the group and did an exercise in clay and music. As they told me about it later, two of the students were particularly affected. Rose had made a little green "niggle" in a blue bowl which initially represented new life to which she had wanted to sing Brahms's "Lullaby." Twenty-four hours later she saw that "the blue was the womb and the green was the foetus." Amidst her tears of recognition of both the pain and the joy, Rose felt deeply grateful that she was continuing to give birth to herself in new ways. After this sharing, Judy showed us the container she had made. It was very deep with a tiny round ball at the bottom. The following conversation ensued:

JOAN: You mentioned in your description how deep you made the container.

JUDY: Well yes! I kept making it deeper and that's how I envisioned myself although I wasn't doing that consciously. I'm a very deep person and I'm really deep at the bottom. I was trying to see how much I want to come out.

JOAN: And you have a distance to go.

JUDY: Yes, a big distance.

JOAN: You'll have to watch out for the bends.

JUDY: That's right. I can only do a little bit at a time.

JOAN: And then you need a decompression chamber.

JUDY: Yeah.

JOAN: I guess that's what the group can be for you.

Judy's repressed libidinal ego would need lots of time and safety and trust to begin to come out again after a lifetime of being ensconced safely "at the bottom." To do this work, Judy would need to experience the group as a very strong container.

Bion was not alone in discovering that being in a small group evoked anxieties reminiscent of returning to the maternal matrix (Foulkes 1964). The influence of a female leader, particularly one who encourages regression either through open expression of feelings, meditative or artistic exercises, articulation of fantasies, or a distancing leadership style, can enrich the group experience by making unconscious material more accessible. Again there is a balance between plunging the group into psychosis and controlling the group so tightly and rationally that it uses all its energy defending itself against any incursion of the unconscious.

> The problem of how a group may gain insight into its
> own processes while at the same time regressing deeply

enough to allow manifestations of the most primitive, psychotic-like undifferentiated group phenomena is precisely the dilemma of the Tavistock consultant (Schermer 1992, 146).

This is also the dilemma of the CPE supervisor as he or she moves between the group experience and the group learning about the group experience.

In the middle of the eighth week of the training unit, Brigid's father died unexpectedly. There was some effort by all of us to attend the wake as a group, but this did not work out. Upon her return and in the midst of her grief, Brigid also expressed disappointment in her attenuated relationship with Judy, from whom she would have liked more caring, particularly at this difficult time. Over the next several SPG sessions it became clear that the two women had very different boundaries and that the work of the group would be to sort this out for the sake of the group's survival.

Judy grew up in a family of boys, had a room to herself and of necessity became quite isolated and self-protective in the face of an older brother's physical and verbal abuse. Brigid grew up in an Irish Catholic family with all the children (boys and girls) in one bedroom throughout the elementary school years. We discovered that Brigid's present life in community includes shared everything– clothing, jewelry, vacations, friends. Given the high degree of enmeshment reflected in her diffuse boundaries, naturally Brigid's expectations for a "good group" would be that everyone did everything together–learning activities, sharing patient work, eating together, recreational activities, etc. Not surprisingly, her favorite role was being "the hostess with the mostest." Judy and Wayne were absolutely appalled at this discovery, since they both preferred tight boundaries, the privacy of their personal lives, and the protected space of their apartments. Rose was also shocked and went on to share at length during this session several examples of the special pairing relationships where she can totally be herself.

Each member of the group then began to review his or her relationship with Brigid over the ten months of the residency program. For the first time it seemed as though they really could *see* one another, and especially Brigid, more clearly. I later discovered that these learnings continued to hit home when the four students went out for Chinese dinner and began to note who shared what food and how. Judy explained: "I even made a little invisible electric fence around the sweet and sour chicken [all laugh]. Don't stick your fork over here!" Brigid, in deference to what she now realized were the boundary needs of the others, ordered four *separate* egg rolls "to make it easier for *them* to share" (her emphasis).

As Brigid loosened up, she also made clear her dislike of process in CPE. She said to the group:

> This whole idea of process, I mean it's not something that ever preoccupied my mind before. I mean relationships just *happen* for me and I never spent time *ever* talking about them!....I never talk process language. That's a new part of me. I'm doing it a little bit now. I feel kind of different, awkward. But I'm aware of it. It's another resource that I never even knew about.

To put it another way, a CPE work group whose task is to engage the central ego in being self-reflective and understanding of group process and interpersonal dynamics was foreign to this student who was enmeshed with her family and religious community. Brigid much preferred the warmth and security of the basic assumption group where one did not have to think or reflect very much. Turquet writes:

> As an individual leaves the BA group way of life, he experiences loss: loss of satisfaction of his needs to belong; loss of a sense of unity, cohesiveness, camaraderie, of being a part of something bigger than himself; loss of a determined, unarguable role; loss...of a sense of vitality and excitement (1974, 369).

If Judy needed a trusting environment to let herself a little more "out" and available to the unconscious forces within herself and the group, Brigid needed to discover how to separate herself from the emotional pull of the group so that she could become more differentiated and flexible in the roles she assumed in her various groupings (family, friends, religious community, CPE). However, another loss on top of all that she had experienced with her father's death was unthinkable. This work would need to wait for another time.

We did our planning for the final evaluation week about ten days before the actual end of the program. This was immediately followed by a very lively SPG session which signaled the beginning of the end of the group. The initial content connected ministry with cancer patients to Judy's fear of her brother's recent diagnosis of melanoma and acknowledgement of Rose's five-year survival from her bout with large-cell lymphoma. As the members of the group talked together, I found myself thinking about the group's impending "death." Then Wayne brought up his negative feelings about a potential new student peer for next year's residency group whom he had shown around the hospital. He said adamantly: "I *mean* I did not *like* the woman. As soon as I met her I did not like her." It was at this point that the group began to play:

> **WAYNE:** I guess part of it for me is not wanting another female ex-nun coming out of....well, more of the same thing!

> **BRIGID:** See! *[all laugh]*

> **WAYNE:** It's a person of the same background in the group *again.*

> **ROSE** *(exaggerated):* What do you mean, Wayne? That we *[women]* are all the same? You are lumping us together?!

> **WAYNE:** Well, you're all nuns or ex-nuns.

> **ROSE:** So that's the big thing that connects us?

> **WAYNE:** No. But that is the same. I didn't say the rest of it is the same. You're all Catholic. She was Anglo-Catholic.

> **ROSE** *(teasing):* So is that a problem for you?

> **WAYNE:** Yes!

> **ROSE:** Why?

> **WAYNE:** Women should stay in their place! *[general laughter]*

> **ROSE:** Why? Where is that coming from?

> **WAYNE:** I'm making it up. It's not the ordained part. I wish I weren't ordained half the time now.

> **JOAN** *(to Wayne):* Did it make you a little bit appreciative of these three?

WAYNE: Damn right it did! Oh Yeah! Yeah! I'm thinking this has been a good group *[more laughter]*. A good group.

From the beginning there had been some talk about the male-female imbalance in the group, and also some honest sharing of sexual feelings. I felt the group as a whole was comfortable with one another, had dealt with the issue of sexuality and sexual orientation at some length, and had over time become accustomed to the close physical proximity of this VSG. It was during this session that Wayne, whose first CPE group had also been all women, went on to make it crystal clear that he did not want this situation for a third time no matter how "good" the group.

Near the end of this "last" session they began to talk about missing the group. There emerged a fascinating dynamic display of valences as the conversation swung around to the reality of my leaving:

BRIGID *(to Joan)***:** I'll tell you one thing, as fun as this is and as serious as this is, I'm really disappointed and angry that you are not going to do your theology of play. Because I was looking forward to that. I feel like I'm being cheated *[said in a little girl voice]*.

JOAN: I didn't know that was such an expectation. I'm sorry I don't have it ready either.

BRIGID: Because I think we could get more out of the dynamic that is happening today if we had those thoughts in your head....and in our head too.

WAYNE: Along the same lines, when you started talking yesterday about the glue and the solvent in pastoral care you said, "Haven't I mentioned that to you?" And we said, "No." And I thought, "You're holding back! We have only two weeks left and you're holding back!" *[semi-hysterical voice on purpose]* I have to make sure I'll get all of this....

ROSE: What's the other one? Fate and....?

JOAN: Guilty man and tragic man. *[subject of a didactic I sometimes do with students]*

BRIGID: What's that? Come on!

JOAN: I think you're trying to hold on to me.

ALL: Yes! Of course!

WAYNE: Or use you up! Come on, Joan. More. More.

BRIGID: Exactly....

The bittersweet feelings involved in realizing the limits of life and the group and time with the supervisor continued as Wayne said: "Usually I start closure way ahead of time. Like today I'm saying ten more sleeps and Joan will be gone." At this point the others chimed in, all except Brigid who had begun to cry. We learned that she, too, had been counting "sleeps"–not of the remaining nights until the end of the group, but of the days since her father had died. The mood shifted from laughter to sadness and then I returned us to the self-reflexive work of the individuals in the SPG:

JOAN *(to Brigid)*: You started by trying to pick a fight with me, so I figured you were having a lot of feelings–your fight valency.

BRIGID: I'd much rather fight than flight. But if fight doesn't work, then I'll flight.

ROSE: I don't want to change the subject, but there's a question I'd like to have you answer sometime, Joan *[others are starting to laugh]*, with regard to the valency thing....

BRIGID *(to Joan)*: Do you feel like toothpaste and we are squeezing?

JOAN: I feel like there are these reins tied to me which each of you is holding.

ROSE *(persisting)*: It was the security thing, where secure attachment ends up with a pairing valency, you know.... I'd like to hear more about that. *[more laughter]*

JOAN: I knew you had perked up on that idea, but I'm only just developing it. You'll have to read the book! *[pause]* Okay Judy, it's your turn.

WAYNE *(to Judy)***:** What was your valency? Dependent/counter dependent?

JOAN: Yeah, that was Judy with a lean on the dependent.

JUDY: I was going to say counterdependent.

WAYNE: That's why she hasn't said anything! *[more laughter]*

JUDY: I was just sitting here trying to...feeling a lot of sadness but I can't really identify it, I'm not sure....

JOAN (to Judy, in jest)**:** We could help you with it.

WAYNE (laughing)**:** She's wicked. *[referring to me]*

ROSE: She's really got her claws out today!

JUDY: Should I be kind or should I be mad?

JOAN: Shall we help you?

JUDY: Sure. *[more laughter]*

WAYNE *(to Judy)***:** You have just been doing such a good job of hiding the fact that you wanted us to help you.

ROSE: That definitely is one of your challenges, Judy, not getting help from others.

BRIGID: Whereas I will solve it first and tell you the results.

JOAN: You fell right into it, Judy.

JUDY *(uncomprehending)*: I don't know. Whatever.

JOAN: Well, have a nice weekend, one and all.

In a sense the group ended here, bringing to life some of the very dynamics they had sought to understand throughout the training unit. Most apparent was their shared resistance (BA dependency group) to letting go of their projections onto me in my role as group leader and supervisor. It was satisfying to watch as what we were learning coalesced and cohered with what we were experiencing in the here-and-now of the group dynamics.

In their final evaluations, each student included a section on the structure of the program and the group work. The totally positive nature of this material was surprising to me and may be suspect, but nevertheless here are a few excerpts:

ROSE: To do everything in group was mind-boggling to me who had my heart set on a third unit of working with Joan in individual supervision. After my initial anger and rage cooled down and I got back on an even keel, I was able to hear the theory behind the changes, accept the "new way" as a potential for growth, and invest myself in the process....I chose to engage rather than pass things off to others as could more easily be done in the other model of CPE....I knew it was my responsibility to be an integral part of the group.

BRIGID: The benefit of doing both peer supervision and interrelational activities in group is that each of us learns from each others' growing edges and issues. It felt like we held all our learning goals in common....In reality, we brought more into the group, we worked harder and we learned much faster in this type of peer group....Being able to choose our own group presentations spoke to the height of an adult learning model. I found that sharing clinical scenarios, spiritual assessments and charting notes in group extremely beneficial. It was such a natural way to grow in peer supervision.

JUDY: Initially I felt both excitement at trying something new and disappointment at not having Joan for individual supervision. This was something I had looked forward to all year and had to let go of....[But] not having individual supervision scheduled encouraged me to take more initiative in utilizing my peer group more fully for my personal and professional growth....I learned more about my dynamics in a group setting, claimed more of my personal authority in the group, and took more responsibility for being assertive and sharing within the group.

WAYNE: I feel much more in touch with what the rest of my peers were doing in their pastoral work than I have in previous units. I feel that I shared more of what was happening in my own work also. I also feel that I came to a much better understanding of my own dynamics and the dynamics of others in the group....I appreciated having Joan engage each of us in group time as she would have in individual supervision. I felt more comfortable sharing with the group in this situation than I have in any other unit of CPE.

In summary, the small process group in CPE offers an unusual opportunity for students to experience *and* understand group-as-a-whole dynamics. By placing the psychotherapeutic and interpersonal models for group work within the larger framework of the group-as-a-whole approach, the SPG maintains its primary focus as a training rather than a treatment experience which works with both conscious and unconscious material in an integrated and balanced way. In doing this work, it is important to realize that because of the strong pull toward regression which is present in every group, and especially in a small peer group, there is constant pressure toward working therapeutically with individuals rather than educationally and dynamically with the role individuals carry in the group-as-a-whole. The *only* other group experience which attempts to hold this unique type of balance in a professional training program is the "experiential group" required in the second and third year of some psychiatric residency training programs (Munich 1993).

PART TWO: DISCUSSION AND FUTURE DIRECTIONS

The preceeding material demonstrates initial efforts to apply the group-as-a-whole approach to the SPG in CPE. By way of evaluation, certain strengths and weaknesses are evident. First, the students' ability to grasp the theoretical ideas on which this approach is based proved to be a source of insight and satisfaction throughout this unit of training. I discovered that it is important to share my theoretical approach with students in order to help them understand the concepts both intellectually and experientially. Group process does not need to be mysterious to students in order to work.

Second, the absence of specific group-as-a-whole supervisory interventions is quite notable. Picking up on the emergence of BA assumption groups as they happen would definitely require more psychological sensitivity and practice. I suspect I am typical of many supervisors in being more comfortable with intrapsychic and interpersonal modes of relating. This may also serve as a defense against the unconscious group process.

> Basic assumption phenomena are most prominent in groups whose leader limits his or her interventions to group level interpretations; they are least prominent in groups with an active leader who...focuses solely on an interpersonal or individual level (Jacobson 1989, 479-80).

Third, there are a number of typical behavior patterns which need to be monitored. The tendency to focus on the one student who is the most interesting, or most defended, or has the most "stuff" raises the suspicion of the scapegoating dynamic. If the group stays stuck in this mode, the basic assumption of dependency needs to be considered. The tendency of two resistant students to pair and form a subgroup needs to be dealt with before it begins to threaten the survival of the small group. In addition, it is often the case in CPE that one student will need "help" and others will try to "supervise" him or her, especially in the apparent absence of a supervisor who stays relatively uninvolved. Finally, splitting into "for" and "against" sides–especially around whether the supervisor is competent–becomes a dynamic for learning the importance of recognizing ambivalence toward authority and the consequent need for further personal integration.

Fourth, until all members are working at a more or less similar level of professional functioning, intrapsychic awareness, and interpersonal trust, it is difficult to move a group forward into a coherent and potentially satisfying process group experience. Thus it remains of critical importance to evaluate the relative ego strength, general life experience, and emotional stability of students new to CPE, and to sort out various levels of student functioning among those doing additional units of training. Because this was a group of CPE chaplain residents who had considerable training and had been working together for nine months, it was definitely easier to establish a shared modus operandi in the SPG.

In my own leadership of the group I was aware that I did not fall into the kind of psychological interpretations which signal psychotherapeutic work with individual group members. Nor did I maintain the kind of distance of a Tavistock consultant. In general my intention was to provide safety for myself and the group by maintaining a teaching and leadership position in the group, staying engaged at the work group (central ego) level, and actively monitoring the group process by using the ups and downs of anxiety and consequent emergence of individual valences and/or one of the BA groups. I am aware that the verbatim material focuses on my active interventions in the group. In actuality much of the time I remained silent, simply by my presence providing a safe space for members to work with one another interpersonally. My growing edge continues to be uncovering my own repressions in order to become more comfortable with experiencing the chaotic underside of my own emotional life as well as the group unconscious experience.

In process-group work based on object relations theory, the concept of projective identification is *the* cornerstone concept of the group-as-a-whole process. It is therefore imperative that the group leader understand how it works. Projective identification is a universal phenomena which is not confined to psychotic functioning but is part of everyday life. It is unique because it is both an intrapsychic defense and an interpersonal mechanism.

> Projective identification is more appropriately described
> as a projection *into* to indicate that it sinks below the
> surface of the target and indeed modifies the target's
> behavior (Horowitz 1983, 275).

Being in any group triggers regression, the desire for relationship with others and consequent feelings of longing and aggression. As a result there is a notable increase in the flow of projections and introjections and an inevitable blurring of some boundaries between subject and object. This becomes a veritable blizzard in the intense and intimate atmosphere of a small process group setting:

> The contagion effect of group emotion, the threats to
> the loss of one's individuality and autonomy, the revival
> of early familial conflicts, and the prevalence of envy,
> rivalry, and competition–all contribute to the regressive
> reactions in a group (Horowitz 1983, 277).

Primitive wishes to dominate, devalue, control, rid one's self of unwanted bad parts, or surround the targeted object (which can be either an individual or the group) with devouring love–all these feelings and more from the repressed libidinal and antilibidinal egos are loosed and coalesce in an inevitable display of either subtle or lively projections onto other people. While enlivening the group process, projective identifications leave both the projector and the projectee emotionally depleted.

The tendency of the target person to receive or fuse with this material and then be manipulated by it is *the* most challenging aspect of group leadership *and* group membership. The signal that this is occurring becomes evident when someone in the group is repeatedly sucked into a certain role or position, becomes the subject for scapegoating (displacement of feelings), or when the group itself is swept up into a certain action or behavior. Much of the work in the group involves the leader and group members learning how to avoid being sucked in and increasing their tolerance for being used by the projector. In this way they can sucessfully contain the projections and then return various metabolized pieces to the owner, sometimes in a slightly different form. When the owner can internalize such feedback and identify with it (rather than introject it as simply another foreign presence in his or her psyche) new emotional growth has occurred. Ogden observes that, "the internalization of the metabolized projection offers the projector the potential for attaining new ways of handling a set of feelings that he could only wish to get rid of in the past" (1979, 361). Thus projective identification is "simultaneously a type of defence, a mode of communication, a primitive form of object relationship, and a pathway for psychological change" (362). The multiplicity of opportunities for this universal phenomenon to occur in a group setting, both between individuals and in the group-as-a-whole, makes the small process group a uniquely exciting opportunity for students training for ministry and for supervisors seeking to use the small group experience for their own and student learning.

The second key concept in doing small process-group work in CPE is realizing that the SPG takes place within, and is surrounded by, a complex set of environmental factors which impinge upon it. Establishing and keeping permeable boundaries which assure enough protection to elicit vulnerability and yet maintain enough openness to keep the group in relationship to its larger context is the primary work of the supervisor as group leader. This includes the supervisor establishing and implementing the self-reflexive task of the group on a consistent basis and relating this task to the other objectives of the educational experience.

There were a number of additional educational and experiential elements which enriched this particular unit of training. For example, in order to enliven concepts from object relations and Bion's group theory, the group found the Nova film entitled "Life's First Feelings" extremely helpful. This film shows various aspects of the relationship between infants and their mothers: different responses which occur during breast feeding including signs of pleasure, frustration and fear; the effects of over- and under-stimulation; and beginning efforts to separate from the safety of the maternal presence. (It occurred to me later that we could have made a field trip to the neonatal and pediatric units to observe some of these behaviors among children and their parents.)

In addition, I presented one teaching session on the attachment theory of John Bowlby, British psychoanalyst and consultant at the Tavistock Clinic. Based on the groundbreaking research of his colleague Mary Ainsworth into how babies respond to strange situations, three modes of attachment to the mother had eventually become evident. *Secure attachment* is present when a baby initially cries when the mother leaves but then is able to take initiative and explore a strange place. When the mother returns, the infant greets her with pleasure, molding his or her body to the mother and thus receiving comfort. *Anxious-ambivalent attachment* occurs when infants are clingy and fearful of exploring a new place, cry and become extremely upset when the mother leaves, and then simultaneously seek contact and arch away from the mother's holding when she returns. *Anxious-avoidant attachment* is present when the child appears independent and unaware when the mother leaves, and snubs her upon her return, refusing all comfort.

It was fascinating to think that there might be some correlation between this work on attachment theory and Bion's initial formulations. For example, it was clear that secure attachment patterns lead to the development of the central ego and the ability to function independently at the work group level. The anxious-ambivalent attachment was reminiscent of the BA dependent/ counterdependent valance, while the anxious-avoidant attachment seemed to correspond to the BA fight/flight valence. It was not exactly clear where the BA pairing valence fit in, but furthering exploration in this area seems promising for the future.

Though I did not share the following ideas with the group, I was aware during our work together of Sheldon Cashdan's *Object Relations Therapy* (1988), which includes a lucid and detailed presentation on the nature of projective identification (PI). As a therapist Cashdan is mainly concerned with pathology which causes illness. As an educator working with a small process group, I am mainly concerned with repetitive roles and patterns of behavior which cause dissatisfaction and miscommunication. Nevertheless, as I thought back on the group members and our experience together, each of Cashdan's four types seemed quite applicable.

In PI Dependency the person honestly believes he or she cannot make it on his or her own. The message conveyed to the targeted object is, "I can't survive without you" (BA dependency). In PI Power the person induces feelings of weakness and incompetence in the targeted object. The message is, "You can't survive without me" (BA counter-dependency). PI Sexuality is specifically designed to evoke an erotic response in the targeted object. The message is, "I am desirable as long as I can excite you" (BA pairing). In PI Ingratiation the projector maintains a position of self sacrifice toward the targeted object. The message is, "You owe me" (BA fight/flight). Though there is no specific mention of Bion's ideas in Cashdan's presentation, I found it easy to make these correlations for myself. Further it is intriguing to wonder which type of projective identification has been active for any of us regarding our choice of CPE supervision and ministry as a profession as well as its influence on how we respond in a group.

Among current practitioners in group work, the one who comes closest to applying and expanding Bion's theoretical ideas is Yvonne Agazarian. Agazarian works as a group therapist in what she calls Systems-Centered Therapy (SCT) in a group-as-a-whole approach. Though her focus is primarily on individual change, her approach emphasizes working on this goal through the dynamics experienced in the group rather than the so-called pathology the individual brings to the group. On a theoretical level Agazarian is making an ambitious attempt to integrate general systems theory (von Bertalanffy), psychoanalytic tradition (Bion), field theory (Lewin), communication theory (Korzybski and Watzlawick), and developmental psychology (Erikson). On a practical level she employs many of Bion's group-as-a-whole concepts and, in running the group, takes an approach similar to the one advocated in this study. She writes:

> The goal of the group is to learn to observe and explain all behavior in the group as a function of group-as-a-whole dynamics. The proposed format for reaching this goal is that each period of experiential group work is either punctuated by, or followed by, a processing period in which the subjective experience will be reviewed objectively and analyzed from the group-as-a-whole perspective (1989, 3).

In addition to her integrative efforts, Agazarian's major contribution is the recognition of the subgroup as the "fulcrum" (1992, 179). Agazarian encourages "functional subgrouping" as a way of containing splits in the group and avoiding the isolation and scapegoating of the "difficult" group member.

> Subgrouping requires being able not to be the center of the group, being able to understand that work in the group requires joining others' work and allowing them to join yours. It requires some understanding of the advantage of not taking things personally, of volunteering to serve as a projective screen for others, and, most important, it means being willing to give up self-defeating roles (181-2).

As people recognize the subgrouping dynamic, members can grow by learning how to integrate both the good and the bad within themselves which they tend to project onto others. Agazarian emphasizes the importance of boundaries which contain the energy of the group, encourage cohesiveness and thus help it work. She also emphasizes the defensive function of some basic assumption behavior (especially fight/flight) which, in her view, becomes apparent through the noise (chaos) of three particular communication patterns: ambiguity, redundancy, and contradictions (201). One of Agazarian's contributions is to reconceptualize BA dependency, not as a defensive maneuver, but rather as a developmental phenomena related to intimacy needs and the eventual maturational work involved in separation and individuation. Overall Agazarian is beginning to make a major contribution which is much needed in group-as-a-whole work. To this end, she has established a series of systems-centered training modules which are available on videotape and in workshops.[3]

At this point it should be clear that the psychoanalytic tradition and object relations theory upon which the group theories of Wilfred Bion were based provide a broad and creative framework for thinking about and doing process-group work in clinical pastoral education. Though all the problems and pitfalls are far from solved, it is the hope of this inquiry that the general approach has been explicated in enough detail to see the possibilities and rationale for continuing to include the open-agenda study group as a primary component in the educational methodology of clinical pastoral education. Based on this conviction, the following set of recommendations are suggested as a stimulus to improving the quality of process-group work and the securing of its rightful place and practice for the future.

---

[3] To obtain information write directly to her at: 553 N. Judson St., Philadelphia, PA 19130.

RECOMMENDATIONS

For CPE Programs

1. That prospective students be informed that doing CPE involves mandatory participation in a group experience which contains both educational and therapeutic elements. The experience will help them understand group dynamics in general and their participation in those dynamics in particular.

2. That students be informed that during each unit of training some sessions of the process group will be videotaped for the supervisor's own learning and peer review.

3. That at least one didactic session on some aspect of the the supervisor's small process group theory be presented to the students during each unit of training.

4. That a debriefing session focused on the small process group experience be held with the students during the last week of each training unit.

5. That students include in their final evaluation a section on what they learned both experientially and conceptually in the small process group experience during CPE.

6. That students not be evaluated on their individual participation in the process group experience, but that the group process itself be described in a general way in the supervisor's final evaluation material.

For Supervisors:

1. That supervisors be able to articulate a clear group theory to students and apply it in their small process-group work in CPE.

2. That sharing parts of a videotaped IPR session of work in a current process group be required in the annual peer review.

3. That there be at least one workshop at each national ACPE meeting on new developments in the theory and practice of process-group work in CPE.

4. That further research into this component of our educational methodology be supported by the National Research Committee of the Association for Clinical Pastoral Education.

5. That supervisors make a request to the National Standards Committee of the Association for Clinical Pastoral Education that standards be developed for doing process-group work in CPE.

For Supervisory Candidates:

1. That all supervisory candidates participate in at least one type of group experience outside of CPE before writing their theory and/or conducting student groups on their own.[4]

2. That a position paper which demonstrates a clear theory for working with the small process group be required for all supervisory candidates seeking certification.

3. That a videotape of a small process group session be analyzed and submitted to the Certification Commission for all certification appearances.

---

[4] These could be variations on the following: psychodynamic group psychotherapy, T-group or psycho-educational group, Tavistock conference, or systems-centered group-as-a-whole (Agazarian).

THEOLOGICAL PERSPECTIVES

PART ONE: OBJECT RELATIONS AND RELIGIOUS FAITH

At one point in Alice Walker's novel *The Color Purple*, the protagonist Celie writes a letter to her missionary sister Nettie. Celie tries to tell Nettie about a conversation she has had with her friend, Shug. The conversation is about God.

> Here's the thing, say Shug. The thing I believe. God is inside you and inside everybody else. You come into the world with God. But only them that search for it inside find it. And sometimes it just manifest itself even if you not looking, or don't know what you looking for. Trouble do it for most folks, I think. Sorrow, lord. Feeling like shit.
>
> It? I ast.
>
> Yeah, It. God ain't a he or a she, but a It.
>
> But what do it look like? I ast.
>
> Don't look like nothing, she say. It ain't a picture show. It ain't something you can look at apart from anything else, including yourself. I believe God is everything, say Shug, including yourself. Everything that is or ever was or ever will be. And when you can feel that, and be happy to feel that, you've found It (1982, 166-7).

Most people know that Sigmund Freud dismissed religious faith as an illusion. In his major work on the subject, *The Future of an Illusion* (1927),

199

Freud made it clear that religious faith originates in an effort to resolve the conflicts which arise during the Oedipal period. By creating the illusion (wish fulfillment) of a benevolent and protective divine father, the child's fears of helplessness in relation to his unconscious instincts (id) as well as in relationship to the world (reality principle) are soothed, if not resolved. Freud did not think much of illusions. In fact, because they are based on irrational human desires, Freud wrote that they "come near to psychiatric delusions" (Freud 1964, 49). In Freud's program of educating a person toward reality, the consolation offered by religious faith was a narcotic which only encouraged "infantilism." Freud preferred to endure "the great necessities of Fate... with resignation" and without the help of any illusions (82). He sought to depend upon reason alone to deal with reality.

Soon after it was published, Freud sent a copy of his essay to his friend, novelist Roman Rolland. Rolland responded positively to Freud's thoughts about religion but with one caveat–Rolland felt Freud "had not properly appreciated the true source of religious sentiments." Rolland pointed specifically to a subjective experience, a "sensation of 'eternity,' a feeling as of something limitless, unbounded–as it were 'oceanic'" which he thought was missing in Freud's account (Freud 1962, 11).

Freud explored the implications of Rolland's comments in the first section of his next essay, *Civilization and its Discontents* (1930). Though Freud could not discover the oceanic feeling within himself, he decided that it may originate in the earliest phase of life, when the ego has not yet separated itself from its larger world (while in the womb or during the earliest experiences of the breast). But, Freud concluded, it is "incontrovertible" that *religious faith* begins in response to the infant's experience of helplessness and felt longing for the father (God). Thus, "the part played by the oceanic feelings, which might seek something like the restoration of limitless narcissism, is ousted from a place in the foreground" (Freud 1962, 19).

As object relations theorists began to focus attention on the infant/mother dyad, interest in Rolland's observation and the psychological origins of religion again surfaced despite Freud's efforts to oust these considerations from a place in the psychological foreground. For instance, W.D. Fairbairn located such antecedents to religion in the earliest experiences of symbiosis with the mother, which he thought were mystical in nature. Harry Guntrip thought initial religious experiences occurred slightly later, when the infant had gained a degree of separation from the mother and a sense of belonging to the mother (and the cosmos). But it was Donald W. Winnicott (1896-1971), British pediatrician and psychoanalyst, who is most responsible for opening the way to further discussion, both by redefining the meaning of illusion and by focussing on the role of the mother.

Winnicott thought that in the relationship between the mother and the infant there was an "intermediate area of experiencing" which lies somewhere in between inner and outer reality. He called this area illusion (1971, 3). It has a special quality and function which can last a lifetime:

> This intermediate area of experience...constitutes the greater part of the infant's experience, and throughout life is retained in the intense experiencing that belongs to the arts and to religion and to imaginative living, and to creative scientific work (14).

Initially this intermediate space is filled by the infant with the illusion of his own, and the mother's, omnipotence. However, through maternal failure the infant is inevitably disillusioned. It was in this intermediate space that the infant began to deal with his consequent anxiety, and his or her own transition toward separation from the mother, by creating and playing with *transitional objects*–usually a toy or blanket. These objects, which are both real *and* illusory, replace the initial perception of the mother's omnipotence and represent the child who is in transition (Winnicott 1971, 14). They are both created and discovered, imbued with a special meaning and purpose which is never to be challenged. One psychologist author waxes eloquent about their importance:

> Both child and parents consider [the transitional object] sacred, and it is put under certain taboos...it is loaded with protonuminous qualities...should not be washed with the rest of the laundry, and the child knows that he may tote it around, finger it, stroke it, stick it into his mouth, and take it to be with him in ways and at times not tolerated in his dealings with ordinary objects. The transitional object is a ceremonial focus of the whole family, surrounded by laughing and crying, holding and sharing, taking and receiving (Pruyser 1974, 207).

Winnicott points out that the usefulness of transitional objects and transitional play is dependent upon the extent to which the infant has already internalized the "good enough" mother–that is, the extent to which the mother had been able to empathically withstand, and not react to, the infant's aggression and thus create a safe *holding environment* for their relationship. Winnicott thought that for the True (noncompliant) Self, the task of self-creation and reality acceptance is never completed. Thus, culture, the arts, and religion are among those constructs or "resting places" or transitional spaces designed to relieve the strain of this lifelong task. Though Winnicott himself was not religious, his sensitive and imaginative reworking of psychoanalytic concepts brought new vigor to exploring the relationship between the mother and child, and the possible origins of Rolland's oceanic feeling.

Prominent among the explorers is Ana-Marie Rizzuto, a psychoanalyst and professor of psychiatry at Tufts University who wrote the groundbreaking *Birth of the Living God: A Psychoanalytic Study* (1979). Rizzuto begins her study by affirming the presence of what Freud called "memory traces" or "imagos" based on the earliest object relations. Through her clinical practice, Rizzuto has discovered that people do indeed "concoct" their own images of God out of a combination of fact and fantasy, fear and hope, based in part on the memory traces from these earliest caretaking relationships. She charmingly concludes, "No child arrives at the 'house of God' without his pet God under his arm" (8).

In the course of her study Rizzuto makes an important distinction between the *image* of God with which one has a largely unconscious relationship and the *idea* of God about which one has conscious thoughts. The first is an internalized object representation formed by primary process while the second is a set of articulated concepts resulting from secondary process. In a sense *faith* is then an unconscious process which grows out of one's feelings about one's earliest object relations, while specific *beliefs* are the result of a later conscious process directed by thought processes and the ego. The first is the God of experience and the mystics while the second is the God of thought and the philosophers (29).

In her study Rizzuto focuses primarily on the object-related nature of religious experience (faith) and the image of God as a transitional object. She thinks such internalized object representations are created during the Oedipal period, but also during the earlier developmental stages. Rizzuto is particularly cognizant of the work of Erik Erikson and points to the earliest stage of basic trust in the infant/mother dyad as the probable locus, in her opinion, for the beginnings of religious experience. Rizzuto points out that object representations can be male or female, devil or savior, malevolent or benign–or a mixture. They are healthy in so far as they help a person deal with reality. This lifelong process of helping a person deal with reality imbues the object with a certain kind of "stuffing":

throughout life God remains a transitional object at the service of gaining leverage with oneself, with others, and with life itself. This is so, not because God is God, but because, like the teddy bear, he has obtained a good half of his stuffing from the primary objects the child has 'found' in his life. The other half of God's stuffing comes from the child's capacity to 'create' a God according to his needs (179).

Despite her efforts to base the genesis of her thinking about religious faith in the early imagos or memory traces mentioned by Freud, in the end Rizzuto is forced to disagree with Freud's dismissal of religion:

> [My] study suggests that Winnicott was accurate in locating religion–and God–in what he called transitional space....That is the place where man's life finds the full relevance of his objects and meaning for himself....Psychic reality–whose depth Freud so brilliantly unveiled–cannot occur without that specifically human transitional space for play and illusion (209).

Rizzuto points out that in this light Freud's creation of the psychoanalytic method as a way of dealing with the relationship between internal and external reality is in fact a type of transitional object in and of itself.

Neither Freud, Rizzuto, nor Winnicott were interested in proving or disproving the existence of God. However, following on their work have been several substantial efforts by theorists in the object relations field to explicate the development of the self in relationship to the dynamics of religious faith and an object named as God. At times these efforts have been met with criticism for the psychologizing of all religious ideas, thereby simply creating a god object who is "a friendly and knowable supporter of human fulfillment" (Steinhoff-Smith 1989, 265). Most of the time these efforts have been stoutly defended:

> Every person is entitled to engage in a project, through which he comes to terms with life's essentials *for him*, on which he can put his stakes, through which he may fulfill himself by taking hold of reality as reality appears and applies to him (Pruyser 1974, 125).

Over time it has become increasingly clear that intellectual work in this field has begun to open up those in the psychoanalytic tradition to more in-depth exploration of religious faith as a significant aspect of self development. It can hopefully also open up those in various faith traditions to a more in-depth consideration of the contribution of psychoanalysis and object relations theory to understanding religious experience.

John McDargh, professor of religion and psychology at Boston College, is among those who have grappled with some of these implications. In his doctoral dissertation, "Psychoanalytic Object Relations Theory and the Study of Religion" (1983), McDargh explores the human longing and need for the transcendent in order to psychologically survive the limits of life and respond to yearnings for the More (William James). McDargh recognizes that the primary issue for the child is solving the problem of how to become a self which is both securely related and separate. This work is done through internalized object representations which are then played out or worked through in transitional spaces (Winnicott). McDargh views the human person as inherently a theological being whose projections based on this type of positive transferential relationship (or faith) result in the growth of human dignity and freedom (111).

McDargh, following Fairbairn, emphasizes the "irreducible centrality of the human need for relationship." Therefore, the question is not so much "*What* is there?" as it is "*Who* is there?" (211). It is as a consequence of the affective tie to the internalized God representation that experiences of conversion and transformation come. Following Rizzuto, McDargh emphasizes that religious faith begins in that internal transitional space where the child deals with "super heroes, devils, monsters, and imaginary companions" (123). McDargh's primary goal is to show that some kind of religious experience, in the broadest sense, is crucial and inevitable in healthy self-development and that it has its own special meaning and import.

One of the helpful aspects of McDargh's work is his exploration of how people approach religious experience. He asks, "Why anchor faith in a transcendent reality?" And he answers, 1) either to protect the self from the threat of dissolution, or 2) to respond to the human yearning for "more and more communion with more and more reality" (108). The first experience approaches such a reality with an awareness of the limitations and restrictions of the human situation; the second approaches such a reality with a longing for connection with it (112). The one seems to emphasize human finitude, separateness, and consequent feelings of awe and helplessness, while the other emphasizes human magnitude, connectedness, and consequent feelings of recognition and responsiveness. It might not be too much to say that the first emphasizes the psychological work of separation and individuation (through aggression), while the second emphasizes the desire to remain empathic and connected (libido).

The work of William W. Meissner, Jesuit priest and psychoanalyst, followed on the heels of McDargh but took a somewhat different tack. In *Psychoanalysis and Religious Experience* (1984), Meissner's initial intent is to show that Freud's treatment of religion was the result of his unresolved conflicts and superstitious fears. Freud's ambivalence toward his own Jewish heritage as well as his persistent attacks against Jung's "mysticism" are among the examples which give evidence for Meissner's case. "It seems clear," Meissner writes, "that Freud's unresolved mystical trends were being projected and dealt with in an externalized form" (55). In addition, religion had no place in the world of scientific positivism into which Freud sought to place psychoanalysis.

In line with other object relations theorists, Meissner himself locates religion in the transitional space between the objective (physical) and subjective (fantasy) world. He explores four expressions of religion as transitional phenomena: faith, God representations, symbols, and prayer. Within these specific activities there is an interpenetration of the external (objective) and internal (subjective) worlds. The result is that these symbols or acts carry special meaning and thus "become part of the transitional realm of the believer's illusory experience" (181). Following Winnicott, Meissner concurs that these activities are transitional both in the sense that they may eventually be either further developed or abandoned, and in the sense that they bridge the two worlds in a special, experiential way.

In all of this work the question persists whether or not the origin of religious experience is in any way separate from the self and its objects. Or, to ask the question slightly differently, is there any point at which the intrapsychic or interpersonal dimension reveals a distinctly nonhuman or numinous element distinct in and of itself? Further, is there any reason to grant the sacred dimension a special status above or different from other life experiences? And if so, what is its special nature? These questions among others continue to tantalize and provoke those in the psychoanalytic tradition who are working at the interface between psychology and religion.

In some ways the most recent contribution is the most unusual because of its forthrightness in making the claim for the existence of an object which is God. Jewish psychologist Moshe Halevi Spero in *Religious Objects as*

Psychological Structures (1992) argues that human beings set aside intrapsychic space specifically for interaction with an object representation of God which is, by its very nature, extrinsic to the human psyche. He claims that even Freud sensed something "further behind" the religious experience of infantile helplessness, something "wrapped in obscurity" (Freud 1962, 19), "a reliable object" through which the self is not just helped but met and understood (Spero 1992, 193-4). Subsequent interaction involving religious experience in a set-aside space continues to occur in varying degrees throughout a lifetime.

Spero asks whether the process of psychotherapy as well as the discipline of religious observance (both of which have much in common) can potentially "fold back the anthropocentric aspects of a god" and thus "allow a glimpse of an objective God" (146). Spero basically answers in the affirmative. He uses such examples from Talmudic exegesis as Moses' initial thought that it was his father Amram calling to him out of the burning bush– until Yahweh identified himself as "God of your father" (154). Likewise in psychotherapeutic work, a mysterious representation in a dream might just as easily be a God or Christ figure as it might be symbolic of the patient's father or the analyst. In Spero's view there is little justification for choosing one interpretation over the other, especially since either might be inaccurate! Spero concludes by pointing out that ultimately the practice of religious faith and the psychotherapeutic experience have the same goal in terms of emotional maturation:

> The interpersonally based transference experience and
> the intrapsychic objects it generates must ultimately be
> relinquished and the divine [or human] object
> differentiated from the endopsychically conceived one
> (154).

James W. Jones, professor of religion at Rutgers University and a clinical psychologist, is also interested in religious experience and the transference relationship, but he works with it in a different way. In *Contemporary Psychoanalysis and Religion* (1991), Jones is intent on exploring a person's affective and interactional relationship to the sacred (transcendent) because this is "the transferential ground of the self" (64). He is not so much interested in "folding back" the transference to discover an "objective God" as he is interested in experiencing the fullness of the transferential relationship in order to discover the uniqueness of the self in relationship to the transcendent and thus to itself.

Jones is convinced that a person does not come to know his or her depths except in relationship with the sacred (or transferential) because these are precisely the experiences which are uniquely personal, individual and transformational. Thus, religion as *relationship* (he underlines it) "resonates to those internalized relationships that constitute the sense of self" (65). For Rudolph Otto this was the experience of the "wholly other"; for Paul Tillich this was the "ground of being"; and for Martin Buber this was the I-Thou relationship. For Jones the task of religion is "to cultivate a richness of consciousness" in the transitional spaces which includes many "religious moments." In this way the self can be fully realized:

> Such religious moments are transitional not only because they transcend subjectivity and objectivity (Meissner) or invoke imagination (Rizzuto) but also because they allow us to enter again and again into that timeless and transforming psychological space from which renewal and creativity emerge (134).

Jones writes in a tradition which grows out of the work of Rudolph Otto in *The Idea of the Holy* (1958) and the psychology of the sacred. Like others before him in the object relations field, Jones places the origin of that awesome and uncanny experience of the numinous or *mysterium tremendum* in the earliest traces of a primal object relationship. In this sense "we are all *homo religiosis* (inherently religious)" (122). In making his case Jones builds on the work of psychoanalyst Christopher Bollas in *The Shadow of an Object* (1987). Bollas emphasizes the primacy of particular transformational objects which lead to metamorphosis of the self and harken back to a "pre-verbal ego memory." Such "holy" objects[1] are recognized when one feels a certain subjective rapport or "uncanny fusion" during an aesthetic moment: listening to symphony, reading a poem, and seeing a sunset. "Such experiences," Bollas writes, "crystallize time into a space where subject and object appear to achieve an intimate rendezvous" (31). He connects this experience of unification to the earliest rapport between mother and infant as "part of the unthought known" (32) and forward to the adult quest for new transformational objects which will assure continued growth in self-knowledge and self-integration.

If Spero tended to look outside the self for some extrinsic transcendent reality, Jones and Bollas search deep within the self for such a reality. Both would receive criticism from feminist Naomi Goldenberg, who eschews any "privileging of the sacred" as either an external or an internal reality. She

---

[1] It is important to keep in mind that this is not an actual object but the internalized affective process of a significant past relational experience.

comments acerbicly, "I feel thought shutting down as theistic awe enters the prose" (1992, 347). In her opinion such an approach goes against the atheism which she considers to be "an important cornerstone of the psychoanalytic epistemology developed by Freud" (348). In particular, Goldenberg feels the search for a special transforming object (inner or outer) is actually a defense against the "masculine anxiety" about existence (ontology). Behind Jones's quest she senses the conjuring up of "an image of God-the-hero, God-the-father, or God-the-benign bureaucrat" (353). Behind his quest for a transformed self she senses a longing for the maternal presence.

Though Goldenberg may be unduly biased in her criticism, she is part of a growing group of feminist thinkers who are returning to the psychoanalytic tradition and in the process making their own contribution to the psychology of religion. The current impetus for such a return was begun by Nancy Chodorow in *The Reproduction of Mothering* (1978) in which she presents a critique and revision of psychoanalytic theories of mothering and gender development based on object relations theory. Chodorow points out that because of our current cultural arrangements based on gender, most primary caretakers of infants are women. This means that in order to achieve gender identity, boys must separate from their mothers to establish their difference while girls must stay in relationship with their mothers to establish their similarity. According to Chodorow this means that boys tend to value autonomy and the quest for individuality more than girls, who tend to value relationality and attachment. Carol Gilligan picked up on this major insight in her book *In A Different Voice* (1982) by documenting the differences in moral development among male and female children. Following Chodorow, Gilligan's research showed that while boys are naturally more concerned about rules and rights and tasks in their relationships, girls are more concerned about care and responsibility and relational empathy.

It is against this background that Goldenberg's criticism of Jones as promoting some kind of uniquely male quest for self- transformation needs to be understood. It is also against this background that she and other feminists begin to talk about the relational return to the past, the body, the earth, and the Goddess. With this return comes a deepening awareness of the maternal matrix as a primary religious concept of interconnection between the self and its objects.

> Since every human life begins in the body of a woman,
> the image of a woman, whether thought of as mother or
> as Goddess, always points to an early history of
> connectedness: Mother-*mater*-matrix. "Woman" is the

stuff out of which all people are made. In the beginning
was her flesh... (202).

According to Goldenberg, it is in the deep memory of this "birth union" that
the genesis of the oceanic feeling resides for both men and women.

All of these efforts attempt to get behind specific beliefs or ideas about
religious experience in order to grasp the nature of faith itself. This work is
difficult and limited because beliefs and cultural influences inevitably shape
and color and mask the More. It is also difficult because, despite the
methodology offered by the psychoanalytic approach, transference is ubiquitous.
One author comments:

> I don't think that any of us are in a position to *get over
> the transference* or to *transcend the transference*, in order
> to finally understand Freud, feminism, or religion. The
> transference, like analysis itself, may in fact, be
> interminable (Jonte-Pace 1992, 373).

Another way to express this situation is to realize that there is always something
of a curtain between ourselves and whatever is on the other side.

From the preceding review of work in the field of psychology of religion
based on object relations theory, it is evident that Freud's dismissal of religion
as an illusion is no longer the last word on the subject. While the Oedipal
period and the relationship with the father presents certain psychological
challenges, it is in the early relationship with the mother that a sense of that
oceanic feeling seems to originate. In response to good-enough mothering, the
infant's ability to contain both good and bad early object introjects as well as
project them without being harmed begins a lifelong process of digestion and
incorporation. It is precisely through the continual process of illusion and
disillusion, begun at birth, that the work of self- creation is accomplished in
that transitional space in between where subject and object meet. This space in
and of itself could be considered sacred:

> The potential space between baby and mother, between
> child and family, between individual and society or the
> world, depends on experience which leads to trust. It
> can be looked upon as sacred to the individual in that it
> is here that the individual experiences creative living
> (Winnicott 1971, 103).

Hidden deep within this space and this process of the self becoming in relationship to its objects (reality), it is evident that there is at times an awareness of something larger than the self or the space, or the process, a Mysterious Other in relationship to which one can feel surprisingly close and similar or disconcertingly distant and different. For a moment here and there the curtain may become transparent or even briefly pulled aside. How does this happen? For some it involves trying to work through the transference to glimpse transcendence directly. For others it involves coming to know the self in its relational core or transferential ground of being. For still others it involves connecting with a primal maternal matrix which nurtures and holds and offers rebirth. For some this may happen in psychotherapy; for others it may occur on a mountaintop or in church. Some come to this religious perception by feeling separate and helpless and overwhelmed. "Trouble do it for most folks....Sorrow, lord. Feeling like shit." Others come through a deep sense of affinity with the wider whole: "I believe God is....Everything that is or ever was or ever will be." But it is also important to note that "sometimes it just manifest itself even if you are not looking, or don't know what you are looking for." And that is probably the most incredible possibility of all.

Part Two: Group Work as Transformative Play

It is my conviction that Wilfred Bion's formulation of the interdependent relationship between the basic assumption group and the work group establishes the foundation for achieving a workable synthesis between the rational and irrational aspects of life as these become available through the small process group experience in CPE. It is my further conviction that by connecting Bion's understanding of group phenomena with D. W. Winnicott's ideas about the psychological relationship between mother and infant, a conceptual view of group process work emerges which is potentially transformative. This transformative possibility achieves expression in the concept of group work as play.

In reflecting on the thought of Wilfred Bion and A.K. Rice regarding their work with groups, Margaret Rioch notes that the concept of play is precisely what is lacking. She comments:

> [Bion and Rice] surely have not been unaware of this
> [lack]. Their theories allow for a basketball team or
> chamber music orchestra which are groups met to play–

the work of such groups is in fact their play (1981, 672).
Rioch wonders whether living in England during the war was just too serious an experience, or whether the Protestant work ethic made the ideal group a working (rational) group for Bion and Rice. She then shares her own conviction–as well as my own:

> It is possible, however, that at another time and another place a man [sic] might find in the concept of play a true synthesis of mature, scientific and primitive fantasy elements without the one being subservient to the other (672-3).

In terms of actual practice, the key to this formulation lies in establishing and maintaining an interdependent and balanced relationship between the (mature, scientific) work group and the (primitive, fantasy) basic assumption group. Fundamental to this effort is educating all group members regarding the major elements of a coherent group theory and its application. In doing this the existence of both the emotional components of the BA group and the self-reflexive task of the work group become understood and available for utilization by group members and their leader throughout the SPG experience.

An understanding of group work as play in clinical pastoral education strikes a particularly timely note in terms of current work in the field of theology, beginning with James Whitehead's article "The Practical Play of Theology" (1987) and more recently John Patton's *From Ministry to Theology* (1990). Both writers pick up on the theme of play as a theological method for fully participating in creation, discovering our true selves, and making correlations between traditional and untraditional human and divine activity.

> In play we imagine reality, and our place in it, anew. We more than imitate or reproduce; we invent....And in this interpretive play we make our lives; we *identify* ourselves...we imagine the next stage of Christian tradition....We play our lives everywhere and all the time. It is what we do (Whitehead 1987, 44).

Whitehead is especially concerned to recognize our biases about play–that it might be considered childish, or remedial, or frivolous, or deceitful. He formulates the theological movement of play which begins with leaping (risking), moves toward testing the leeway (making correlations), and ends in falling or coming back to earth (failure). Based on these ideas, Whitehead concludes:

> What if creation is imagined as God's leap of delight?
> What if in creation God tests the leeway between God
> and non-God, pushing the limit until something non-
> God breaks off, existing separately now as creature?
> Then Adam and Eve's fall can be imagined as a
> subsequent but necessary part of that divine play–as
> creation coming down to earth (1987, 51).

Both Whitehead and Patton stress the importance of this type of theological reflection being done in community. Whitehead calls such activity when done at close range a "contact sport" but does not delve into it further (52). Patton focuses on "doing theology" in the context of a group of ministers and CPE students whose theological reflection is directed toward renewed engagement in pastoral activity and personal faith. Though Patton is more interested in theological method and outcome than he is in group dynamics as such, he is aware that being part of a group is of crucial importance because it emboldens members to work both theologically and politically:

> Reflection and sharing in the community of ministers
> validates the members of that community as persons who
> can risk handling the faith and interpreting it in the light
> of their experience. These meanings, shared in
> relationship with other members of the community of
> ministers, contributes to the life of that community and,
> sometimes, to the larger community of faith to which
> the members are accountable (Patton 1990, 112).

While theological reflection in a group context is familiar to students and supervisors in clinical pastoral education, thinking through the larger implications of participation in the self-reflexive task of the small process group experience itself is not as self-evident. In an effort to accomplish this, the final section of this inquiry seeks to integrate the thought of Bion with that of Winnicott in order to explore more fully the concept of group work as transformative play. The initial connections between the two theorists are found in the interrelationship between Bion's internal concept of the mother as container and Winnicott's external concept of the holding environment–that in-between, illusory space between mother and infant. In fact, it is in the reciprocal relationship between the mother as container and the external holding environment that the earliest psychological dynamics of human development begin:

> It is the process outside, namely the holding environment, that sets the stage for the internal process, . namely containment, to occur inside the mother and later to be taken in by the baby. *Both internal and external processes have to occur at the same time for the baby to handle anxiety well* and so have a maximal chance of undisturbed development (Scharff 1992, 41; italics added).

Put another way, in object relations theory the earliest experiences of interpersonal relations (the holding environment provided by the transitional space) get translated into intrapsychic structures (the infant's container into which feelings about part objects are introjected) which in turn affect all subsequent interpersonal relations and become especially activated later on in a group situation.

It is the point of view of this study that the small process group experience in CPE occupies this holding environment or transitional space between the student (internal reality) and the world (external reality) in an unique and unforgettable way. It is here that the student has an opportunity to process his or her experiences in CPE and ministry. It is in this space that he or she can receive feedback from peers and supervisor. It is here that students can learn to work with their own introjections and others' projections and identifications. It is through interpersonal experiences in this space that individual participation in both the conscious and unconscious workings of the group-as-a-whole process becomes evident. It is here that some perception of the human/divine dimension, a Mysterious Other, may even occur.

There are a variety of intermediary ways to use and talk about this aspect of the group experience (Schlachet 1986, 36-7). Sometimes the group itself forms a psychic envelope where the subjective world of each member touches that of the other members. Sometimes the group serves as an empathic bridge between two members. At other times the group provides a buffer zone between incongruent or warring camps within one individual or between people. It can be a filter or screen through which to view the self or the world. Sometimes it becomes a moat which keeps the inner world of self or group relationships separate and protected from the outer world of demands and responsibilities. Perhaps it serves as a telescope to see the world more clearly or a microscope to be used for self-examination. Yet all of these metaphors are subsumed under the overarching understanding of the process group as occupying a transitional space in which relationships between the self and other are "played out" in a unique way:

> The group helps the individual to delineate and clarify
> that border between reality and illusion, and the sense
> of a shared but clearly circumscribed transitional arena
> of a created psychic world makes the definition very
> compelling (Schlachet 1986, 47).

In order to make optimal use of this transitional space, group members must be able to share and process their here-and-now experiences of self and the other (peers, supervisor, patients, learning goals) in the group. They must not only agree that this is a requisite for membership in the group, they must also be aware that by participating they will automatically contribute to the emotional life of the group-as-a-whole and that this latter process is largely unconscious. For it is when the "cross fire of multilateral projective identifications" in a dyadic relationship becomes a "veritable blizzard" in a group (Gosling 1981, 628) that the possibility of what Winnicott calls "shared playing" can begin to happen:

> There is a direct development from transitional
> phenomena to playing, and from playing to shared
> playing, and from this to cultural experience (1971, 60).

Winnicott's great contribution to psychology was his development of the idea that the creation of illusion through play is *the* chief way in which the infant psyche gains a healthy foothold on reality. Rizzuto calls this process the "illusory transmutation of reality" which is "the indispensable and unavoidable process all of us *must* go through if we are to grow normally and acquire psychic meaning and substance" (1979, 228). It is "the key to coming to terms with reality" (Pruyser 1974, 241). Meissner adds:

> It is not by bread alone that man lives. Man needs to
> create, to shape and transform his environment [in order
> to express] the constant commerce between the ongoing
> worlds of his external experience and his inner psychic
> reality (1984, 177).

For some people this work-that-is-play in the small process group in CPE will prove difficult and forbidding. Those who have depended on the facticity of the physical world will find this experience highly subjective and may judge it as unreliable. Those who believe that there are certain correct religious doctrines or scientific truths or ways to run a group will find this experience disconcerting at best, certainly imprecise, and even frightening at worst. On the other hand, for those who have a highly-developed inner fantasy world, the process group experience will force them to come into contact with more reality–through the presence of other group members–than they may have ever wanted or imagined existed! Most people are somewhere in between these extremes in processing their relationship between the (subjective) self and the (objective) world. But when the group experience begins, they will all discover–hopefully sooner rather than later–that as contact and trust increase between group members so will their ability to create a transitional group space where both work and play can occur.

How can the nature of this work-which-is-play best be described? Or, how can we understand that "the route of mother space to self space is the root of play" (Howe 1990, 47)? One of the most effective metaphors is the image of a child on a beach who moves away from his or her family and is forcefully drawn to the water's edge. With bucket and shovel and the utmost concentration, the child digs and shapes and builds in the sand to his or her heart's content. No one has told the child to make sand castles or that the tide will eventually come in and destroy his or her creation. Rather it is as if each player–child and beach–quietly but distinctly calls to the other to be in creative relationship:

> To the child, the sand cries for his shoveling and his muscles itch for the sand. His fantasies lust for the resistance of the grainy matter, and the beach demands to be molded by his hand. Child and beach present themselves to each other, beach appealing to child and child appealing to beach. It is not far-fetched to say that both engage each other in play (Pruyser 1974, 242).

Such activity is a temporary, spontaneous contract in which subject and object, the child and the beach, human and nature, self and the group are temporarily and totally engaged. In the process the child is working out separation and difference from the mother; in the process the individual is working out relationship with reality (the group). Concentration is total; the child and beach literally meet–in the profoundest sense. It is not the content but rather the process which is totally engaging. This is the work of play. It is an experience of deeply congruent outer/inner communication. The experience is so notable that "the memory will linger" (Pruyser 1974, 242).

In order to better understand the qualities of play, Johan Huizinga's classic study *Homo Ludens* (1950) is helpful. At the outset Huizinga notes that the word *illusion* comes from the Latin *inlusio*, *illudere*, and *inludere* which literally mean "in-play" (1950, 11). Huizinga lifts up the four major characteristics of play. First, he points out that play is voluntary and free, and thus can be suspended at any time. It is never a task, but it always means something. "The need for [play]," he writes, "is only urgent to the extent that the enjoyment of it makes it a need" (8). Second, play is not real as such. That is, it involves a stepping out of ordinary life into a pretend sphere of activity, like an intermezzo or interlude in our daily lives. Yet because "play turns to seriousness and seriousness turns to play" it "interpolates" itself back into real life again and again (8).

Third, Huizinga points out that play is secluded and limited. It uses its own marked-off space (playground, magic circle, beach), and its own time and rules. As a result, it is eminently repeatable and, thus quickly becomes a tradition which is handed on to others. Finally, play creates order or rather "*is* [its own] order" (19). "Into an imperfect world and the confusion of life it brings a temporary, limited perfection" (10). There is a tension inherent in play, not as to who will win, but rather as to who will play the game and how. The spoil sport who refuses to play (and destroys the illusion) is worse (and will be extruded) than is the cheat who breaks the rules. There is also a secrecy about play because "inside the circle of the game the laws and customs of ordinary life no longer count" (11).

All of these characteristics ring particularly true in terms of the small group process in clinical pastoral education. In fact, Huizinga's ideas help explicate the reasons why such group work, or rather play, in CPE is replete with its own special norms and rules, and has persisted and been handed down through the generations of supervisors and students without much effort or reflection at all. Huizinga's insights also help to understand why this tradition is exceedingly intuitive and experiential–even "sacred"–and thus not particularly amenable to being examined, researched, or understood in a scientific way.

In presenting Huizinga's work, one important clarification needs to be made. Unfortunately, Huizinga tends to think of play as purely "irrational" amidst "the determinism of the Cosmos":

> The very existence of play continually confirms that
> supralogical nature of the human situation....We play
> and know that we play, so we must be more than merely
> rational beings, for play is irrational (3-4).

It is more accurate to say that play brings out and expresses the irrational (unconscious) side of life as it is in relationship and in contrast with the rational or conscious. Huizinga himself seems somewhat cognizant of this dialectic when he points out that there are actually two basic aspects of play, or ways in which it functions: "as a contest *for* something or a representation *of* something" (13). The first seems to point to a conscious use of play while the second points to its more symbolic or unconscious meaning. It is with the dialectical relationship between the conscious (work group) and unconscious (basic assumption group) in mind, as well as the relationship between the thought of Bion and Winnicott, that a number of different ramifications of the group experience point toward its transformative potential.

First, the development of the basic assumption group is the first sign that the group is claiming the transitional space and creating a distinct entity for people to join. Through establishing its own language and norms, a unitary concept of the group comes into being, forming its own temporary society which transcends individual differences (Jacobson 1989, 476). This occurs through negotiation about what the group represents or means–what each person unconsciously wishes the group to be and fantasizes about how the group will solve its problems. According to Bion this unconscious material organizes itself around one of three primary patterns: protective (fight/flight), productive (pairing), or nurturing (dependency). Winnicott confirms this general phenomena in his own language:

> If we wish we may collect together and form a group on
> the basis of the similarity of our illusory experiences.
> This is a natural root of grouping among human beings
> (1971, 3).

An important aspect of this development is its irrational (basic assumption) nature. For this reason the small process group is often viewed, especially initially, as the *only* place in the larger context of a professional training program and institutionalized setting where feelings and relational connections are valued (Krantz 1991). For some this is threatening and for others it comes as a welcome relief.

Second, one of the most compelling experiences of a BA dependency group is of the group as maternal matrix, a theme touched on at several different points in this study. It was S.H. Foulkes who first used the term *group matrix* to describe the actual communicational web of relationships between group members (1964). Interestingly, the word *matrix* or *matter* derives from the Latin for "womb," which literally means "the place which brings forth life." Through these associations such a basic assumption group comes to represent the feminine, darker, and chthonic elements out of which new life grows. One feminist writer specifically notes that the "collective body" is remembered as the "maternal body."

> A maternal body is always, I think, a relational body, experienced as a matrix alive in herself and yet, at the same time serving as a physical and communal context for other human living (Goldenberg 1990, 36).

In an effort to claim the universal significance of this experience, these ideas are sometimes extended into the body politic and even the wider world: "The entire earth is conceptualized as the body of the Goddess and thus is sacred" (Goldenberg 1990, 201).

Third, the need for authority and leadership in a small process group, especially at the beginning stages, is similar to the need for the "good enough mother" (either male or female). Winnicott observes that "there is no possibility whatever for an infant to proceed from the pleasure principle to the reality principle...unless there is a good-enough mother" (1971, 10). For the infant or the group the illusory space in which to do this work cannot be created without "the *overlap* between what the mother supplies and what the child might conceive" (Winnicott 1971, 12; italics added). If the group leader does not supply enough of this "good enough" stuff (warmth and empathy along with structure and discipline), the group will try to both defend itself against its angry feelings about this lack *and* meet its own needs through the ascendancy of the basic assumption mode of relating and an alternative leader (mother). In fact, "Bion saw the basic assumptions as fantasies about a sort of shadow group mother" (Jacobson 1989, 478). Under these circumstances, the group in order to survive (and not fragment and die) may create its own irrational and defensive way of being in the transitional space. Thus

> basic assumption groups are defenses against death, but like all psychological defenses, BA groups have a content

which in fact is death. All non-conforming members
die of exclusion in the cold world outside (Turquet 1974,
370).

When disconnected from the work group or rational aspect of its existence, the
basic assumption group with its inherent warmth and seductiveness is by nature
a fickle and "mindless" phenomenon, a closed system with a hatred for learning
(Bion 1961). This development might be best described as regression in service
of the id.

Fourth, it is of critical importance that the group leader be able to work
within the dialectic between illusion and disillusion as good-enough mother. It
is through learning to live within this tension that the group comes to accept the
leader's inevitable failures which are necessary for the incremental growth of
the group's acceptance of reality. These failures, which represent a kind of
weaning, initially depend on the mother's ability to contain the hateful feelings
of the child (Winnicott 1971)–or achieve a state of reverie (Bion 1962)–and
still remain in contact with the infant. In this way she keeps her head while
continuing to give away her heart. In a group situation, the disillusionment
experience in relationship to the good-enough leader would lead to the formation
of a basic assumption group, but one which is able to stay connected to the
work group because there has been sufficient overlap. This could be described
as regression in service of the ego. It is important to understand this basis for
determining the difference between a connected (functional) versus a
disconnected (dysfunctional) basic assumption group.

By receiving the negative feelings of the group and then being able to
give them back in such a way that they are digestible (through reinterpretation
or reframing), the leader avoids getting sucked into the projective identifications
and is able to return the projections in a new form. This new emotional material
is then internalized by group members; that is, it becomes palatable and
nourishing through the process of the (adult) ego's identification (with whole
objects) rather than the (infant) ego's introjection (of part objects). It is through
this gradual process that the individual and group ego (or self) is strengthened
and becomes increasingly able to take over the dialectical task of the good-
enough mother function for themselves/itself. In this way the group literally
grows up. In the small process group in CPE this is actually begun when the
individuals who are adult learners agree to being part of the group in the first
place:

> One could say the group members are their own mother
> in the group. They fulfill the original maternal role of

> preserving the paradox that the "group" and what it
> contains is neither self nor other but both...the maternal
> function is really a part of the very fabric of group
> dynamics (Jacobson 1989, 492).

Fifth, there comes a point at which the group itself becomes a transitional object for its various members. In this way the group is used for the purpose of experimentation and reality testing and then put aside–much like a painting is enjoyed or a book read or a piece of music performed.

> Group members can use the "group" as a medium in
> which to *play* with an issue before committing
> themselves to engaging with it as individuals. More
> exactly, the "group" is the frame or constraint within
> which playing can happen (Jacobson 1989, 488).

As new behaviors are tried, or deeper personal feelings are shared, or problems in interpersonal relating are faced, the group provides a context for working on individual change. But the group *as a group* also presents a unique opportunity to work on the larger, lifelong task of staying connected with others while at the same time becoming and remaining an autonomous self. Herein lies the central tension inherent in a small process group experience between belonging versus integrity, compliance versus the possibility of isolation. By being a member *and yet* being one's self, sitting within the circle *and also* alongside it, both the public (interpersonal and social) and private (personal and singular) realms of the human situation are held together (Jacobson 1989, 495). This is potentially *the* most fruitful and challenging aspect of the group experience. It is no wonder that for awhile the group itself becomes like a blanket used to comfort in a new situation, or a toy held close to the body, or a piece of string[2] which both joins *and* separates the self from the other (mother/group). Not only does the group itself embody the inherent paradox of itself as a transitional object but also the inherent paradox of being in transition as it deals with creating or maintaining the crucial balance between what might finally be recognized as *the* major dialectics of life: separation and connection, masculine and feminine, conscious and unconscious, aggression and libido.

---

[2] At one point in his work, Winnicott tells about a seven-year-old boy whose obsession with string belied his anxiety about separation from his mother (Winnicott 1971, 108).

Conclusion

Over fifty years ago Anton Boisen, the founder of clinical pastoral education, looked for the key to emotional and spiritual healing in the pain and mystery of his own and others' mental illness. He was convinced that if he could but understand "human documents in all their complexity and elusiveness" (1938, 248), he would be able to illumine the nature of the relationship between the human and divine. His search for an empirical theology through efforts to understand the living human document became the basis for doing pastoral ministry and provided an agenda which has influenced both practical theologians and religious practitioners ever since. Though Boisen knew that there was no royal road to the reading of these documents or the doing of this kind of theology, it nevertheless became his life's work.

This inquiry has examined the small process group in clinical pastoral education as a living human document. It has explored the complex historical origins of this particular component of the CPE methodology. It has verified the varieties of both theory and practice which supervisory candidates and CPE supervisors presently consider as relevant to the nature and purpose of the small process group in CPE. This inquiry has affirmed the historic and current influence of both the psychoanalytic and the humanistic psychology traditions in CPE. It has proposed that in order to ground and improve the small process-group work in CPE there needs to be a recovery of certain elements from the psychoanalytic tradition related to group work, particularly as these were initially formulated by Wilfred Bion and object relations theorists. The study contends that as a result of the recovery of the self-reflexive group task as the primary framework for group work, the balance between the CPE group experience as therapeutic and the CPE group experience as educational can be redressed. This study has then demonstrated an effort to apply this new/old approach to group process work through a presentation and discussion of an actual case study.

Over forty years ago Reuel Howe, practical theologian and seminary professor, laid out a challenge to supervisors in clinical pastoral education. In his speech to the annual national gathering in 1952, he said that he wanted his students taking CPE "dunked–plunged deeply into life, brought up gasping and dripping." He went on to explain:

> I want my students to lose, as soon as possible, their
> easy faith, their ready answers; and I want them to lose

any hope of ever again having an easy faith or a ready
answer. I want them to lose their personal conceits and
their illusions about themselves, their illusions about
their fellow men, and their illusions about God (5-6).

As part of this dunking experience in CPE, Howe went on to name the small
process group as a unique resource for learning because "man cannot face the
truth about himself as long as he is alone" (8). Because the small process
group experience in CPE contains an unusual opportunity to not be alone and
thus face the truth about the human situation, by extension it also contains the
possibility of discovering something of the truth about the human/divine
situation. Or, to put it another way, by examining its own case or nature as a
living human document, the SPG experience becomes the potential means
through which an empirical or clinical theology can discovered.

To lay the groundwork for these concluding thoughts, the last section of
this study has delineated a psychology of religion based on the relationship
between object relations and religious experience. It has proposed, through
integrating the thought of Wilfred Bion with that of D.W. Winnicott, that the
work of the small process group in CPE is actually a type of transformative
play. Through this work/play the individuals and the group engage in a process
of self/group creation and self/group reflection which involves both staying
connected and separating from each other and the group. The experience is
both an agent for individual change and a process for learning about such change.
It happens in the group through awareness of individual or group basic
assumptions, or working with the projective identifications, or letting go of the
good-enough mother (individual or group). This kind of transformative play is
totally engaging and riveting–perhaps because it has the potential for not only
revealing the deeper parts of the self but also for revealing a Deeper Order or
Mysterious Other beyond itself. For a short while CPE group members become
like the sand for the child on the beach. They are drawn to play together in an
intense and focused way. The experience of self-discovery and group creation
can be so compelling that, even though their castles eventually disappear with
the tide, the memory lingers forever.

Selected Bibliography

Abstracts in Pastoral Care and Counseling. 1971-1991. Volumes 1-21. Richmond, VA: Virginia Institute of Pastoral Care.

ACPE Anniversary Celebration Play Premieres. 1993. *ACPE News.* 26 (1): 7-8.

ACPE Certification Pursuit Game. 1985. *ACPE News.* 18 (2):11-17.

ACPE Standards Committee Study Document. 1984. *ACPE News.* 17 (5): 11-15.

Aden, Leroy and J. Harold Ellens, eds. 1990. *Turning Points in Pastoral Care.* Grand Rapids: Baker Book House.

Agazarian, Yvonne and Richard Peters. 1981. *The Visible and Invisible Group.* London: Tavistock/Routledge.

Agazarian, Yvonne M. 1989. Reframing the group-as-a-whole from a human systems perspective. Unpublished paper presented at the ninth scientific meetings of the A.K. Rice Institute, New York City.

_____. 1992. Contemporary theories of group psychotherapy. *International Journal of Group Psychotherapy* 42 (2): 177-302.

_____, ed. 1993. Systems-centered training. *News* 1(1).

Ahlskog, Gary. 1992. 'They had to beg us to pray': reflections on the undesirability of clinical pastoral education. *The Journal of Pastoral Care* 2 (Summer): 179-87

Alonso, Anne. 1985. *The Quiet Profession*. New York: Macmillan.

_____. 1987. Discussion of women's groups led by women. *International Journal of Group Psychotherapy* 37 (2): 155-62.

Anderson, Herbert and C. George Fitzgerald. 1977. The use of family therapy as preparation for ministry within CPE and seminary context. 1977 ACPE Conference. New York: Association for Clinical Pastoral Education.

Anon. 1992. Bion: an appreciation. In *Bion and Group Psychotherapy*, ed. Pines, 386-9. London: Tavistock Publications.

Anthony, E. James. 1971. The history of group psychotherapy. In *Comprehensive Group Psychotherapy*, eds. Kaplan and Sadock,3-31. Baltimore: Williams & Wilkins.

Argyris, Chris and Donald A. Schoen. 1974. *Theory in Practice: Increasing Professional Effectiveness*. San Francisco: Jossey-Bass Publishers.

Ashbrook, James B. 1970. The small group as an instrument in personal growth and organizational change. *The Journal of Pastoral Care* 24 (September): 178-92.

A Student. 1951. Clinical pastoral training as a religious experience. *The Journal of Pastoral Care* 5 (Spring): 31-5.

Asquith, Glenn H., ed., 1992. *Vision From A Little Known Country: A Boisen Reader*. Decatur, GA: Journal of Pastoral Care Publications, Inc.

Batchelder, Richard L. and James M. Hardy. 1968. *Using Sensitivity Training and the Laboratory Method*. New York: Association Press.

Beatty, Donald C. 1965. Reflections on the early beginnings of the clinical training movement. *Pastoral Psychology* 6 (May): 27-30.

Benne, Kenneth D. 1964. History of the T group in the laboratory setting. In *T-Group Theory and Laboratory Method*, eds. Bradford, Gibb and Benne, 80-135. New York: John Wiley & Sons.

Bennis, Warren G. 1964. Patterns and Vicissitudes in T-group development. In *T-Group Theory and Laboratory Method*, eds. Bradford, Gibb and Benne, 248-78. New York: John Wiley & Sons.

Berne, Eric. 1964. *Games People Play*. New York: Ballantine Books.

_____. 1966. *Principles of Group Treatment*. New York: Grover Press.

Bion, Wilfred R. 1961. *Experiences in Groups*. London: Tavistock.

_____. 1962. *Learning from Experience*. New York: Basic Books

_____. 1965. *Transformation*. New York: Jason Aronson.

_____. 1970. *Attention and Interpretation*. New York: Jason Aronson.

_____. 1982. *The Long Week-End 1897-1919*. Abingdon: Fleetwood.

Bogia, Benjamin Preston. 1987. Group supervision versus group psychotherapy. *The Journal of Pastoral Care* 41 (September): 252-7.

Boisen, Anton T. 1930. Theological education via the clinic. In *Vision From a Little Known Country*, ed. Glenn Asquith, 25-31. Decatur, GA: Journal of Pastoral Care Publications, Inc.

_____. 1936. *The Exploration of The Inner World: A Study of Mental Disorder and Religious Experience*. Philadelphia: University of Pennsylvania Press.

_____. 1948. The service of worship in a mental hospital. In *Vision From a Little Known Country*, ed. Glenn Asquith, 89-107. Decatur, GA: Journal of Pastoral Care Publications, Inc.

_____. 1950. The period of beginnings. *The Journal of Pastoral Care* 4 (Fall/Winter): 13-16.

_____. 1954. Group therapy: the Elgin Plan. *Pastoral Psychology* 5 (March): 35-8.

_____. 1960. *Out of the Depths: An Autobiographical Study of Mental Disorder and Religious Experience*. New York: Harper & Brothers.

Bollas, Christopher. 1987. *The Shadow of the Object: Psychoanalysis of the Unknown Thought*. New York: Columbia University Press.

Bowlby, John. 1988. *A Secure Base*. New York: Basic Books.

Boyd, Robert D. 1991. *Personal Transformation in Small Groups*. New York: Routledge, 1991.

Bradford, Leland P. and Jack R. Gibb and Kenneth D. Benne, eds. 1964. *T-Group Theory and Laboratory Method*. New York: John Wiley & Sons.

Brinkman, Robert E. 1945. Standards for a full-time program in the light of the experience of the council for clinical training. In *Clinical Pastoral Training*. ed. Seward Hiltner, 23-30. New York: Commission on Religion and Health, Federal Council of Churches of Christ in America.

Bruder, Ernest E. 1952. Clinical training and the student. *The Journal of Pastoral Care* 6 (Spring): 13-16.

_____. 1954. Some theological considerations in clinical pastoral education. *The Journal of Pastoral Care* 8 (Fall): 135-46.

_____ and Marion L. Barb. 1956. A survey of ten years of clinical pastoral training at Saint Elizabeths Hospital. *The Journal of Pastoral Care* 10 (Summer): 86-94.

_____., eds. 1958. *Clinical Education for Pastoral Ministry* (proceedings of Fifth National Conference on Clinical Pastoral Education, 1956). Washington, DC: Advisory Committee on Clinical Pastoral Education.

Buber, Martin. 1958. *I and Thou*. New York: Charles Scribner's Sons.

Burck, James L. 1969. A corrective use of reality group therapy within the institutional ministry. *The Journal of Pastoral Care* 23 (March): 15-25.

Burton, Anne L. and Charles A. Weinrich. 1990. So great a cloud of witnesses. *The Journal of Pastoral Care* 44 (Winter): 331-41.

Cabot, Richard C. and Russell L. Dicks. 1936. *The Art of Ministering to the Sick.* New York: Macmillan.

Callahan, Rachel and Robert F. Davenport. 1987. Group counseling: a model for teaching and supervision. In *The Art of Clinical Supervision*, eds. Estadt, Comptom and Blancette, 149-59. New York: Paulist Press.

Cashdan, Sheldon. 1988. *Object Relations Therapy.* New York: Norton and Company.

Cedarleaf, Lennart. 1987. Anton Boisen--A Memoir. (Unpublished manuscript): 1-9.

Chodorow, Nancy. 1978. *The Reproduction of Mothering.* Berkeley and Los Angeles: University of California Press.

Close, Henry T. 1975. Play in CPE. *Journal of Pastoral Care* 29 (4): 241-7.

_____. 1981. A visit with Milton H. Erickson: The grandfather of CPE. *The Journal of Pastoral Care* 35 (March): 52-7.

Cohen, A.M. and R.D. Smith. 1976. *Critical Incidents in Growth Groups.* La Jolla, CA: University Associates.

Coleman, Arthur D. and W. Harold Bexton. 1975. *Group Relations Reader.* Sausalito, CA: GREX.

Corey, Gerald. 1990. *Theory and Practice of Group Counseling.* Pacific Grove: Brooks/Cole Publishing.

Coulson, William R. 1972. *Groups, Gimmicks and Instant Gurus.* New York: Harper & Row.

Criswell, Grover E. 1982. The paradox of paradoxical thinking. 1982. In *Re-visioning Supervision: ACPE Conference*, 115-18. New York: Association for Clinical Pastoral Education

DeArment, Daniel C. 1987. Families and groups. *The Journal of Pastoral Care* 41 (June): 111-18.

Dies, Robert R. 1992. Models of group psychotherapy: sifting through the confusion. *International Journal of Group Psychotherapy* 42 (1): 1-17.

Duncombe, David C. 1988. The trivial nature of clinical pastoral education. *The Journal of Pastoral Care* 42 (Spring): 46-56.

Durkin, James E. ed. 1981. *Living Groups*. New York: Brunner/Mazel Company.

Egan, Gerard. 1973. *Face to Face*. Monterey, CA: Brooks/Cole Publishing Company.

Eichenbaum, Louise and Susie Orbach. 1983. *Understanding Women*. New York: Basic Books.

Estadt, Barry and John Compton and Melvin C. Blanchette, eds.1987. *The Art of Clinical Supervision*. New York: Paulist Press.

Ettin, Mark F. 1988. 'By the crowd they have been broken, by the crowd they shall be healed': the advent of group psychotherapy. *International Journal of Group Psychotherapy*. 38 (2): 139-67.

Fairbanks, Rollin J. 1945. Standards for full-time clinical training in the light of the New England experience. In *Clinical Pastoral Training*, ed. Seward Hiltner, 36-40. New York: Commission on Religion and Health, Federal Council of Churches of Christ in America.

Farley, Edward. 1983. *Theologia: The Fragmentation and Unity of Theological Education*. Philadelphia: Fortress Press.

Fedele, Nicolina and Elizabeth Harrington. 1990. *Women's Groups: How Connections Heal*. No. 47. Wellesley, MA: Stone Center Publication.

Feilding, Charles, ed. 1966. *Education for Ministry*. Dayton, OH: American Association of Theological Schools.

_____. 1975. The Journal of Pastoral Care: A historical perspective. *The Journal of Pastoral Care* (29) 3: 204-6.

Fitchett, George. 1982. A coherent theory of education relevant for CPE. In *Re-Visioning Supervision: ACPE Conference*, 73-114. New York: Association for Clinical Pastoral Education.

Fitzgerald, C. George. 1970. Report on a leaderless group. *Pastoral Psychology* 21 (December): 21-8, 60.

Florell, John L. 1975. After fifty years: analysis of the national ACPE questionnaire. *The Journal of Pastoral Care* 29 (December): 221-32.

Foster, Arthur L. 1972. The use of encounter groups in the church. *The Journal of Pastoral Care* 26 (September): 148-55.

Foulkes, S. H. 1964. *Therapeutic Group Analysis*. New York: International Universities Press.

_____. 1975. *Group-Analytic Psychotherapy*. London: Gordon and Breach.

Frank, Jerome. 1964. Training and Therapy. In *T-Group Theory and Laboratory Method*, eds. Bradford, Gibb and Benne, 442-51. New York: John Wiley & Sons.

Freud, Sigmund, 1950. *Totem and Taboo*. New York: W. W. Norton & Company (copyright 1950 by Routledge and Kegan Paul Ltd.).

_____. 1959. *Group Psychology and the Analysis of the Ego*. New York: W. W. Norton & Company (copyright 1922 by the Institute of Psycho-analysis and Angela Richards).

_____. 1960. *A General Introduction to Psychoanalysis*. New York: Washington Square Press (copyright 1920, Edward L. Bernays).

_____. 1962. *Civilization and its Discontents*. New York: W.W. Norton & Company (copyright 1961, James Strachey).

_____. 1964. *The Future of an Illusion*. Garden City: Doubleday & Company (copyright 1961, James Strachey).

Gainor, Kathy. 1992. Internalized oppression as a barrier to effective group work with Black women. *The Journal for Specialists in Group Work* 17 (November): 235-42.

Galloway, Albert L. 1991. Memorandum (May 23, 1991).

Gazda, George M., ed. 1968a. *Basic Approaches to Group Psychotherapy and Group Counseling*. Springfield, IL: Charles C. Thomas.

_____. 1968b. *Innovations in Group Psychotherapy*. Springfield, IL: Charles C. Thomas.

Gebhart, James E. and Grover E. Criswell. 1974. The 24-hour marathon. *The Journal of Pastoral Care* 28 (December): 221-40.

Gibb, Jack R. 1964. Climate for trust formation. In *T-Group Theory and Laboratory Method*, eds. Bradford, Gibb and Benne, 279-309. New York: John Wiley & Sons.

Gibbard, G.S. and J.J. Hartman and R.D. Mann. 1974. *Analysis of Groups*. New York: Jossey-Bass.

Gibbons, Graeme D. 1987. Clinical pastoral education: seasons of a group's life. *The Journal of Pastoral Care* 41 (September): 241-50.

Gibbons, James L. and David C. Myler. 1978. Research as a curricular component in CPE. *Journal of Supervision and Training in Ministry* 1 (Winter): 36-45.

Gillette, Jonathon and Marion McCollom. 1991. *Groups in Context*. Reading: Addison-Wesley Company.

Gilligan, Carol. 1982. *In A Different Voice*. Cambridge:Harvard University Press.

Goldenberg, Naomi R. 1990. *Returning Words to Flesh: Feminism, Psychoanalysis, and the Resurrection of the Body*. Boston: Beacon Press.

_____. 1992. Psychoanalysis and religion: the influence of theology on theory and therapy. *Pastoral Psychology* 40 (6): 343-54.

Gordon, Thomas. 1955. The challenge of a new conception of leadership. *Pastoral Psychology* 6 (April): 15-24.

Gosling, Robert. 1981a. A study of very small groups. In *Dare I Disturb the Universe?* ed. Grotstein, 633-45. Beverly Hills: Caesura Press.

_____. 1981b. Interview. In *Dare I Disturb the Universe?* ed. Grotstein, 627-31. Beverly Hills: Caesura Press.

Greenberg, Jay R. and Stephen A. Mitchell. 1983. *Object Relations in Psychoanalytic Theory*. Cambridge: Harvard University.

Grotstein, James S., ed. 1981. *Do I Dare Disturb the Universe? A Memorial to Wilfred R. Bion*. Beverly Hills: Caesura Press.

Guiles, Philip A. 1945. Standards for clinical training during the school term in the light of the New England Group. In *Clinical Pastoral Training*, ed. Seward Hiltner, 43-9. New York: Commission on Religion and Health, Federal Council of Churches of Christ in America.

Guntrip, Harry. 1971. *Psychoanalytic Theory, Therapy and The Self*. New York: Basic Books.

Gynther, Malcolm D. and J. Obert Kempson. 1958. Personal and interpersonal changes in clinical pastoral training. *The Journal of Pastoral Care* 12 (Winter): 210-19.

Habermas, Jurgen. 1971. *Knowlege and Human Interests*. Boston: Beacon Press.

Haines, Denise. 1988. Problems of leadership relative to authority. In The Power to Heal (unpublished manuscript): 124-48.

Hall, Calvin S. and Gardner Lindzey. 1957. *Theories of Personality*. New York: John Wiley & Sons.

Hall, Charles E. 1966. Elsa Leichter, The Interrelationship of Content and Process in Therapy Groups. *The Journal of Pastoral Care* 20 (December): 243.

_____. 1986. New thrusts for the Association for Clinical Pastoral Education. *The Journal of Pastoral Care* 22 (December): 203-5.

_____. 1992. *Head and Heart: The Story of the Clinical Pastoral Education Movement.* Decatur, GA: Journal of Pastoral Care Publications, Inc.

Hammett, Jenny Yates. 1975. A second drink at the well. *The Journal of Pastoral Care* 29 (June):86-9.

Harris, Maria. 1991. *Teaching and the Religious Imagination.* San Francisco: HarperCollins.

Harris, Thomas A. 1967. *I'm Okay--You're Okay.* New York: Harper & Row.

Hartl, Emil M. 1960. The constitutional base of personality as a dimension for investigation in the study of group. In *Objectives of Clinical Pastoral Training*, ed. John I. Smith, 93-106. Cambridge: Institute of Pastoral Care.

Hemenway, Joan E. 1982. Position Paper on CPE Supervision and Learning. *The Journal of Pastoral Care* 36 (September): 194-202.

Herrick, Everett C. 1945. The place of clinical training in the theological curriculum. In *Clinical Pastoral Training*, ed. Seward Hiltner, 79-81. New York: Commission on Religion and Health, Federal Council of Churches of Christ in America.

Hiemstra, William L. 1962. A history of clinical pastoral training in the United States. *Reformed Review* 10 (May): 30-47.

Higgins, Richard T. 1976. Group maintenance: a common theme in group psychotherapy and pastoral leadership. *The Journal of Pastoral Care* 30 (March): 46-9.

Hiltner, Seward, ed. 1945. *Clinical Pastoral Training.* New York: Commission on Religion and Health, Federal Council of Churches of Christ in America.

_____. 1958. *Preface to Pastoral Theology*. Nashville: Abingdon Press.

_____. 1966. The debt of clinical pastoral education to Anton T. Boisen. *The Journal of Pastoral Care* 20 (September): 129-35.

_____. 1970. The contribution of liberals to pastoral care. In *Pastoral Care and the Liberal Churches*, ed. James Luther Adams and Seward Hiltner, 221-43. Nashville: Abingdon Press.

_____. 1975. Fifty years of CPE. *The Journal of Pastoral Care* 29 (June): 90-8.

_____. 1980. Doggerel days in CPE. *Fantasy and Festivity in the Church* (ACPE 1980 Conference Proceedings). New York: Association for Clinical Pastoral Education.

Hirschhorn, Larry. 1993. *The Workplace Within: Psychodynamics of Organizational Life*. Cambridge: The MIT Press.

Holifield, Brooks E. 1980. Ethical assumptions of clinical pastoral education. *The Journal of Pastoral Care* 34 (March): 39-53.

_____. 1983. *A History of Pastoral Care in America: From Salvation to Self-Realization*. Nashville: Abingdon Press.

Holt, Herbert and Charles Winick. 1963. Group pastoral counseling. *Pastoral Psychology* 14 (June): 13-22.

Hopper, Earl. 1985. The problem of context in group analytic psychotherapy. In *Bion and Group Psychotherapy*, ed. Pines, 330-53. London/New York: Tavistock.

Horowitz, Leonard. 1983. Projective identification in dyads and groups. *International Journal of Group Psychotherapy* 33(3): 259-79.

Hough, Joseph C. and Barbara G. Wheeler. 1988. *Beyond   Clericalism: The Congregation as a Focus for Theological Education*. Atlanta: Scholars Press.

_____. and John H. Cobb. 1985. *Christian Identity and Theological Education*. Atlanta: Scholars Press.

Howard, Jane. 1970. *Please Touch*. New York: McGraw-Hill.

Howard, Judson D. 1955. Pastoral experiences in the interpersonal group. *Pastoral Psychology* 6 (April): 25-30.

_____. 1958. Group dynamics seminar at Boston State Hospital. In *Clinical Education for Pastoral Ministry*, eds. Bruder and Barb, 112-20. Advisory Committee for Clinical Pastoral Education.

_____. 1960a. Interpersonal group seminar: A training method in the pastoral care of groups. *The Journal of Pastoral Care* 14 (Fall): 160-6.

_____. 1960b. Some reflections on the pilot efforts in research in the pastoral care of groups carried on in the clinical pastoral education program at Boston State Hospital. In *Objectives of Clinical Pastoral Training*, ed. John I. Smith, 82-3. Cambridge: Institute of Pastoral Care.

Howe, Leroy T. 1990. Crises of belief: an object relations perspective. *Journal of Pastoral Care* 44 (1):42-53.

Howe, Reuel. 1952. The role of clinical training in theological education. *The Journal of Pastoral Care* 6 (Spring): 1-12.

Hulme, William E. 1973. General pastoral care and the future of ministry. In *Dynamic Interpersonalism for Ministry*, ed. O. Strunk, 285-303. Nashville: Abingdon Press.

Hunter, Rodney, ed., 1990. *Dictionary of Pastoral Care and Counseling*. Nashville: Abingdon Press.

Hyde, Robert W. 1952. Communication of feeling in group psychotherapy. *The Journal of Pastoral Care* 6 (Fall): 26-33.

_____ and Robert C. Leslie. 1952. Introduction to group therapy for graduate theological students. *The Journal of Pastoral Care* 6 (Summer): 19-27.

Jackson, Edgar N. 1950 The therapeutic function in preaching. *Pastoral Psychology* 1 (June): 36-9.

Jacobson, Lawrence. 1989. The group as an object in the cultural field. *International Journal of Group Psychotherapy* 39(4): 475-97.

Jaeckle, Charles and William Clebesch. 1964. *Pastoral Care in Historical Perspective*. Englewood Cliffs: Prentice-Hall.

James, Colin D. 1984. Bion's "Containing" and Winnicott's "Holding" in the context of the group matrix. *International Journal of Group Psychotherapy*, 34 (2): 201-13

James, William. 1958. *The Varieties of Religious Experience*. New York: Mentor Books.

Johnson, Paul E. 1968. Fifty years of clinical pastoral education. *The Journal of Pastoral Care* 22 (December): 223-31.

Jones, James W. 1991. *Contemporary Psychoanalysis & Religion: Transference and Transcendence*. New Haven: Yale University Press.

_____. 1992. Psychoanalysis, feminism and religion. *Pastoral Psychology* 40 (6): 355-67.

Jonte-Pace, Diane. 1987. Object relations theory, mothering, and religion: towards a feminist pyschology of religion. *Horizons* 14 (2): 310-27.

_____. 1992. Which feminism? Whose Freud? *Pastoral Psychology* 40 (6): 369-74.

Jorgensen, Danny L. 1989. *Participant Observation: A Methodology for Human Studies*. London: Sage Publications.

Kanzer, Mark. 1971. Freud: the first psychoanalytic group leader. In *Comprehensive Group Psychotherapy*, eds. Kaplan and Sadock, 32-46. Baltimore: Williams & Wilkins.

Kaplan, Harold I. and Benjamin J. Sadock. 1971. *Comprehensive Group Psychotherapy*. Baltimore: Williams & Wilkins.

Karen, Robert. 1990. Becoming attached. *Atlantic Monthly* (February 1990): 35-70.

Keeley, Terry D. and James E. Burgin and Kevin Kenney. 1971. The use of sensitivity training in a unit of professional education. *The Journal of Pastoral Care* 25 (September): 188-95.

Kemp, Charles F. 1947. *Physicians of the Soul: A History of Pastoral Counseling*. New York: Macmillan.

Kemp, C. Gratton. 1971. *Small Groups and Self-Renewal*. New York: Seabury Press.

Kenny, Dennis. 1980. Clinical pastoral education: exploring covenants with God. *The Journal of Pastoral Care* 34 (June): 109-13.

Kew, Clifton and Clinton Kew. 1951. Group psychotherapy in a church setting. *Pastoral Psychology* 1 (January): 31-7.

_____. 1955. Principles and values of group psychotherapy under church auspices. *Pastoral Psychology* 6 (April): 37- 48.

_____. 1963. Countertransference and the group therapist. *The Pastoral Counselor* 1 (Fall): 9-18.

_____. 1965. An experiment in teaching group psychotherapy through a group experience. *The Journal of Pastoral Care* 19 (September): 129-40.

Khaleelee, Oyla and Eric Miller. 1992. Beyond the small group. In *Bion and Group Psychotherapy*, ed. Pines, 354-85. London/New York: Tavistock Publications.

Klein, Edward B. and Boris M. Astrachan. 1971. Learning in groups: a comparison. *The Journal of Applied Behavioral Science* 7(6): 659-83.

Klein, Melanie. 1990. *Envy and Gratitude and Other Works 1946-1963*. London: Virago Press.

Klink, Thomas A. 1958. How is supervision carried out? In *Clinical Education for Pastoral Ministry*, eds. Bruder and Barb, 104-10. Washington, DC: Advisory Committee for Clinical Pastoral Education.

Klinkman, Myron F. 1960. The emotional growth of students in clinical pastoral education. In *Objectives in Clinical Pastoral Training*, ed. John I. Smith, 60-8. Institute of Pastoral Care.

Knights, Ward A. 1970. A gestalt approach in a clinical training group. *The Journal of Pastoral Care* 24 (September): 193-8.

_____. 1972. Concerning clinical pastoral education and the group experience. *The Journal of Pastoral Care* 26 (September): 190-2.

Knowles, Malcolm and Hulda Knowles. 1972. *Introduction to Group Dynamics*. New York: Association Press.

Krantz, James. 1991. Group relational training in context. In *Groups in Context*, eds. Jonathon Gillette and Marion McCollom, 216-34. Reading: Addison-Wesley.

Kuether, Frederick C. 1945. The place of clinical training in the theological curriculum as training supervisors see it. In *Clinical Pastoral Training*, ed. Seward Hiltner, 88-93. New York: Commission on Religion and Health, Federal Council of Churches of Christ in America.

_____. 1958. How are supervisory skills transmitted to new supervisors? In *Clinical Education for Pastoral Ministry*, eds. Bruder and Barb, 76-92. Advisory Committee for Clinical Pastoral Education.

Lacoursiere, Roy. 1980. *The Life Cycle of Groups*. New York: Human Sciences Press.

Lawrence, Raymond. 1992. Editorial. In *Underground Report #32*. 432 West 47th St., New York, NY 10036.

Lawrence, W. Gordon. 1992. Beyond the frames. In *Bion and Group Psychotherapy*, ed. Pines, 306-29. London and New York: Tavistock/Routledge.

Leslie, Robert C. 1951. Growth through group interaction. *The Journal of Pastoral Care* 5 (Spring): 36-45.

_____. 1952a. Pastoral group psychotherapy. *The Journal of Pastoral Care* 6 (Spring): 56-61.

_____. 1952b. The role of the chaplain in patient relationships: group counseling. *Journal of Pastoral* Care 6 (Winter): 43-46.

_____. 1955. Group therapy: a new approach for the church. *Pastoral Psychology* 6 (April): 9-14.

_____. 1958. The goals of clinical pastoral education. In *Clinical Education for Pastoral Ministry*, eds. Bruder and Barb, 16-23. Washington, DC: Advisory Committee for Clinical Pastoral Education.

_____. 1967. Education in group methods: a working paper. *The Pastoral Counselor* 5 (Winter): 54-9.

_____. 1974. Small groups in the church: a bibliography. *The Journal of Pastoral Care* 28 (December): 241-4.

Lieberman, Morton, Irvin Yalom and Matthew Miles. 1973. *Encounter Groups: First Facts*. New York: Basic Books.

Liff, Zanvel. 1984. Editorial. *International Journal of Group Psychotherapy* 34 (4): 515.

Lubin, Bernard and William B. Eddy. 1972. The laboratory training model. In *Progress in Group and Family Therapy*, eds. Sager and Kaplan, 819-51. New York: Brunner/Mazel.

Lyth, Isabel Menzies. 1981. Bion's contribution to thinking about groups. In *Dare I Disturb the Universe?*, ed. Grotstein, 662-6. Beverly Hills: Caesura Press.

Madara, Edward J. and Barrie Alan Peterson. 1987. Clergy and self-help groups. *The Journal of Pastoral Care* 41 (September): 213-20.

Manual of the Certification Commission. 1989. Decatur, GA: Association for Clinical Pastoral Education.

Marrow, Alfred J. 1969. *The Practical Theorist: The Life and Work of Kurt Lewin.* New York: Basic Books.

Maslow, Abraham H. 1962. *Toward A Psychology of Being.* Princeton: Van Nostrand.

McDargh, John. 1983. *Psychoanalytic Object Relations Theory and the Study of Religion.* New York: University Press of America.

McKay, Matthew and Kim Paleg, eds. 1992. *Focal Group Psychotherapy.* Oakland, CA: New Harbinger Publications.

McNeill, John T. 1951. *A History of The Cure of Souls.* New York: Harper & Row.

McWilliams, Nancy and Jill Stein. 1987. Women's groups led by women. *International Journal for Group Psychotherapy* 37 (2):139-62.

Meissner, W. W. 1984. *Psychoanalysis and Religious Experience.* New Haven and London: Yale University Press.

Miller, E.J. and A.K. Rice. 1967. *The Control of Task and Sentient Boundaries.* London: Tavistock.

Miller-McLemore, Bonnie and William R. Myers. 1989. The Doctorate of Ministry as an exercise in practical theology. *Journal of Supervision and Training in Ministry* 11: 4-24.

Moore, Mary Elizabeth Mullino. 1991. *Teaching from the Heart.* Minneapolis: Fortress Press.

Moreno, J. L. 1971. Psychodrama. In *Comprehensive Group Psychotherapy*, eds. Kaplan and Sadock, 460-500. Baltimore: Williams and Wilkins.

Morgan, Robert. 1989. Issues and Concerns Confronting the Certification Commission (memo), 1-4.

Morris, Robert D. 1951. Report to the dean. *The Journal of Pastoral Care* 5 (Spring): 27-30.

Mowrer, O. Hobart. 1972. Is the small-group movement a religious revolution? *Pastoral Psychology* 23 (March): 19-22.

Munich, Richard L. 1993. Varieties of learning in an experiential group. *International Journal for Group Pschotherapy* 43 (3): 345-61.

Myers, William R. and Bonnie J. Miller-McLemore. 1990. Can one be faithful while teaching research methods to D.Min. students? *Journal of Supervision and Training in Ministry*. 12: 15-29.

Napier, Rodney W. and Matti K. Gershenfeld. 1985. *Groups: Theory and Experience*. Boston: Houghton-Mifflin.

Nichols, Michael P. and Richard C. Schwartz. 1991. *Family Therapy: Concepts and Methods*. Boston: Allyn and Bacon.

Niebuhr, H. Richard and Daniel D. Williams and Sydney E. Ahlstrom. 1980. *The Ministry in Historical Perspective*. New York: Harper & Row.

Nouwen, Henri. 1968. Anton T. Boisen and theology through living human documents. In *Vision from a Little Known Country*, ed. Glenn Asquith, 157-75. Decatur, GA: Journal of Pastoral Care Publications, Inc.

Oates, Wayne C. 1958. The goals of clinical pastoral education. In *Clinical Education for Pastoral Ministry*, eds. Bruder and Barb, 36-9. Washington, DC: Advisory Committee for Clinical Pastoral Education.

Oden, Thomas C. 1972. *The Intensive Group Experience*. Philadelphia: Westminster Press.

Ogden, Thomas H. 1979. On projective identification. *International Journal of Psychoanalysis* (60): 357-73.

Ormont, Louis R. 1992. *The Group Therapy Experience, From Theory to Practice:* New York: St. Martin's Press.

Otto, Rudolph. 1958. *The Idea of the Holy.* New York: Oxford University Press.

Palmer, Barry. 1992. Ambiguity and paradox in group relations conferences. In *Bion and Group Psychotherapy*, ed. Pines, 274-305. London and New York: Tavistock/Routledge.

Parker, Duane. 1978. Student-directed CPE. *The Journal of Pastoral Care* 32 (September): 161-9.

_____. 1992. A question of paradigm. *ACPE News* 25 (January-February): 6.

Patton, John. 1990 *From Ministry to Theology*. Nashville: Abingdon Press.

Patton, Michael Quinn. 1980. *Qualitative Evaluation and Research Methods*. London: Sage Publications.

Peck, Scott. 1987. *A Different Drum*. New York: Simon & Schuster.

Perls, Frederick S. 1969. *Gestalt Therapy Verbatim*. New York: Bantam Books.

Pines, Malcolm, ed. 1992. *Bion and Group Psychotherapy*. London and New York: Tavistock/Routledge.

Plummer, Stuart A. 1984. Clinical pastoral education and the future: through a glass darkly. In *Agendas for Education and Ministry: ACPE Conference*, 24-33. New York: Association for Clinical Pastoral Education.

Pohly, Kenneth H. 1977. *Pastoral Supervision*. Houston: Institute of Religion.

_____. 1993. *Transforming the Rough Places: The Ministry of Supervision*. Dayton: Whaleprints.

Poling, James N. and Donald E. Miller. 1985. *Foundations for a Practical Theology of Ministry*. Nashville: Abingdon Press.

Powell, Robert C. 1975a. *CPE:Fifty Years of Learning Through Supervised Encounter With Living Human Documents.* New York: Association for Clinical Pastoral Education, Inc.

_____. 1975b. Questions from the past on the future of clinical pastoral education. In *Fiftieth Anniversary: ACPE Conference Proceedings*, 1-21. New York: Association for Clinical Pastoral Education.

Pruyser, Paul W. 1967. Anton T. Boisen and the psychology of religion. In *Vision from a Little Known Country*, ed. Glenn Asquith, 145-56. Journal of Pastoral Care Publications, Inc.

_____. 1974. *Between Belief and Unbelief.* New York: Harper and Row.

Ramsden, William E. 1960. The Boston State Hospital and a sociometric approach to the study of group processes. In *Objectives in Clinical Pastoral Training*, ed. John I. Smith, 84-92. Institute of Pastoral Care.

Redlich, R. C. and Boris M. Astrachan. 1975. Group dynamic training. In *Group Relations Reader*, ed. Coleman and and Bexton, 225-50. Sausalito, CA: GREX

Reed, Melinda. 1992. The road to Emmaus: a new model for supervision. *ACPE News* 25 (November-December): 7-8.

Regional Directors' Consultation. 1988. Discussion of New Certification Process (3/30/88; unpublished paper).

Research in Ministry. 1983-92. Evanston: American Theological Library Association.

Rice, A. Kenneth. 1965. *Learning for Leadership.* London: Tavistock.

Rioch, Margaret J. 1972. The work of Wilfred Bion on groups. In *Progress in Group and Family Therapy*, eds. Sager and Kaplan, 18-32. New York: Brunner/Mazel.

_____. 1975. All we like sheep. In *Group Relations Reader*, eds. Coleman and Bexton, 159-78. Sausalito, CA: GREX.

_____. 1981. The influence of Wilfred Bion on the A.K. Rice Group Relations Conferences. In *Dare I Disturb the Universe?* ed. Grotstein, 668-73. Beverly Hills: Caesura Press.

Rizzuto, Ana-Maria. 1979. *The Birth of the Living God.* Chicago: University of Chicago Press.

Rogers, Carl. 1942. *Counseling and Psychotherapy.* Boston: Houghton Mifflin.

_____. 1970. *Carl Rogers on Encounter Groups.* New York: Harper & Row.

Rogers, William F. 1960. Clinical training program - Fulton State Hospital. In *Objectives of Clinical Pastoral Training*, ed. John I. Smith, 44-59. Institute of Pastoral Care.

Rosenbaum, Max. 1971. Co-therapy. In *Comprehensive Group Psychotherapy*, eds. Kaplan and Sadock, 501-14. Baltimore: Williams & Wilkins.

Rutan, J. Scott and Walter N. Stone. 1984. *Psychodynamic Group Psychotherapy.* Lexington: Collamore Press.

Sager, Clifford J. and Helen Singer Kaplan, eds. 1972. *Progress in Group and Family Therapy.* New York: Brunner/Mazel.

Scharff, Jill Savage and David Scharff. 1992. *Scharff Notes: A Primer of Object Relations Therapy.* London: Jason Aronson.

Schermer, Victor L. 1992. Beyond Bion: the basic assumption states revisted. In *Bion and Group Psychotherapy*, ed. Pines, 139-50. London and New York: Tavistock/Routledge.

Schilling, Paul. 1973. Dynamic interpersonalism and contemporary theology. In *Dynamic Interpersonalism in Ministry*, ed. O. Strunk, 43-66. Nashville: Abingdon Press.

Schlachet, Peter J. 1986. The concept of group space. *International Journal of Group Psychotherapy* 36 (1): 33-53.

Schoen, Donald A. 1983. *The Reflective Practitioner: How Professionals Think in Action*. New York: Basic Books.

Schutz, William C. 1967. *Joy: Expanding Human Awareness*. New York: Grove Press.

Shephard, Herbert. 1964. Exploration in observant participation. In *T-Group Theory and Laboratory Method*, eds. Bradford, Gibb and Benne, 379-94. New York: John Wiley & Sons.

Skaggs, Bruce. 1989. Group supervision. In *The Supervision of Pastoral Care*. Steere, ed. 172-82. Louisville: Westminster/John Knox Press.

Slater, Philip E. 1966. *Microcosm*. New York: John Wiley & Sons.

Slavson, S. R. 1950. *Analytic Group Psychotherapy*. New York: Columbia University Press.

Smith, Alexa. 1989. Student responses to clinical pastoral education. In *Supervision of Pastoral Care*, ed. Steere, 129-45. Louisville: Westminster/ John Knox Press.

Smith, John I., ed. 1960. *Objectives in Clinical Pastoral Training*. Cambridge: Institute of Pastoral Care.

Snyder, Ross. 1968. The Boisen heritage in theological education. In *Vision From a Little Known Country*, ed. Glenn Asquith, 177-84. Journal of Pastoral Care Publications, Inc.

Special Study Committee Report 1978-1980. New York: Association for Clinical Pastoral Education.

Spehn, Mel R. 1972. The small-group religion. *Pastoral Psychology* 23 (January): 50-8.

Spero, Moshe Halevi. 1992. *Religious Objects As Psychological Structures*. Chicago: University of Chicago Press.

Spotnitz, Hyman. 1971. Comparison of different types of group psychotherapy. In *Comprehensive Group Psychotherapy*, eds. Kaplan and Sadock, 72-103. Baltimore: Williams and Wilkins.

Stackhouse, Max L. 1988. *Apologia: Contextualization, Globalization and Mission in Theological Education*. Grand Rapids: William B. Eerdmans.

Standards of The Association for Clinical Pastoral Education. 1993. Decatur, GA: Association for Clinical Pastoral Education, Inc.

Stange, Otto. 1990. Clinical pastoral education for theological students: A Dutch short-term model. *Journal of Supervision and Training in Ministry*. 12:89-95.

St.Clair, Michael. 1986. *Object Relations and Self Psychology*. Monterey, CA: Brooks/Cole.

Steinhoff-Smith, Roy Herndon. 1989. The denial of mystery: object relations theory and religion. *Horizons* 16 (2): 243-65.

_____. 1992. The tragedy of clinical pastoral education. *Pastoral Psychology*. 41(1): 45-54.

Steere, David A. 1989. *The Supervision of Pastoral Care*. Louisville: Westminster/ John Knox Press.

Stewart, Charles W. 1972. The plus and minus of encounter groups. *The Journal of Pastoral Care* 26 (September): 145-7.

Stock, Dorothy. 1964. A survey of research on T groups. In *T-Group Theory and Laboratory Method*, eds. Bradford, Gibb andBenne, 395-441. New York: John Wiley & Sons.

_____ and Herbert A. Thelen. 1958. *Emotional Dynamics and Group Culture*. New York: New York University Press.

Stollberg, Dietrich. 1973. Some specifics about psychoanalytic group work with theologians. *The Journal of Pastoral Care* 27 (June): 77-82.

Stokes, Allison. 1985. *Ministry After Freud*. New York: Pilgrim Press.

Strunk, Orlo, ed. 1973. *Dynamic Interpersonalism for Ministry*. Nashville: Abingdon Press.

Student "A". 1951. The student evaluation. *The Journal of Pastoral Care* 6 (Spring): 17-20.

Student "B". 1951. The student evaluation. *The Journal of Pastoral Care* 6 (Spring): 21-5.

Student "C". 1951. The student evaluation. *The Journal of Pastoral Care* 6 (Spring): 26-8.

Student "D". 1951. The student evaluation. *The Journal of Pastoral Care* 6 (Spring): 29-33.

Sullivan, Harry Stack. 1953. *The Interpersonal Theory of Psychiatry*. New York: W. W. Norton (copyright: William Alanson White Psychiatric Foundation).

_____. 1954. *The Psychiatric Interview*. New York: W.W. Norton & Co. (copyright: William Alanson White Psychiatric Foundation).

Thelen, Herbert. 1992. Research with Bion's concepts. In *Bion and Group Psychotherapy*, ed. Pines, 114-38. London and New York: Tavistock/ Routledge.

Thornton, Edward E. 1968. Some hard questions for clinical pastoral educators. *The Journal of Pastoral Care* 22 (December): 194-202.

_____. 1970. *Professional Education for Ministry: A History of Clinical Pastoral Education*. Nashville: Abingdon Press.

_____. 1990. Clinical Pastoral Education. *Dictionary of Pastoral Care and Counseling*, ed. Hunter, 177-82. Nashville: Abingdon Press.

Tillich, Paul. 1948. *The Shaking of the Foundations*. New York: Charles Scribner's Sons.

_____. 1952. *The Courage to Be*. New Haven: Yale University Press.

_____. 1958. The theology of pastoral care. In *Clinical Education for Pastoral Ministry*, eds. Bruder and Barb, 1-6. Advisory Committee for Clinical Pastoral Education.

Trist, Eric. 1992. Working with Bion in the 1940s. In *Bion and Group Psychotherapy*, ed. Pines, 1-46. London and New York: Tavistock/Routledge.

Turquet, Pierre. 1974. Leadership: the individual and the group. In *Analysis of Groups*, eds. G.S. Gibbard, J.J. Hartman, and R.D. Mann, 349-71. New York: Jossey-Bass.

VandeCreek, Larry. 1988. *A Research Primer for Pastoral Care and Counseling*. Decatur, GA: Journal of Pastoral Care Publications.

VandeCreek, Larry and Jerry Royer. 1975. Education for interdisciplinary teamwork. *The Journal of Pastoral Care* 29 (September): 176-84.

Van Wagner, Charles A. and Quentin L. Hand and Allison Stokes, ed., 1991. *In Historical Perspective: A History of the American Association of Pastoral Counselors (1963-1991)*. Fairfax, VA: American Association of Pastoral Counselors.

Walker, Alice. 1982. *The Color Purple*. New York and London: Harcourt Brace Jovanovich.

Wedel, Theodore O. 1954. Group dynamics and the church. *The Journal of Pastoral Care* 9 (Winter): 203-12.

Weston, John H. 1990. Ethics in CPE: A consumer's report. *Journal of Supervision and Training in Ministry*. 12: 175-83.

Whitaker, Dorthy Stock and Morton A. Lieberman. 1964. *Psychotherapy through the Group Process*. New York: Atherton Press.

Whitehead, James, D. 1989. The practical play of theology. In *The Promise of Practical Theology*, eds. Lewis S. Mudge and James N. Poling, 36-54. Philadelphia: Fortress Press.

Whitman, Roy M. 1964. Psychodynamic principles underlying T-group processes. In *T-Group Theory and Laboratory Method*, eds. Bradford, Gibb and Benne, 310-35. New York: John Wiley & Sons.

Wieand, David John. 1968. The philosophy, goals, and methodology of sensitivity training. *New Thrusts in Clinical Pastoral Education* (proceedings from 1968 meeting in Chicago). New York: Association for Clinical Pastoral Education.

Williams, Dean. 1990. In praise of manipulation. *Journal of Supervision and Training in Ministry*. 12: 213-16.

Williams, Daniel Day. 1961. *The Minister and The Care of Souls*. New York: Harper & Row.

Winnicott, D.W. 1971. *Playing and Reality*. London and New York: Routledge.

Wise, Carroll A. 1968. Dealing with defenses in clinical pastoral education. *The Journal of Pastoral Care* 22 (September): 171-72.

Yalom, Irvin. 1985. *The Theory and Practice of Group Psychotherapy*. New York: Basic Books.

Yoder, Walter. 1955. Solving personal problems in a church group. *Pastoral Psychology* 6 (April): 31-6.

INDEX

249